"Ensuring left-behind places can catch up with richer regions is among the most severe challenges our economies and polities face. This book is a comprehensive compendium of evidence on both regional inequalities and corrective policies in the European Union. This valuable analysis uncovers new facts and sheds light on the EU's remaining challenges."

—Dani Rodrik,
Harvard University.

"Increasing regional disparities in income across the regions of the European Union are a major concern to us all. However, effective policy responses remain elusive. This book makes an excellent contribution as to what can be done. It provides a valuable review of relevant theory, a robust empirical analysis of key data and the contribution of policy. A core finding is that there is an urgent need to deliver new policy initiatives to improve the productivity of Europe's left behind regions. It should be a core reader for students, academics and policy makers in the field."

—Professor Peter Tyler,
Emeritus Professor University of Cambridge.

Lagging Regions in the European Union

Unequal distribution of income is one of the most important socio-economic issues. The processes of globalisation and integration are accelerating economic growth; however, at the same time, imbalances between regions are growing. Reducing inequalities within regions and national economies, as well as around the world, is important for individual and societal well-being and cohesion, and for effective state policies.

This book investigates the problem of left-behind regions in the European Union (EU). It first introduces the reader to the theories of regional imbalances and problems with measuring them. It then explores imbalances in the EU using a variety of indicators and describes the EU's regional policy for reducing regional disparities. It uses an empirical shift-share analysis to assess the productivity of EU regions which are lagging behind. The book also provides an empirical analysis of the effectiveness of EU funds in increasing labour productivity performed with DEA methodology.

This book can be used as a teaching resource for undergraduate and postgraduate students and can serve as reference material for academics and researchers, as well as policymakers at the European, national and local levels.

Paweł Dobrzański is an Associate Professor of Economics and a Faculty Member of the Department of Mathematical Economics at Wrocław University of Economics and Business (WUEB), Wrocław, Poland.

Routledge Advances in Regional Economics, Science and Policy

Smart Cities in Europe and Asia
Urban Planning and Management for a Sustainable Future
Edited by Prana Krishna Biswas and Robert Dygas

Sustainable Regional Development
Revitalizing Regions Through Innovation
Michael P. Clair

Governance and Leadership in Shrinking Cities
Strategies for Managing Urban Decline
Edited by Stanisław Mazur

Regional Policy in the Southern African Development Community
Edited by J. Ernst Drewes and Mariske van Aswegen

Regional Cooperation and Resilience in East Asia
Edited by Sebastian Bobowski

The Business of Affordable Housing
Case Studies of the Commercial Supply of Affordable Homes
Alexander Styhre

Spatial Planning and the European Union
Europeanisation from Within
Eva Purkarthofer

Economic Resilience and Pandemic Response
Edited by Agnieszka Rzepka and Artur Paździor

Lagging Regions in the European Union
Structural, Productivity and Efficiency Aspects
Paweł Dobrzański

For more information about this series, please visit: www.routledge.com/series/RAIRESP

Lagging Regions in the European Union

Structural, Productivity and Efficiency Aspects

Paweł Dobrzański

Routledge
Taylor & Francis Group
LONDON AND NEW YORK

First published 2025
by Routledge
4 Park Square, Milton Park, Abingdon, Oxon OX14 4RN

and by Routledge
605 Third Avenue, New York, NY 10158

Routledge is an imprint of the Taylor & Francis Group, an informa business

British Library Cataloguing-in-Publication Data
A catalogue record for this book is available from the British Library

Library of Congress Cataloging-in-Publication Data
Names: Dobrzański, Paweł, author.
Title: Lagging regions in the European Union : structural, productivity and efficiency aspects / Paweł Dobrzański.
Description: Abingdon, Oxon ; New York, NY : Routledge, 2025. | Series: Routledge advances in regional economics, science and policy | Includes bibliographical references and index.
Identifiers: LCCN 2024021774 (print) | LCCN 2024021775 (ebook) | ISBN 9781032615462 (hardback) | ISBN 9781032615493 (paperback) | ISBN 9781032615516 (ebook)
Subjects: LCSH: Regional economic disparities—European Union countries. | European Union countries—Economic conditions—Regional disparities. | European Union countries—Economic policy. | European Union countries—Social policy.
Classification: LCC HC241.2 .D55 2025 (print) | LCC HC241.2 (ebook) | DDC 337.1/42—dc23/eng/20240709
LC record available at https://lccn.loc.gov/2024021774
LC ebook record available at https://lccn.loc.gov/2024021775

ISBN: 978-1-032-61546-2 (hbk)
ISBN: 978-1-032-61549-3 (pbk)
ISBN: 978-1-032-61551-6 (ebk)

DOI: 10.4324/9781032615516

Typeset in Times New Roman
by codeMantra

Contents

Figures

Tables

Appendices

About the author

Paweł Dobrzański is an Associate Professor of Economics and a Faculty Member in the Department of Mathematical Economics at Wrocław University of Economics and Business (WUEB), Wrocław, Poland, as well as a Past Visiting Scholar with the Department of Land Economy at the University of Cambridge, UK, and a Past and Current Visiting Scholar with the Minda de Gunzburg Center for European Studies (CES) at Harvard University, USA. He graduated with a master's degree in Economics and Administration from the Faculty of Law, Administration and Economics at the University of Wrocław. He is a member of Regional Studies Association (RSA), the Center for Research in Global Business, Economics, International Development and Social Movements (CEDIMES) and the Editorial Board of the Proceedings of Rijeka Faculty of Economics: *Journal of Economics and Business*. He has authored and co-authored over 50 research papers in Polish, English, French and Russian, published in journals such as *Cambridge Journal of Regions, Economy and Society* (Oxford University Press) and *Applied Economics* (Taylor & Francis).

Professor Paweł Dobrzański has carried out many research projects. He was a project lead at the National Science Center (NCN) and five other projects funded by the Ministry of Science and Higher Education, and a contractor on the international Ekonomski Fakultet U Rijeci & Sveučilište U Rijeci (EFRI&UNIRI) project.

His research has been presented in 63 international conferences in the USA, Canada, Singapore, France, Italy, Russia, Ukraine, Austria, Croatia, Latvia, Czechia, Slovenia and others. He has moderated seven panels, including at the Western Economic Association International (WEAI) and CEDIMES conferences in the USA. Paweł Dobrzański has completed many research internships at well-known foreign universities, including Visiting Scholar at the CES (USA); Visiting Scholar at the University of Cambridge (UK); Post-doc at Université de Laval (Canada); Visiting Scholar at the State University of New York (USA); Post-doc at Université de Bordeaux (France); Post-doc at the CEDIMES Institute (Paris, France); and Post-doc at Université Paris Dauphine (France).

He has received 25 outstanding scientific awards. These include the Scholarship of the Minister of Science and Higher Education for Outstanding Young Researchers in 2019, which is the most important award for young scientists in Poland; the CEDIMES Institute's award for the best PhD dissertation in 2015 ('Efficiency and competitiveness of market economies: USA, Japan and Germany', written under the supervision of Full Professor Leon Olszewski); the 'Iuvenes Wratislaviae' Award of the Wrocław Branch of the Polish Academy of Sciences in 2018 for outstanding scientific or artistic achievement; the Award for the best presentation at the International Conference 'Innovation economics / Big data in business and economics' in Opatija, Croatia; numerous Rector's Awards from Wrocław University of Economics and Business for scientific and research achievements; and a teaching award based on student surveys with a congratulatory letter from the Dean of the University of Economics in Wrocław in 2019.

His primary research interests lie in regional development, economic growth, productivity, dominant and left-behind regions, effectiveness, international competitiveness, inequality, the automotive industry and innovation.

Acknowledgements

My first debt is to my long-time mentor, Professor Leon Olszewski (University of Wrocław), for his substantive support and the hundreds, if not thousands, of hours spent on scientific projects and articles – also for pointing out good directions for the development of my scientific career.

I thank the Minda de Gunzburg Center for European Studies (CES) at Harvard University for allowing me to do a Research Internship as a Visiting Scholar on Left-behind regions in the European Union. In particular, I thank Laura Falloon, Program Coordinator at CES, Dr. Albana Shehaj, Program Manager at CES, and Directors Professor Daniel Ziblatt (Harvard University), Elaine Papoulias (Harvard University), and Professor Grzegorz Ekiert (Harvard University). In addition, I thank all CES Visiting Scholars for their valuable comments and support, especially Dr. Ayca Arkilic (Victoria University of Wellington) and Professor Spyros Economides (London School of Economics and Political Science). I also thank Professor Edward Glaeser (Chair of the Department of Economics, Harvard University) for providing constructive comments whilst chairing the New Research on Europe Seminar at CES. Special thanks to Professor Robert J. Barro (Harvard University) for his substantive support and intellectual stimulus and advice during my stay at Harvard University. Lastly, I thank Professor Dani Rodrik (Harvard University) for the constructive discussion about productivity, which has outlined interesting new research areas for me.

I also feel grateful to Professor Peter Tyler (University of Cambridge), Professor Philip Arestis (University of Cambridge) and Professor Alan Barrell (Cambridge Innovation Academy, Cambridge Learning Gateway) for hosting me at the University of Cambridge as a Visiting Scholar in 2019. This research stay was a career breakthrough for me and helped me develop in my research work. In addition, it inspired me to conduct research about regional inequality.

In addition, I feel grateful to Kristina Abbotts, Senior Editor, Economics, Finance and Accounting in Routledge (Taylor & Francis), and Christiana Mandizha, Editorial Assistant, Economics in Routledge (Taylor & Francis), for all the support at every stage of creating the book. It's hard to find someone as supportive as them. The author is also grateful to two referees for their constructive comments and suggestions and to Eric Hilton, who did the language proofreading for my book.

I also feel grateful to Professor Sebastian Bobowski from Wrocław University of Economics and Business (Poland) and Dr. Karenjit Clare form the University of Cambridge (UK) for their helpful comments and suggestions – and for taking the time to prepare joint scientific articles, which support the development of my scientific career.

I thank Professor Bogusława Drelich-Skulska, Professor Ewa Stańczyk-Hugiet, Professor Maria Piotrowska and Professor Bogusław Fiedor from Wrocław University of Economics and Business (Poland) for supporting my projects, and Ewelina Turlej-Szyjka, Beata Bielecka, Joanna Marcinkowska and Justyna Morawska-Ploskonka for all their help since the beginning of my work at the university.

I am grateful to Professor Zhan Su (Laval University, Canada) and Professor Elie Chrysostome (Ivey Business School at Western University [Canada]; State University of New York [USA]) for giving me the opportunity to do research in the USA and Canada and for their valuable lessons, which strongly influenced my scientific career. Likewise, I thank Professor Sasa Drezgic (University of Rijeka), Emil Velinov (Skoda Auto University) and Igor Cvecic (University of Rijeka) for allowing me to do joint research at the international level.

Finally, I would like to acknowledge with gratitude the support and love of my family – my wife Elizabeth, my daughters Natalie and Alice, my parents Barbara and Wladyslaw and my brother Raphael. They all kept me going, and this book would not have been written without them.

Selected abbreviations

CEE	Central Eastern Europe
CF	Cohesion Fund
COMPET	Competitiveness Council
COVID-19	Coronavirus disease
CRII	Coronavirus Response Investment Initiative
CRS	Constant returns to scale
DEA	Data envelopment analysis
DMU	Decision-making units
EAFRD	European Agricultural Fund for Rural Development
EaSI	EU Programme for Employment and Social Innovation
EEC	European Economic Community
EMFAF	European Maritime, Fisheries and Aquaculture Fund
ERDF	European Regional Development Fund
ESF	European Social Fund
ESIF	European Structural and Investment Funds
EU	European Union
EUR	Euro
FEAD	Fund for European Aid to the Most Deprived
FDI	Foreign direct investment
FIFG	Financial Instrument for Fisheries Guidance
GDP	Gross domestic product
GNI	Gross national income
GVA	Gross value added
HDI	Human Development Index
IT	Information technology
JTF	Just Transition Fund
MPI	Multidimensional Poverty Index
NACE	Nomenclature of Economic Activities
NUTS	Nomenclature of Territorial Units for Statistics
PO	Programming objective
PPP	Purchasing power parity
PPS	Purchasing power standard
RCI	Regional Competitiveness Index

R&D	Research and development
RDPs	Rural development programmes
REACT-EU	Recovery Assistance for Cohesion and the Territories of Europe
SEA	Single European Act
SME	Small and medium-sized enterprises
TAI	Technological Achievement Index
TEN-T	Trans-European Transport Network
UK	United Kingdom
VRS	Variable returns to scale
WEF	World Economic Forum
YEI	Youth Employment Initiative

Introduction

Unequal distribution of income is one of the most important socio-economic issues. The processes of globalisation and integration are accelerating economic growth; however, at the same time, imbalances between regions may grow. Reducing inequalities within regions and national economies, as well as around the world, is important for individual and societal well-being and cohesion, and for effective state policies. The subject of this monograph belongs to the economics growth studies, and, more specifically, it is related to development at the regional level. The analysis focusses primarily on lagging European Union (EU) regions. The monograph also addresses structural and productivity changes and the efficiency of EU regional funds.

The main objective of the analysis is to identify left-behind regions in EU countries and to analyse the structural and productivity changes within them. The aim is to verify the research hypothesis, which states that lagging regions have similar economic structures with a high share of agriculture. Another hypothesis is that EU regional funds are spent inefficiently, so an increase in funds does not produce proportional productivity growth in the region. The research period covers 2000–2020 using data from the Eurostat database.

The primary goals of this monograph are as follows:

- establish comparative characteristics of the European regions in terms of productivity and economic structure
- identify lagging regions throughout the EU and analyse the relationship between economic structure and productivity growth with shift-share analysis
- analyse convergence processes within EU regions
- assess the EU's regional policy in supporting the development of left-behind regions
- validate whether subsidising economic activity within lagging regions is the right approach
- systematise and update the research concerning the problem of regional imbalances in different research streams.

Therefore, the monograph is divided into five chapters.

DOI: 10.4324/9781032615516-1

Chapter 1 describes the essentials of the theory for regional imbalances and convergence. The starting point for the research is understanding the different theories of regional disparities, e.g. growth pole theory, core and periphery model, cumulative causation model, Hirschman's model, etc. I also focus on different criteria for identifying lagging regions and discuss the problem of measuring regional disparities.

In Chapter 2, a comparative analysis is carried out for the EU countries and regions to determine their inequality. The comparative analysis is supplemented with descriptive statistics methods. Such an analysis can indicate similarities and differences between European countries. This research is also supplemented with an examination of competitiveness and findings from the literature regarding imbalances in the EU.

In Chapter 3, I describe the evolution of the EU's regional policy and its main objectives and instruments. I also discuss the functioning of the European Regional Development Fund, Cohesion Fund and European Social Fund. In the last section of this chapter, I present achievements in the implementation of the EU's regional policy in recent years.

I analyse the structural and productivity changes in the left-behind EU regions in Chapter 4. In the first phase, I analyse employment, GVA and productivity data for 1,166 EU NUTS 3 regions. Left-behind regions are defined as those with low productivity and growth rates. The analysis identified 30 regions with the worst productivity per employee in 2020 and 21 regions that recorded a decline in productivity per employee in the study period. The analysis answered whether all left-behind regions in the EU have similar economic structures.

Finally, Chapter 5 assesses the effectiveness of EU policy in the left-behind regions in order to verify whether EU funds have been spent efficiently and whether there is a positive correlation between increased funds and regional development indicators. Effectiveness is measured using the data envelopment analysis (DEA) methodology. The input indicators are the EU funds received by the region, while the output indicators are key statistics related to the level of development and standard of living in EU regions.

Paweł Dobrzański

1 Regional imbalances – left-behind places

1.1 Theories of regional disproportions

The inequality theory explains why there are areas of poverty and backwardness with no prospects for development – and at the other extreme, areas of increasing wealth. Some theories of regional imbalances clearly emphasise root causes and development factors, while others focus on the interrelationships between regions and the economic environment. Theoretical achievements in regional development are the basis for numerous publications explaining regional disproportions in development, their genesis and the possibilities of levelling out the differences.

Various global and country- or region-specific factors, which reinforce each other, have been proposed in theory and the empirical literature to explain regional inequality. The main root causes affecting regional disparities are shown in Table 1.1.

Landes (1998) includes territorial expansion and access to rare resources among the root causes of inequality, between both countries and regions. Expansion means an armed invasion, usually short term at first and consisting of annexing everything of any value and retreating to one's own country. Over time, territorial expansion began to take the form of occupying the seized territory and systematically exploiting it economically. The main risk of this form of wealth building was that the wealth seized from conquered territories discouraged self-construction of wealth. Another cause of wealth creation and, thus, of inequality, which is more relevant to our times is access to specific, usually scarce resources. These are inequalities which nature itself creates. It is not just about access to natural resources, as with oil-rich countries. Landes (1998) also points to the example of the United States, which developed rapidly in the 19th century, having unlimited resources for two basic factors of production: land and cheap labour constantly flowing from Europe. The third factor, capital, was beginning to shape the stock of wealth.

In the 20th century, and especially the second half, another factor appeared and shaped the global structure of wealth and poverty. This factor was and still is technical progress (Fagerberg, 1994). It also allowed those who had almost no natural resources to join the world's wealth elite, as exemplified by Japan. Traditional economic theory holds that specialisation is beneficial because it leads to a more efficient use of available resources. However, Fagerberg (2001) points

DOI: 10.4324/9781032615516-2

Table 1.1 Root causes of regional disparities

Global factors	*Country- or region-specific factors*
Technological progress	Access to resources
Globalisation	Wealth from territorial expansion
Commodity price cycles	Government policy

Source: Author's own elaboration based on literature review

out that it will only lead to higher growth in the long run if it positively affects technological progress. What is important for growth and competitiveness is not an overall increase in specialisation but the ability to take advantage of areas of strong technological opportunity (Begg et al., 1999). The slow growth is mainly due to the inability to take advantage of the technological opportunities inherent in new and rapidly evolving technologies. The main problem is not the absence of competition in the production of computers or other products that integrate information and communication technologies but the development of new technologies throughout society. Regional disparities have been exacerbated by the highly unequal diffusion of new technologies that have hitherto disproportionately favoured high-income, research-intensive and highly developed areas that specialise in high-tech manufacturing and, above all, in the service sector. In contrast, traditional agricultural regions or regions in the Rust Belt have benefited little. To benefit from technological progress achievements, it is necessary to constantly invest and conduct extensive research, which is only affordable for some regions or countries. Therefore, technical progress inevitably leads to the emergence of centres of wealth and poverty, i.e. it creates and perpetuates inequalities.

Another factor that appeared in the second half of the 20th century, creating inequalities, is globalisation. The integration of economic activities in the world through the development of international trade and investment is certainly one of the most important trends in the modern global economy. From one perspective, globalisation is generally anticipated to alleviate poverty through accelerated expansion in more interconnected economies. Developing countries have faced fierce international competition with other countries since the 1980s, when almost all countries began to participate in the globalisation process. Wood (1998) claims that this falsifies the predictions of international trade theory. Lee (2014) concludes that historical events and empirical research show that the growth impacts of globalisation, particularly financial globalisation, are inconsistent. Globalisation may exacerbate income inequality through various means. The expansion of outsourcing, increased trade in intermediate products and a rapid rise in FDI could heighten income inequality in advanced nations. Globalisation could also lead to higher income inequality in developing nations through various mechanisms, such as disparities in initial resources and the negative consequences of financial instability. Feenstra (2007) concentrates on the initial resource differences associated with global outsourcing and the trade in intermediate goods. Higher skilled and more prosperous workers in developing countries produce goods previously produced by low-skilled workers in developed countries. Thus, the growth of international trade and outsourcing may exacerbate the situation of low-skilled workers in developed countries – and vice versa for highly skilled workers in developing countries – leading to increased income inequality in both countries. However, it is important to recognise that although globalisation's effects on distribution may differ, they rather depend on various factors, such as education and institutional initiatives.

Mohtadi and Castells-Quintana (2021) investigated the relation between changes in international commodity prices and the evolution of income inequality. A high dependence on natural resources can slow down structural change and hamper economic development. Commodity price shocks affect income inequality. However, the impact depends on the type of commodity, with non-agricultural (capital-intensive) price shocks increasing inequality more significantly. Mohtadi and Castells-Quintana also note heterogeneity between countries: the inequality-enhancing effects of non-agricultural price shocks are most felt in countries with high initial inequality and low institutional quality. Agricultural (labour-intensive) price shocks reduce wage inequality, while non-agricultural (capital-intensive) price shocks increase capital income inequality. As international commodity prices have shown great volatility in recent decades, it is important for policymakers to understand how changes in different prices can have different effects, including on the internal distribution of income.

Institutional theories (Powell & DiMaggio, 1991) draw attention to the fact that institutions can steer the economy in a way that uses and develops its resources. Where institutional capacity is unevenly distributed in space, the institutional factor contributes to the agglomeration of economic activity, strengthening the concentration of more advanced activities in the most developed areas. According to Stiglitz (2015), the weakness of the political system has a significant impact on increasing inequalities. The growth in inequality is mainly a result of the actions of governments, economic players and institutions. The changes that have taken place in the last decades of the market economy assumed that lowering taxes would liberalise the economy and stimulate economic growth. However, such a decision leads to greater inequality. According to Stiglitz, we can still reverse this course by changing the rules with more investment in public goods, better corporate governance, antitrust and anti-discrimination laws, a better regulated financial system, stronger workers' rights and more progressive tax and transfer policies. The economy must be restructured to restore fairer conditions and to run the Fourth Industrial Revolution in a more sustainable way, distributing or redistributing the benefits of technology and avoiding an increase in inequality.

There is no single theory that explains the occurrence of regional disparities. From the classical economic point of view, market forces automatically lead to equilibrium. Adam Smith, the father of modern economics, is often seen as having a positive view of economic inequality and being more interested in reducing absolute poverty than inequality. He believed that the flows of factors/market forces will automatically lead to equilibrium, and he argued that labour will move from the low-wage sector (migrants) to the high-wage sector, while capital will flow in the opposite direction (Smith, 2012). According to Walraevens (2021), Smith's view of economic inequality is concerned more with the causes of inequality than with its magnitude. The system of natural freedoms and its sustained economic growth will lead to low levels of economic inequality and more efficiency and equity. This benefits the poor by increasing wages and providing them with a decent standard of living. It also provides greater social mobility, independence and equal opportunity for the poor by eliminating barriers to the free movement of labour and education. Wage and profit inequalities are 'natural', 'fair' and essential to the economy and to the dynamism and progress of society because they reward individual effort, talent, education, innovation and risk-taking. The state's direct and substantial redistribution of income and wealth is not necessary to achieve the 'right' level of economic inequality.

Holland (1976) emphasises that many factors that were later included in the theory of regional imbalances of the Myrdal and Perroux type were anticipated by Marx. In general, from the Marxist point of view, regional disparity is a characteristic feature of capitalism. It is exacerbated by competition and the goal of maximising production profit through private ownership of the means of production. One of the key factors that Marx recognised was the degree of spatial concentration of production in regions, which was not primarily due to resource deposits or the need to reduce transport costs, but due to sectoral concentration of production. Marx also drew attention to the labour displacement introduced by large-scale machine production in the capitalist system. Furthermore, Marx also pointed out that the modern capitalist industry creates jobs by opening new global markets for raw materials and finished products and by promoting the demand for labour to create new infrastructure. Marx highlights labour transfer from the countryside to the city in his general explanation of economic history. He sees in it a spatial basis for the division of labour, upon which progress in the efficiency of the means of production is based.

The extant literature on the theory of regional imbalances emphasises the interrelationships between regions. The theory of growth poles by Perroux (1955) explains why economic development occurs differently in each region. Perroux assumes the existence of a spatial imbalance that accompanies economic growth. The emerging economic growth in each region must lead to an imbalance in other regions. The dominant region may sometimes influence the neighbouring areas, but can also cause the opposite effects, contributing to stagnation or recession. According to this theory, economic development is polarised, meaning that due to development forces, economic activity becomes concentrated and growth and imbalances occur between geographical areas. The dominant region modifies the structure of the surrounding regions. The result of its impact is regionally diverse in terms of population, innovation and the institutions present in a given territorial system.

Myrdal (1957), the founder of the regional polarisation theory, distinguished the interaction between more developed regions and underdeveloped regions as either positive (spreading or trickle-down effects) or negative (polarised or backwash effects). The level of differences in development between regions is determined by positive or negative development effects in their centres. If the desired effects of the economic activity in the centres are transferred to the periphery, spreading development occurs. Consequences of the backwash effect will be migration between cities and the countryside, cumulative development in centres, etc. Myrdal was convinced that the effects of individual cumulative mechanisms are related and lead to a growth spiral, i.e. the outflow of growth sources (capital and labour) from underdeveloped to more developed regions. Because of economic, social, political and cultural factors, a diversification between regions can be indicated: rich areas develop faster and underdeveloped ones become stagnant.

Hirschman (1958) pointed out that spatially balanced development is impossible to achieve in practice, although sometimes there is a spread of growth from centres to neighbouring areas. Hirschman stated that economic growth does not occur everywhere at the same time. Once development starts, powerful forces create a spatial concentration of economic activity and development of the regions, which have initial advantages. Hirschman's economic transmission theory is similar to Myrdal's cumulative causal theory. The transmission of economic growth takes place and can be explained by the trickle-down and polarisation effects. A trickle-down effect refers to transmitting goods and services from the centre to the periphery. A polarising effect refers to transmitting goods and services from the periphery to the centre. Polarising effects can be positive or negative on peripheral development. However, despite many similarities with Myrdal's theory of the economic growth process, Hirschman's theory is fundamentally different. Hirschman argues that growth is inherently unbalanced and a natural part of the growth process. To him, natural resources are unevenly distributed, and some places are rich in resources, while others have little. Growth only starts in some resource-rich regions that are well located. Hirschman argues that once growth begins at the centre, its benefits flow down to the periphery. Flow also leads to the growth and development of the periphery. Here, Hirschman argues against Myrdal that this trickling is automatic and that the government should not interfere in the growth process because the income trajectories of developed and underdeveloped regions will eventually converge.

Friedmann (1967), in his core–periphery model, underscores the social aspect of the growing regional differences. Centres, creating the investment climate, stimulate the development of modern systems of innovation and R&D centres, and through them it is possible to increase per capita income despite increasing population density. Therefore, in centres, a cumulative process of growth and development can be observed, for which the peripheral regions cannot keep up in the short term. In the long term, however, the core region expands the demand for raw materials and labour force to the periphery. Exceeding the absorption capacity of the core region leads to new economic capacities being located in the peripheral regions. The periphery can become a part of the core or it can arrange concentrated service activities for companies from the core region. Although various theories describe interactions between regions, these theories do not specifically define the left-behind regions or any criteria for identifying them.

According to the theory of endogenous growth (Romer, 1986; Lucas, 1988; Grossman & Helpman, 1991), the concentration of human capital and research and development takes place in central, not peripheral areas, and is the result of integration processes. The degree of concentration of economic activity is associated with an increase in the economies of scale. Models, including those based on innovations such as Schumpeter's growth theory, take into account effective, adaptive changes, and, to a much lesser extent, match optimal allocations from specific locations, with a focus on integration and trade. Therefore, economic growth at the regional level is based on the reinforcement of the labour-responsive process of innovative learning/knowledge assimilation.

1.2 Convergence

Section 1.1 identified the main causes and theories of inequality between countries and regions. The next question that arises is whether inequalities between regions can decrease. How quickly does this catching-up process take place? Or will backward regions stay behind forever? Convergence theories provide answers to these questions.

The convergence hypothesis has been present in growth theories since the 1950s, but intensive research in this field only developed in the 1990s. Initially, convergence resulted from the neoclassical growth theory and was understood as economies levelling up per capita production levels. The main assumptions of these theories were the decreasing marginal productivity of capital per capita and the exogenous nature of technological progress. Capital accumulation was the main factor causing the convergence of various economies, while any influence of technological progress on the convergence process was excluded (Solow, 1956). In the 1960s, Hagen (1962), Schulz (1962) and Lewis (1966), among others, noticed that the accumulation of physical capital is an insufficient factor for economic development. Their work showed that the effectiveness of using the components of physical capital depends on equipping employees with knowledge and qualifications, i.e. with so-called human capital. Becker's theory of human capital (1975) and the later work of Romer (1986) and Lucas (1988), which constituted the endogenous direction of research on economic growth, made a special contribution to the dissemination of the important role of the human capital factor in economic growth and development. Endogenous growth models explain that human capital has a stronger impact on the growth rate and its convergence in the long run than the stock of physical capital. Human capital directly and indirectly affects economic growth by accumulating other growth factors, i.e. physical capital and technical progress. The human factor is also credited with effects on economic structural and demographic changes.

The approach to convergence popularised in the economic literature since the 1980s stems from the achievements of the theory of economic growth. The main message of the precursors of the neoclassical theory was to eliminate the instability of the process of bringing the economy towards sustainable growth. In turn, the creators of endogenous growth sought to capture the theoretical mechanisms responsible for widening the income gap between economies moving towards and along the path of sustainable growth. The assumptions of the Solow (1956) growth model treat the convergence of the economy on the path of economic growth as a matter of time. Regardless of the initial conditions, the economy will strive to achieve a constant growth rate that corresponds to sustainable development. Moreover, in the long term, all countries will follow a common, sustainable path. In turn, Ramsey's neoclassical model made it possible to lead the mechanism of moving the economy to new paths of sustainable growth. Differences in the output level per employee between countries result from different structural parameters of the economies; hence, countries follow different economic growth paths (Newbery, 1990). On the other hand, endogenous growth, contrary to the conclusions of neoclassical growth models, suggests that convergence between poor and rich countries may not occur. While these models explain the mechanisms of the economy shifting to a higher individual sustainable growth path with higher outputs and per capita income, they do not describe the catching-up mechanism. This applies, in particular, to the models based on increasing marginal benefits resulting from the factors of production, mainly human capital, knowledge and technology. Models assuming multiple paths of sustainable growth prove that countries with different initial levels of human capital, knowledge and technology will show convergence in the growth rate of these resources, but cannot equalise their levels (Caballe & Santos, 1993).

Sala-i-Martin (1990) presented two concepts of convergence in his doctoral dissertation: sigma convergence and beta convergence. Sigma convergence occurs when the dispersion of per capita income (or another phenomenon under study) between regions or countries decreases over time. Beta convergence occurs when poor economies/regions grow faster than rich ones. Beta convergence can be additionally described as unconditional (absolute) or conditional convergence. Unconditional convergence assumes that countries (or regions) become similar regardless of initial conditions. Poor areas record a faster growth rate than rich ones, and the lower their initial gross domestic product (GDP) per capita, the greater the growth of their real GDP per capita. Therefore, poorer countries or regions catch up in terms of development. Conditional convergence means that those with similar structural parameters become similar, and thus, those with different characteristics converge to different long-term income levels. Baumol et al. (1994) suggest that there may exist a 'club of convergence', i.e. a subset of converging countries, while countries outside the 'club' do not necessarily converge. Only countries with sufficient initial human capital can leverage modern technology to exploit the potential for converged growth.

Barro and Sala-i-Martin (2004) emphasised that explaining convergence is a prerequisite for keeping a given theory or model of economic growth up to date. Therefore, in the literature, there are many empirical studies dealing with convergence issues using different empirical approaches. A summary of selected studies on convergence in European regions can be found in Table 1.2.

The beta convergence framework is used especially often. Beta convergence was introduced to empirical studies by Barro and Sala-i-Martin (1991), who analysed a sample of 73 Western European regions over the period 1950–1985. They estimated that beta convergence was roughly 2% a year for 35 years. Armstrong (2005) tested a sample of 85 European Union (EU) regions from 1950 to 1990 and found that between-country absolute convergence was about 1% per year. Cuadrado-Roura (2001) and López-Bazo (2003) examined the absolute beta

Table 1.2 Literature review of studies about convergence

Author/year	*Type of convergence*	*Period*	*Sample*	*Indicator*	*Convergence Yes/No*	*Main findings*
Barro and Sala-i-Martin (1991)	Beta, sigma	1950–1985	73 Western European regions	GDP per capita	Yes	Convergence at a speed of 2% per year. Poorer regions within a country tend to grow faster than richer regions.
Armstrong (2005)	Beta	1950–1990	85 EU regions	GDP per capita	Yes	Convergence at a speed of 1% per year. He pointed out that the results depended on the selected data set.
Cuadrado-Roura (2001)	Beta	1977–1994	107 EU regions	GDP per capita and GDP per worker	Yes	Convergence at a speed of less than 2% per year. Regions with lower initial levels of GDP per capita tend to grow faster than regions with higher GDP per capita. There are national and differential effects.
López-Bazo (2003)	Beta	1975–1996	108 EU regions	GDP per capita and GDP per worker	Yes	Convergence at a speed of less than 2% per year. A reduction in speed was observed during the study period.
Martin (2001)	Beta	1975–1998	195 EU regions	GVA per worker	Yes	Worker productivity shows weak convergence, while regional employment growth was sharply divergent. The convergence rate was diminishing.
Fagerberg and Verspagen (1996)	Beta	1950–1990	70 EU regions	GDP per capita	Yes	The convergence rate was diminishing. They also found some support for the idea of a 'Europe at different speeds', with at least three different 'growth clubs' characterised by different dynamics, productivity and unemployment levels.

Yin et al. (2003)	Beta, sigma	1960–1995	EU15 countries	GDP per capita	Yes	The empirical findings support the hypothesis of economic convergence within the EU except for the 1980–1985 sub-period, where weak divergence was indicated.
Niebuhr and Schlitte (2004)	Beta, sigma	1950–1995	EU25 and EU15 countries	GDP per capita	Yes	There was a pronounced decline in disparities between new and old Member States since the mid-1990s. A high convergence rate marked the second half of the 1990s.
Geppert et al. (2005)	Beta	1980–2000	167 EU regions	GDP per capita	Yes	The process of convergence was interrupted in the first half of the 1980s but regained strength thereafter.
Neven and Goymte (1995)	Beta, sigma	1975–1989	107 northern and southern European regions	GDP per capita	Yes, but not in all regions and periods	There are strong differences in the pattern of convergence across sub-periods and across subsets of regions. If the south of Europe seemed to catch up in the early 1980s, it stagnated, at best, in the second part of the decade. At the opposite end, the regions in the north of Europe tended to stagnate or diverge in the first part of the 1980s but to converge strongly thereafter.
Baumont et al. (2003)	Beta; Convergence club	1980–1995	138 EU regions	GDP per capita	Yes, but not in all regions and periods	There is no beta convergence process for northern regions, and only a weak one for southern regions. Using spatial econometric tools has helped to integrate predictions from ‘new’ economic geography theory, leading to the estimation of a spatial spillover effect in the framework of spatial convergence clubs. This effect appeared to be enormously significant.

(Continued)

Table 1.2 (Continued)

Author/year	*Type of convergence*	*Period*	*Sample*	*Indicator*	*Convergence Yes/No*	*Main findings*
Olejnik (2008)	Beta	2004	228 EU NUTS 3 regions	GDP per capita	Yes	The levels of per capita income in the neighbouring regions positively influence the level in a given location. A presence of spatial convergence forces in the European economic system was noted.
Tselois (2009)	Beta	1995–2000	102 regions	GDP per capita	Yes	The results reveal the presence of conditional convergence in income per capita after controlling for educational attainment, unemployment, sectoral composition, spatially lagged growth of income per capita, regional fixed effects and unconditional convergence in income inequality.
Azomahou et al. (2011)	Beta	1998–2007	255 EU regions	GDP per capita	Yes for medium-income regions No for high-income and low-income countries	The estimation results indicate both country heterogeneity and nonlinearity in the convergence process. The findings suggest that low-income regions, particularly those from new adhesion countries, diverge while medium-income regions converge. There is no evidence of convergence for high-income regions.
Petrakos et al. (2011)	Beta	1990–2003	249 NUTS 3 regions	GDP per capita	Yes, at earlier levels of development	A mirror-image, J-shaped relationship was detected between regional growth and regional development levels. This type of relationship indicates that regional divergence factors are getting stronger and will eventually dominate at more advanced levels of development.

Hegerty (2016)	Beta	2000–2013	233 NUTS 3 regions	GVA per capita	No	A regression of growth in per capita gross value added (GVA) based on initial levels indicated no evidence for beta convergence, except for in the construction sector at the country level in a few cases.
Boldrin and Canova (2001)	Beta, Sigma	1980–1996	EU15 (185/101 regions)	GDP per capita, labour productivity	No	The results are mixed, but certainly not supportive of β-convergence for regional per capita income and clear sigma convergence. Strong phenomena of either divergence or convergence are not taking place. The data do not suggest that further polarisation and increasing inequality are occurring.
Fingleton (2003)	Sigma	1987–1997	200 EU regions	GDP per capita	Yes	There were slightly reducing inter-regional disparities. If we look at the PPS-adjusted series, following the peak of 1990, there has been a reduction in dispersion but no evidence of convergence post 1992. The Gini coefficient series are remarkably similar, with the exception that ongoing convergence is more evident through 1997 for the PPS data. The inter-quartile range for the unadjusted series provides only limited evidence of a systematic convergence process and follows a fairly uneven path.
Barrios and Strobl (2005)	Sigma	1975–2000	EU15	GDP per capita	No	Regional inequalities inevitably rise as economic development proceeds, but then tend to decline once a certain level of national economic development is reached.

(Continued)

Table 1.2 (Continued)

Author/year	*Type of convergence*	*Period*	*Sample*	*Indicator*	*Convergence Yes/No*	*Main findings*
Cappelen et al. (2003)	Sigma	1980–1997	163 NUTS 2 regions	GDP per capita	No	To the extent that there has been any tendency towards convergence, it has been at the country level, related to the catching-up of the relatively poor southern countries that joined the community during the 1980s. Within countries, however, there has at best been a standstill, if not divergence.
Ertur et al. (2006)	Convergence club	1980–1995	138 EU regions	GDP per capita	Yes	The estimation of the appropriate spatial error model shows that the convergence process is different across regimes. The authors also estimate a strongly significant spatial spillover effect: the average growth rate of per capita GDP of a given region is positively affected by the average growth rate of neighbouring regions.
Canova (2004)	Convergence club	1980–1992	144 EU regions	GDP per capita	Yes	There are heterogeneities in European regional per capita income and a tendency of the steady-state distribution to cluster around four poles of attraction characterised by different dynamics, different posterior mean steady states and different mobility features.

Corrado et al. (2005)	Convergence club	1975–1999	77 NUTS 1 regions	GVA per capita	Yes	The results suggest that processes of regional convergence across the EU are complex and vary over time. All four analysed sectors (agriculture, manufacturing, market services and non-market services) revealed quite large numbers of regional convergence clusters, suggesting that there is no single EU-wide convergence process, but rather different convergence paths in different economic sectors and different parts of the EU.
Le Gallo and Dall'erba (2006)	Convergence club	1980–1999	145 EU regions	GDP per capita	Yes	The assumption of temporal independence between two sub-periods is rejected, and the estimation results points to the presence of spatial error autocorrelation in both sub-periods and spatial instability in the second sub-period, indicating the formation of a convergence club between the peripheral regions of the European Union.
Alcidi (2019)	Beta, sigma	2000–2015	EU28 countries and NUTS 2 regions	GDP per capita	Yes in the case of counties No in the case of regions	First, there was a strong convergence since the turn of the century across Member States, which is essentially driven by East–West dynamics. Second, many southern regions struggled or failed to keep pace with the rest of the EU. In the case of southeastern countries, a very strong internal income divergence was noted across the regions: capital regions outperformed the rest of the country.

(*Continued*)

Table 1.2 (Continued)

Author/year	*Type of convergence*	*Period*	*Sample*	*Indicator*	*Convergence Yes/No*	*Main findings*
Cabral and Castellanos-Sosa (2019)	Beta	1973–2012	EU25	GDP per capita	Yes	The results show that the global financial crisis has brought a greater absolute convergence rate rather than divergence, has affected richer members more heavily and, presumably, has allowed less developed members to recover more quickly. Evidence was found that creating the European Union has contributed towards economic growth and convergence. Meanwhile, no similar evidence was found concerning the European Monetary Union.
Glawe and Wagner (2021)	Convergence club	2002–2018	EU27	GDP per capita	Yes	Both income and institutional convergence clubs are formed, mainly based on the geographic region. Northern and western European countries are typically in the higher institutional/income clubs, whereas the lower institutional/income clubs comprise primarily eastern and southern European countries.

Source: Author's own elaboration based on literature review

convergence for EU12 regions for the periods 1977–1994 and 1975–1996. They used the income per capita of EU regions and concluded that a low absolute convergence rate was observed for these economies, which is slower than 2% yearly. They also found that regions with an initial value below the average income per capita tended to have an above-average growth rate. Moreover, the convergence rate was diminishing, which was also reported in other empirical studies by Martin (2001) and Fagerberg and Verspagen (1996). A diminishing convergence rate was not confirmed in studies by Yin et al. (2003), Niebuhr and Schlitte (2004) or Geppert et al. (2005), who stated that convergence speed is U-shaped, with the minimum values corresponding to the beginning of the 1980s. A study by Neven and Goymte (1995) conducted separate estimations for 107 northern and southern European regions for the period 1980–1988. They indicated that if country-specific variables are not included in the equations, neither group could demonstrate a significant convergence rate. The same was confirmed in a study by Baumont et al. (2003) for northern European regions from 1980 to 1995. Olejnik (2008) used a spatial autoregressively distributed lag model for 228 EU NUTS 3 regions only for one year, 2004. Tselois (2009) analysed 102 regions from 1995 to 2000 and estimated an expanded model, including spatial effects. His study confirmed convergence in income per capita in the region. Azomahou et al. (2011) analysed 255 EU regions in a semiparametric analysis for the period 1998–2007 and noticed that richer and poorer regions exhibited different convergence processes. Petrakos et al. (2011) applied the techniques of linear and non-linear ordinary least squares (OLS) and weighted least squares (WLS) to test regional convergence models for 249 NUTS 3 regions from 1990 to 2003. The main conclusion from their research is that convergence occurs at an early stage of development and divergence at a later stage of development. A study by Hegerty (2016) tested 233 NUTS 3 regions and four sectors using spatial statistical methods from 2000 to 2013. A standard regression of GVA growth on initial levels found no evidence of beta convergence. Alcidi (2019) analysed beta convergence for EU28 Member States for the period 2000–2015 and confirmed the hypothesis of β-convergence. Analyses for NUTS 2 regions paint a different picture. Many southern regions in both the old and new EU Member States have struggled or failed to keep up with the rest of the EU. In the case of the Southeast Member States, very strong internal income divergences were noted. Capital city areas were disproportionately superior to the rest of the country, pushed by strong agglomeration forces around urban areas. Cabral and Castellanos-Sosa (2019) studied the impact of the global financial crisis on the convergence process for EU25 countries by analysing GDP per capita for the period 1973–2012. They found that the financial crisis reduced the convergence rate across the EU rather than leading to divergence. While the financial crisis undoubtedly harmed growth in Europe, it reduced the EU members' output per capita gap. This is explained mainly by the wealthier members – principally the 15 oldest EU members – who were not just the most affected but also those that recovered less rapidly. Studies show that the recent incorporation of countries into the EU seems to have contributed to absolute and conditional convergence across all its members.

Another framework used in empirical studies is sigma convergence, which refers to a reduction in the dispersion of levels of income across economies. Sigma convergence only occurs if beta convergence takes place. However, the existence of beta convergence is not a sufficient condition for sigma convergence. Boldrin and Canova (2001) analysed the standard deviation of labour productivity, income per capita and GDP per capita for the EU15 and did not confirm sigma convergence for the period 1980–1996. Yin et al. (2003) verified sigma convergence for the period 1960–1995 using the standard deviation of GDP per capita. Moreover, countries were divided into several groups to detect different patterns of convergence. The measures of concentration are also used to examine sigma convergence. Fingleton (2003) compared the coefficient of variation, the Gini coefficient and the inter-quartile range among European regions. His studies confirmed a slight reduction of disparities between 1987 and 1997. Studies by Neven and Goymte (1995), Barrios and Strobl (2005) and Cappelen et al. (2003) rejected the sigma convergence hypothesis for all European regions.

Another concept of convergence is the club convergence hypothesis. Convergence clubs are regions which will converge to a similar steady-state value. Ertur et al. (2006) analysed a sample of 138 EU regions for the period 1980–1995 and found that per capita income levels were highly spatially correlated. Exploratory spatial data analysis (ESDA) confirmed no convergence in the Northern club and a convergence rate of 2.9% per year for the Southern club. Canova (2004) assumed a predictive density approach to indicate convergence clubs from 144 EU regions from 1980 to 1992. He identified four homogeneous clubs, with different convergence rates and steady-state values highlighting North–South or poor–rich dimensions and the initial conditions influencing the probability of belonging to a club. Corrado et al. (2005) employed the cluster method to analyse convergence clubs. They investigated sectoral convergence from 1975 to 1999 and concluded that the highest degree of convergence was found in the service sector and the lowest in the manufacturing sector. The results also indicated that the convergence clubs varied over time to only a limited extent. Le Gallo and Dall'erba (2006) identified a convergence club by testing the seemingly unrelated regression model with spatial autocorrelation for 145 European regions for the period 1980–1999. Glawe and Wagner (2021) analysed convergence in institutions and in per capita income across the European Union. They found that income and institutional convergence clubs are formed mainly based on the geographic region. Northern and Western European countries are typically in the higher institutional/income clubs, whereas the lower institutional/income clubs comprise primarily eastern and southern European countries. This suggests that the underlying institutional clusters could determine the formation of income clubs.

1.3 The problem with measuring regional disparities

Measuring inequality is inextricably linked to the problem of comparability between elements. This comparison concerns specific characteristics that can be measured using appropriate indicators or indices. Thus, the analysis of inequality boils down to examining the differences between the individual values of the studied phenomenon for different units. Starting the analysis of regional disproportions, the basic research question is to define what the examined differences will concern. Economists tend to focus mainly on income disparities, but studying disparities in other areas such as productivity, innovation, human capital and infrastructure is also important to learn more about the different paths of the economic growth process in different regions.

Mills (2009) states that contradictory results from inequality research can arise from four key methodological issues: operationalisation of inequality, data availability and quality, population-weighted versus unweighted estimates and the technique one uses to calibrate income to a single currency in the income survey. The choice of these methodological assumptions is crucial for the results one obtains. The basic assumption in the study of inequality is the conceptual choice and the method of measuring inequality. All methodological assumptions are interrelated, so when deciding to consider a given research problem, we must verify whether data for our study are available and what their quality is. There are many measures used to study regional inequalities. The most frequently cited in the literature can be found in Table 1.3, divided into quantitative and qualitative indicators.

Disparity is a multifaceted concept that encompasses dimensions such as convergence, inequality and polarisation. Thus, measuring regional disparities is closely related to research needs. Difficulties in measuring inequality may arise when the phenomenon under study concerns quantitative and qualitative measures, which require judgment in evaluating a given phenomenon. Measuring inequality usually involves measuring per capita income, wealth and consumption differences. The problem arises when the comparison concerns qualitative measures, such as the standard of living of individuals in a particular society. There is no single accepted definition of or way to measure an individual's standard of living, due to the difficulty in accurately capturing the well-being of a given person. Quantitative measures do not take into account health, freedom or success. They do not measure happiness unless we assume it is equivalent to income or consumption. Also, what people consider happiness is influenced by culture and personal preferences, and varies from person to person. Income, consumption and wealth tell us about resource potential in the case of income and wealth – and actual trends in the case of

Table 1.3 Selected measures of regional imbalances

Quantitative measures	*Qualitative measures*
Income per capita	Human Development Index (HDI)
Consumption per capita	Multidimensional Poverty Index (MPI)
Gross domestic product	Technological Achievement Index (TAI)
Gross national product	
Labour productivity per employee	
Wages	

Source: Author's own elaboration based on literature review

consumption – but do not tell us about personal well-being (Goodman et al., 1997). Thus, the standard of living of an individual is, in fact, a multidimensional concept. Analyses devoted to the study of inequality tend to have a standardised scale that allows different population groups to be compared (Wratten, 1995). The problem with using too many indices to describe inequality is that they can produce conflicting results. Cowell and Jenkins (1995) draw attention to the fact that empirical studies of inequality aim to unambiguously answer the question, 'Has inequality increased or decreased?' with the words 'yes' or 'no'. Thus, multivariate analyses carry a high probability of providing ambiguous answers. Using a standard indicator provides a uniform scale with which comparisons can be made in different populations, such as urban and rural populations and populations living in different regions of the country. Therefore, in practice and for policy purposes, income, consumption and wealth remain the key measures of inequality despite the serious shortcomings of compressing the various characteristics of inequality into a single indicator of well-being, which gives only a partial picture of reality.

Often, the choice of a representative variable is determined by the availability of data from a long time series. If long time series data are not available for the most representative variable, it would be preferable to use an alternative closely matched variable for which suitable data can be found (Villaverde & Maza, 2009). In international comparisons, it is also necessary to decide whether the studied countries/regions should be weighted by population size or treated merely as equal units in cross-national comparisons. Another problem with measuring inequality is data at the regional level. For example, European integration has stimulated numerous studies of economic convergence at the country and regional levels in the scholarly literature. One of the main problems with analysing convergence in the EU is that official statistics are only available at the NUTS level, which results from historical factors of the countries and has no relationship to socio-economic variables. Studies by Cheshire and Carbonaro (1995) and Corrado et al. (2005) indicated that these regions are neither internally homogenous nor uniform in size. A final methodological problem that arises when income serves as the main measure is calibrating income to a common comparator currency. The two main techniques used to calibrate income to a common currency across countries are purchasing power parity (PPP) and unadjusted exchange rates. The results obtained from these conversion factors may be contradictory (Mills, 2009). Therefore, the results of the research depend on the period of analysis, data sets, methodological approaches and variables included. To obtain meaningful results, it is important to be clear about the hypotheses and limitations of the various indicators and to be aware that regional borders vary greatly both within and between countries (Spiezia, 2003).

References

Alcidi, C. (2019). Economic integration and income convergence in the EU. *Intereconomics*, *54*(1), 5–11. https://doi.org/10.1007/s10272-019-0783-6

Armstrong, H. W. (2005). Convergence among regions of the European Union, 1950–1990. *Papers in Regional Science*, *74*(2), 143–152. doi:10.1111/j.1435–5597.1995.tb00633.x

Azomahou, T. T., El Ouardighi, J., Nguyen-Van, P., & Pham, T. K. C. (2011). Testing convergence of European regions: A semiparametric approach. *Economic Modelling, 28*(3), 1202–1210.

Barrios, S., & Strobl, E. (2005). The dynamics of regional inequalities. *Economic Papers of the European Commission*, No. 229. Brussels.

Barro, R. J., & Sala-i-Martin, X. (1991). Convergence across states and regions. *Brookings Papers on Economic Activity, 1991*(1), 107. doi:10.2307/2534639

Barro R. J., & Sala-i-Martin, X. (2004). *Economic growth.* Cambridge, MA–London: The MIT Press.

Baumol, W. J., R. R., Nelson, & Wolff, E. N. (Eds.). (1994). *Convergence of productivity.* New York: Oxford University Press.

Baumont, B., Ertur, C., Le Gallo, J. (2003). Spatial convergence clubs and the European regional growth process, 1980–1995. In B. Fingleton (Ed.), *European regional growth* (pp. 131–158). Springer.

Becker, G. (1975). *Human capital: A theoretical and empirical analysis, with special reference to education.* Chicago: University of Chicago Press.

Begg, I., Dalum, B., Guerrieri, P., & Pianta, M. (1999). The impact of specialization in Europe. In F. Fagerberg, P. Guerrieri, & B. Verspagen (Eds.), *The economic challenge for Europe: Adapting to innovation based growth* (pp. 21–45).

Boldrin, L., & Canova, F. (2001). Inequality and convergence in Europe's regions: Reconsidering European regional policies. *Economic Policy, 16*(32), 207–253.

Caballe, J., & Santos, M. S. (1993). On endogenous growth with physical and human capital. *Journal of Political Economy, 101*(6), 1042–1067.

Cabral, R., & Castellanos-Sosa, F. A. (2019). Europe's income convergence and the latest global financial crisis. *Research in Economics, 73* (1), 23–34, doi:10.1016/j.rie.2019.01.003

Canova, F. (2004). Testing for convergence clubs in income per capita: A predictive density approach. *International Economic Review, 45*(1), 49–78.

Cappelen, Å., Castellacci, F., Fagerberg, J., Verspagen, B. (2003). Regional disparities in income and unemployment in Europe. In B. Fingleton (Ed.), *European regional growth* (pp. 323–350). Springer.

Cheshire, P., Carbonaro, G. (1995). Convergence–divergence in regional growth rates: An empty black box? In H. W. Armstrong & R. W. Vickerman (Eds.), *Convergence and divergence among European regions* (pp. 89–111), London: Pion

Corrado, L., Martin, R., & Weeks, M. (2005). Identifying and interpreting regional convergence clusters across Europe. *Economic Journal, 115*(3), C133–C160.

Cowell, F. A., & Jenkins, S. P. (1995). How much inequality can we explain? A methodology and an application to the United States. *The Economic Journal, 105*(429), 421–430. https://doi.org/10.2307/2235501

Cuadrado-Roura, J. R. (2001). Regional convergence in the European Union: From hypothesis to the actual trends. *The Annals of Regional Science, 35*(3), 333–356. doi:10.1007/s001680100054

Ertur, C., Le Gallo, J., & Baumont, C. (2006). The European regional convergence process, 1980–1995: Do spatial regimes and spatial dependence matter? *International Regional Science Review, 29*, 3–24.

Fagerberg, J. (1994). Technology and international differences in growth rates. *Journal of Economic Literature, American Economic Association, 32*(3), 1147–1175.

Fagerberg, J. (2001). Europe at the crossroads: The challenge from innovation-based growth. In Archibugi D, Lundvall B.-Å. (Eds.). *The Globalizing Learning Economy* (pp. 45–60). Oxford University Press.

Fagerberg, J., & Verspagen, B. (1996). Heading for divergence? Regional growth in Europe reconsidered. *Journal of Common Market Studies*, *34*(3), 431–448.

Feenstra, R. (2007). Globalization and its impact on labour. *wiiw Working Papers*, No. 44. The Vienna Institute for International Economic Studies, 1–24.

Fingleton, B. (2003). Models and simulations of GDP per inhabitant across Europe's regions: A preliminary view. In B. Fingleton (Ed.), *European regional growth* (pp. 11–53). Springer.

Friedmann, J. (1967). *A general theory of polarized development*. Santiago: Ford foundation.

Geppert, K., Happich, M., & Stephan, A. (2005). Regional disparities in the European Union: Convergence and agglomeration. *DIW Working Paper*, No. 525.

Glawe, L., & Wagner, H. (2021). Convergence, divergence, or multiple steady states? New evidence on the institutional development within the European Union. *Journal of Comparative Economics*, *49*(3), 860–884. doi:10.1016/j.jce.2021.01.006

Goodman, A., Johnson, P., & Webb, S. (1997). *Inequality in the UK*. Oxford–New York: Oxford University Press.

Grossman, G. M., & Helpman, E. (1991). Trade, knowledge spillovers, and growth. *European Economic Review*, *35*(2–3), 517–526.

Hagen, E. F. (1962). *The theory of social change: How economic growth begins*. Homewood, IL: Richard D. Irwin, Inc.

Hegerty, S. W. (2016). Regional convergence and growth clusters in Central and Eastern Europe: An examination of sectoral-level data. *Eastern European Business and Economics Journal*, *2*(2), 95–110.

Hirschman, A. (1958). *The strategy of economic development*. New Haven: Yale University Press.

Holland, S. (1976). *Capital versus the regions*. London: Macmillan.

Landes, D. (1998). *The wealth and poverty of nations: Why are some so rich and others so poor*. New York: W. W. Norton.

Lee, K.-K. (2014). Globalization, income inequality and poverty: Theory and empirics. *Social System Studies*, *28*, 109–134

Le Gallo, J., & Dall'erba, S. (2006). Evaluating the temporal and spatial heterogeneity of the European convergence process, 1980–1999. *Journal of Regional Science*, *46*(2), 269–288. doi:10.1111/j.0022–4146.2006.00441.x

Lewis, A. (1966). *Developing planning*. New York: Harper & Row.

López-Bazo, E. (2003). Growth and convergence across economies: The experience of the European regions. In B. Fingleton, A. Eraydin, & R. Paci (Eds.), *Regional economic growth, SMEs and the wider Europe* (pp. 49–74), London: Routledge.

Lucas, R. E. (1988). On the mechanics of economic development. *Journal of Monetary Economics*, *22*, 3–42.

Martin, R. (2001). EMU versus the regions? Regional convergence and divergence in Euroland. *Journal of Economic Geography*, *1*(1), 51–80.

Mills, M. (2009). Globalization and inequality. *European Sociological Review*, *25*(1), 1–8. https://doi.org/10.1093/esr/jcn046

Mohtadi, S., & Castells-Quintana, D. (2021). The distributional dimension of the resource curse: Commodity price shocks and income inequality. *Structural Change and Economic Dynamics*, *59*, 63–78, https://doi.org/10.1016/j.strueco.2021.08.002

Myrdal, G. (1957). *Economic theory and underdeveloped regions*. Gerald Duckworth.

Neven, D., & Goymte, C. (1995). Regional convergence in the European Community. *Journal of Common Market Studies*, *33*(1), 47–65. doi:10.1111/j.1468–5965.1995.tb00516.x

Newbery, D. M. (1990). Ramsey model. In J. Eatwell, M. Milgate, & P. Newman (Eds.), *Capital theory*. London: Palgrave Macmillan. https://doi.org/10.1007/978-1-349-20861-6_20

Niebuhr, A., & Schlitte, F. (2004). Convergence, trade and factor mobility in the European Union: Implications for enlargement and regional policy. *Intereconomics*, *39*(3), 167–176.

Olejnik, A. (2008). Using the spatial autoregressively distributed lag model in assessing the regional convergence of per-capita income in the EU25. *Papers in Regional Science*, *87*(3), 371–384.

Perroux, F. (1955). Note sur la notion de poles croissance. *Economic Appliquee*, *8*(1–2), 307–320.

Petrakos, G., Kallioras, D., & Anagnostou, A. (2011). Regional convergence and growth in Europe: Understanding patterns and determinants. *European Urban and Regional Studies*, *18*(4), 375–391.

Powell, W. W., & DiMaggio, P. (Eds.). (1991). *The new institutionalism in organizational analysis*. University of Chicago Press. http://catdir.loc.gov/catdir/toc/uchi051/91009999.html.

Romer, P. (1986). Increasing returns and long run growth. *Journal of Political Economy*, *94*, 1002–1037.

Sala-i-Martin. (1990). *On growth and states* [PhD Dissertation, Harvard University].

Schultz, W. (1962). Reflections on investment in man. *Journal of Political Economy*, *70*, 1–8.

Smith, A. (2012). *Wealth of nations*. Wordsworth Editions.

Solow, R. M. (1956). A contribution to the theory of economic growth. *Quarterly Journal of Economics*, *70*, 65–94.

Spiezia, V. (2003). *Measuring regional economies*. Organisation for Economic Co-operation and Development. Retrieved August 6, 2023 from https://www.oecd.org/sdd/15918996.pdf

Stiglitz, J. (2015). Inequality and economic growth. *The Political Quarterly*, *86*, 134–155. 10.1111/1467–923X.12237

Tselios, V. (2009) Growth and convergence in income per capita and income inequality in the regions of the EU. *Spatial Economic Analysis*, *4*(3), 343–370.

Villaverde, J., & Maza, A. (2009). Measurement of regional economic disparities. *UNU-CRIS Working papers*, W-2009/12. Retrieved August 6, 2023 from https://cris.unu.edu/measurement-regional-economic-disparities

Walraevens, B. (2021). Adam Smith's view of economic inequality. *Cambridge Journal of Economics*, *45*(1), 209–224. https://doi.org/10.1093/cje/beaa024

Wood, A. (1998). Globalisation and the rise in labour market inequalities. *The Economic Journal*, *108*(450), 1463–1482. doi:10.1111/1468-0297.00354

Wratten, E. (1995). Conceptualizing urban poverty. *Environment and Urbanization*, *7*(1), 11–38. https://doi.org/10.1177/095624789500700118

Yin, L., Zestos, G. K., & Michelis, L. (2003). Economic convergence in the European Union. *Journal of Economic Integration*, *18*(1), 188–213.

2 How unequal is the EU?

2.1 Key macroeconomic indicators

2.1.1 GDP per capita (current USD) and GDP per capita growth (annual %) for EU countries

This section presents selected macroeconomic indicators for the period 2000–2022. GDP per capita is one of the most commonly used economic indicators for assessing the competitiveness of a country or region, in both the academic literature and policymaking (Aiginger, 2006).

Table 2.1 presents the statistics of GDP per capita in the EU27 for the period 2000–2022. The highest GDP per capita in 2022 can be observed in Luxembourg (125,000 USD). The country's statistics for the average of the 23 periods look similar: the average for Luxembourg was more than 100,000 USD. In the second place in 2022 was Ireland, for which the value of GDP per capita was almost 104,000 USD. It is worth noting that the country's average for the whole study period was significantly lower, at 59,000 USD. The indicator in Ireland proved to be very high, as in the starting period it was only 26,000 USD. The next places in 2022 belong to Denmark, the Netherlands, Sweden, Austria and Finland. All these countries exceeded a GDP per capita of over 50,000 USD. The growth rate varied from 90% in Sweden to 120% in Denmark. In contrast, countries from Central and Eastern Europe (CEE) fared the worst – especially Bulgaria, whose indicator in 2022 was close to only 14,000 USD. Not much higher values were achieved by Romania (15,700 USD), Hungary (18,400 USD), Croatia (18,600 USD) and Poland (18,700 USD). It is worth mentioning, however, that the values for Romania and Bulgaria in 2000 were significantly lower, amounting to about 1600 USD. Hence, the growth in the period under study was very high, amounting in both countries to of 800%. Very high growth rates in GDP per capita were also recorded in the three Baltic States: Lithuania (661%), Latvia (547%) and Estonia (593%). Italy and Greece recorded the lowest growth in all the countries under study. The increase over the 23 years was only around 73%. Weak growth rates of GDP per capita, below 100%, were also recorded in France (82.39%) and Sweden (90.29%). The average for the Eurozone countries over the period under review was 35,000 USD, while for the EU countries it was 31,000 USD. The GDP per capita in 2022 for the Eurozone and the EU27 were 41,000 USD and 37,500 USD, respectively.

DOI: 10.4324/9781032615516-3

Table 2.1 GDP per capita in EU countries (current USD)

Country code	*2000*	*2001*	*2002*	*2003*	*2004*	*2005*	*2006*	*2007*	*2008*	*2009*	*2010*	*2011*	*2012*	*2013*	*2014*	*2015*	*2016*	*2017*	*2018*	*2019*	*2020*	*2021*	*2022*
AUT	24626	24559	26528	32294	36889	38417	40669	46915	51920	48153	46904	51442	48565	50731	51786	44196	45308	47429	51467	50068	48789	53518	52085
BEL	23099	23015	25006	30655	35429	36810	38705	44319	48303	44760	44185	47411	44671	46758	47764	41008	42013	44198	47545	46642	45609	51850	49927
BGR	1621	1771	2093	2719	3390	3900	4523	5889	7271	6988	6864	7857	7431	7688	7912	7079	7571	8382	9448	9874	10148	12219	13974
CYP	14388	14821	16093	20252	23793	24959	26729	31245	35397	32109	31023	32396	28911	27728	27162	23408	24605	26609	29335	29420	28281	32746	32048
CZE	6029	6637	8061	9819	11750	13431	15262	18467	22805	19862	19960	21871	19871	20133	19891	17830	18575	20636	23424	23665	22993	26823	27223
DEU	23695	23628	25197	30310	34107	34520	36354	41640	45613	41650	41572	46706	43856	46299	48024	41103	42136	44653	47939	46805	46749	51427	48718
DNK	30744	30752	33229	40459	46512	48800	52027	58487	64322	58163	58041	61754	58508	61191	62549	53255	54664	57610	61592	59593	60837	69269	67790
ESP	14750	15369	17107	21511	24907	26429	28389	32591	35511	32170	30532	31678	28323	29077	29514	25754	26537	28185	30380	29582	26984	30489	29675
EST	4071	4506	5342	7204	8914	10413	12639	16745	18205	14712	14663	17488	17403	19056	20261	17402	18295	20438	23166	23424	23595	27944	28247
FIN	24346	24968	26998	32928	37772	39055	41223	48476	53773	47481	46505	51149	47708	49892	50327	42802	43814	46412	49988	48630	49170	53560	50916
FRA	22416	22449	24288	29628	33797	34768	36470	41558	45516	41738	40676	43846	40871	42603	43069	36653	37063	38781	41558	40495	39180	43671	40886
GRC	12073	12549	14178	18518	21995	22560	24822	28864	32128	29829	26717	25484	21913	21788	21617	18084	17924	18582	19757	19144	17617	20311	20867
HRV	4952	5364	6219	8192	9723	10446	11505	13762	15899	14421	13694	14656	13440	13979	14001	12099	12580	13592	15040	15121	14270	17809	18570
HUN	4624	5276	6655	8419	10302	11223	11490	13941	15772	13077	13218	14234	12985	13715	14294	12717	13105	14621	16425	16786	16126	18753	18390
IRL	26335	28282	32705	41204	47754	50933	54329	61396	61353	52133	48664	52220	48944	51497	55753	62179	62784	70151	79447	80848	85973	102002	103983
ITA	20138	20501	22376	27526	31317	32055	33530	37871	40945	37227	36036	38650	35052	35560	35566	30242	30961	32407	34622	33674	31923	36449	34776
LTU	3293	3526	4142	5499	6700	7855	9231	12285	14945	11821	11988	14377	14368	15730	16551	14264	15008	16885	19186	19616	20382	23850	25065
LUX	48660	48440	53006	65689	76545	80988	90789	107475	120422	109420	110886	119025	112585	120000	123679	105462	106899	110193	116787	112726	116905	133712	125006
LVA	3362	3578	4137	5145	6379	7595	9723	14114	16467	12332	11421	13339	13847	15007	15742	13786	14332	15695	17865	17883	18096	20930	21780
MLT	10432	10402	11290	13669	15197	15888	16724	19486	22205	21083	21799	23155	22527	24770	26753	24922	25624	28813	31786	31727	29598	34881	34128
NLD	26214	26897	29343	35751	40437	41995	44901	51799	57880	52722	51000	54230	50070	52199	52901	45193	46039	48675	53045	52476	52163	58728	57025
POL	4501	4991	5207	5702	6681	8022	9036	11254	13996	11526	12504	13776	13011	13558	14182	12560	12379	13815	15505	15700	15817	18050	18688
PRT	11526	11735	12937	15798	18064	18780	19839	22811	24949	23151	22521	23217	20564	21653	22104	19250	19992	21490	23563	23331	22242	24661	24515
ROU	1660	1825	2120	2679	3495	4618	5758	8360	10435	8548	8398	9560	8931	9497	10031	8977	9404	10728	12494	12958	13047	14947	15787
SVK	5427	5722	6565	8732	10691	11690	13171	16106	18754	16597	16909	18510	17498	18276	18720	16391	16563	17585	19486	19382	19552	21768	21257
SVN	10201	10480	11777	14849	17233	18099	19673	23818	27596	24792	23532	25128	22642	23503	24247	20890	21678	23514	26124	26042	25558	29331	28439
SWE	29625	27248	29899	37322	42822	43437	46594	53700	56153	46947	52869	60756	58038	61127	60020	51545	51965	53792	54589	51939	52838	61418	56374
Eurozone	20215	20450	22212	27193	31005	31948	33795	38715	42353	38579	37605	40657	37593	39119	39914	34390	35162	37159	40048	39185	38194	42808	41037
EU27	16948	17198	18760	22968	26307	27342	29090	33587	37044	33481	32966	35767	33169	34565	35282	30487	31174	33091	35752	35080	34357	38722	37433

Source: Author's own elaboration based on the World Bank database

Note: AUT-Austraia, BEL-Belgium, BGR-Bulgaria, CYP-Cyprus, CZE-Czech Republic, DEU-Germany, DNK-Denmark, ESP-Espania,EST-Estonia, FIN-Finland, FRA-France, GRC-Greece, HRV-Croactia, HUN-Hungary,IRL-Irleand, ITA-Italy, LTU-Lithuean a, LUX-Luxemburg, LVA-Latvia, MLT-Malta, NLD-Netherlands, POL-Poland, PRT-Portugal, ROU-Romania, SVK-Slovakia, SVN-Slovenia, SWE-Sweden

Table 2.2 shows the annual changes in GDP per capita for the period 2000–2022. The highest averages in the study period were in Lithuania (5.0%), Latvia (4.6%), Romania (4.6%), Bulgaria (4.5%) and Ireland (4.2%), while the lowest were below 1% – in Italy (0.3%), Greece (0.6%), France (0.8%), Portugal (0.9%) and Spain (0.9%). The highest amplitudes were mainly observed in countries with the highest GDP growth, i.e. Ireland (29.7%), Malta (29%), Croatia (26.9%), Lithuania (26.3%) and Latvia (25.8%), or those with the lowest GDP growth, i.e. Greece (19.7%), Spain (19.9%) and Italy (17.4%), where the average amplitude for EU countries was 16.3%. The lowest amplitudes in this indicator were seen in Poland (9.8%), the Netherlands (10.1%), Sweden (10.7%), Austria (10.8%) and Germany (11.3%). Poland, which has the lowest amplitude, even recorded additions to its 2009 GDP score of 2.8%. This is surprising since no other country in the EU recorded a positive rate after the 2008 subprime crisis, during which the small Baltic countries of Lithuania (−13.9%), Latvia (−12.8%) and Estonia (−14.5%) fared worst. During the COVID-19 pandemic in 2020, Ireland's economy managed best and was the only one to record positive GDP growth (5.5%). A good lesson from the previous crisis was learnt by the Baltic countries, which recorded a minimal decline in Lithuania (−0.1%), Estonia (−0.7%) and Latvia (−2.8%). Similar to the previous crisis, Poland also ranked among the top EU countries with a decline of 1.8%. EU countries have a specific correlation in this indicator, namely, in the periods 2001–2007 and 2010–2019, one could observe a good performance in GDP per capita. Of course, there were a few exceptions. Countries like Greece, Cyprus and Italy struggled long after the 2008 subprime crisis. They only started to achieve positive GDP per capita values from 2015 onwards. The figure for Ireland in 2015, at 23.3%, was also surprising. The high growth in GDP per capita did not transfer to the population's wealth. No Western country has achieved such a growth rate in this century. In the case of Ireland, the very fast growth rate was the result of tax inversion, a phenomenon in which companies from abroad move their headquarters because of low taxes. This shows that GDP growth cannot be the only tool for evaluating certain governmental economic policies. There are certainly question marks over the indicator of GDP, but it will remain essential, mainly due to the lack of reliable alternatives.

2.1.2 GINI index – income inequality

Table 2.3 shows the differences in the level of income distribution as measured by the national Gini coefficient. The Gini coefficient is a number from 0 to 1, where 0 corresponds to full equality (everyone has the same income) and 1 corresponds to absolute inequality (one person has all the income, and all the others have zero income). Although the Gini coefficient takes values in the range of [0; 1], it is often expressed in international statistics as a percentage. Taking a 20-year average (2000–2020), the least social stratification was observed in Slovenia (24.8%), Slovakia (26.1%), Czechia (26.1%), Denmark (26.9%), Finland (27.5%), Sweden (27.8%), Belgium (28.3%) and the Netherlands (28.5%). By contrast, social stratification was highest in Bulgaria (37.4%), Romania (36.1%), Portugal (36%),

Table 2.2 GDP per capita growth in EU countries (annual %)

Country code	*2000*	*2001*	*2002*	*2003*	*2004*	*2005*	*2006*	*2007*	*2008*	*2009*	*2010*	*2011*	*2012*	*2013*	*2014*	*2015*	*2016*	*2017*	*2018*	*2019*	*2020*	*2021*	*2022*
AUT	3.1	0.9	1.2	0.5	2.1	1.5	2.9	3.4	1.1	−4	1.6	2.6	0.2	−0.6	−0.1	−0.1	0.9	1.6	1.9	1	−7	3.8	3.8
BEL	3.5	0.8	1.3	0.6	3.1	1.8	1.9	2.9	−0.3	−2.8	1.9	0.4	0.1	0	1.1	1.5	0.8	1.2	1.3	1.7	−5.7	6.4	2.1
BGR	5.1	5.9	8.2	6.1	7.3	7.9	7.6	7.4	6.9	−2.7	2.2	2.7	1.3	0	1.5	4.1	3.8	3.5	3.4	4.8	−3.4	8.5	10.6
CYP	4.8	2.8	2.5	1.4	3.6	3.4	3	2.9	1.1	−4.6	−0.4	−2.1	−4.9	−6.4	−0.7	4	6.1	4.8	4.4	4.1	−5.5	5.6	4.6
CZE	4.3	3.4	1.8	3.6	4.8	6.5	6.5	5	1.8	−5.2	2.1	1.6	−0.9	−0.1	2.2	5.2	2.3	4.9	2.9	2.6	−5.7	5.4	0.8
DEU	2.8	1.5	−0.4	−0.8	1.2	0.8	3.9	3.1	1.2	−5.5	4.3	5.9	0.2	0.2	1.8	0.6	1.4	2.3	0.7	0.8	−3.9	3.1	1.1
DNK	3.4	0.5	0.1	0.1	2.4	2.1	3.6	0.5	−1.1	−5.4	1.4	0.9	−0.1	0.5	1.1	1.6	2.4	2.2	1.5	1.1	−2.7	6.4	1.9
ESP	4.8	3.2	1.3	1.1	1.4	1.9	2.4	1.7	−0.7	−4.6	−0.3	−1.2	−3	−1.1	1.7	3.9	3	2.7	1.8	1.3	−11.6	6.3	5
EST	9.6	6.7	7.4	8.3	7.4	10.2	10.4	8.1	−4.9	−14.5	2.7	7.6	3.6	1.8	3.3	1.8	3.1	5.7	3.4	3.4	−0.7	7.9	−2.6
FIN	5.6	2.4	1.5	1.8	3.7	2.4	3.6	4.9	0.3	−8.5	2.7	2.1	−1.9	−1.4	−0.8	0.2	2.5	3	1	1.1	−2.5	3	1.3
FRA	3.2	1.2	0.4	0.1	2.1	0.9	1.7	1.8	−0.3	−3.4	1.4	1.7	−0.2	0.1	0.5	0.8	0.8	2	1.5	1.5	−7.8	6.1	2.1
GRC	3.5	3.6	3.5	5.5	4.8	0.3	5.3	3	−0.6	−4.6	−5.6	−10	−6.6	−1.8	1.1	0.5	−0.1	1.3	1.9	2	−9.1	9.7	7
HRV	4	7.2	5.8	5.6	4.2	4.2	5.1	5.1	2	−7.1	−1	0.3	−2	−0.1	0	3.4	4.3	4.6	3.7	4	−8.2	18.7	7
HUN	4.8	4.3	5	4.4	5.2	4.5	4.1	0.4	1.2	−6.5	1.3	2.2	−0.7	2.1	4.5	4	2.5	4.5	5.5	4.9	−4.3	7.5	5.3
IRL	8	3.6	4.1	1.3	4.9	3.5	2.2	2.3	−6.4	−6.1	1.1	0.8	−0.6	0.6	8	23.3	0.6	8.1	7.1	3.9	5.5	14	7.4
ITA	3.7	1.9	0.1	−0.3	0.8	0.3	1.5	1	−1.6	−5.7	1.4	0.5	−3.2	−3	−0.9	0.9	1.5	1.8	1.1	1.6	−8.5	8.9	4.1
LTU	4.4	7.4	7.6	11.5	7.8	9.5	9.1	12.4	3.7	−13.9	3.8	8.5	5.2	4.6	4.4	3	3.8	5.8	5	4.9	−0.1	6.1	1.3
LUX	5.5	1.9	2.1	1.4	2.8	0.9	4.3	6.4	−2.1	−5	1.9	−1.2	−0.8	0.8	0.2	−0.1	2.7	−1.1	−0.7	0.9	−2.5	5.6	−0.6
LVA	6.7	7.7	8.3	9.5	9.5	11.9	13	10.8	−2.2	−12.8	−2.4	4.5	8.4	3.1	2.9	4.7	3.3	4.2	4.8	1.3	−2.8	7.6	3.6
MLT	18.9	−1.9	1.8	3.4	−0.5	2.7	2.1	4.4	3.2	−1.9	5	0	3.2	4	5.5	7	1	7.9	3.7	2.9	−10.1	11.6	4.4
NLD	3.5	1.6	−0.4	−0.3	1.6	1.8	3.3	3.5	1.8	−4.2	0.8	1.1	−1.4	−0.4	1.1	1.5	1.6	2.3	1.8	1.3	−4.4	5.6	3.3
POL	5.7	1.3	2.1	3.6	5	3.6	6.2	7.1	4.2	2.8	3.2	5	1.5	0.9	3.9	4.5	3	5.1	5.9	4.5	−1.8	7.4	7.9
PRT	3.1	1.2	0.2	−1.3	1.5	0.6	1.4	2.3	0.2	−3.2	1.7	−1.6	−3.7	−0.4	1.3	2.2	2.3	3.8	3	2.7	−8.4	5.1	6.3
ROU	2.6	6.7	7.7	3.1	11.1	5.3	8.7	8.8	11.1	−4.7	−3.3	5	2.4	0.6	4.5	3.6	3.4	8.8	6.7	4.4	−3.1	6.5	5
SVK	1.3	3.4	4.5	5.6	5.3	6.6	8.5	10.8	5.5	−5.6	6.6	2.5	1.1	0.5	2.6	5.1	1.8	2.8	3.9	2.4	−3.4	5	2
SVN	3.4	3.1	3.4	2.9	4.3	3.6	5.4	6.4	3.3	−8.4	0.9	0.7	−2.8	−1.2	2.7	2.1	3.1	4.7	4.1	2.8	−4.9	7.9	2.3
SWE	4.6	1.2	1.9	1.9	3.9	2.4	4.1	2.7	−1.2	−5.2	5.1	2.4	−1.3	0.3	1.6	3.4	0.8	1.2	0.8	1	−2.9	5.5	2.1
Eurozone	3.5	1.8	0.4	0.1	1.7	1.2	2.8	2.5	−0.1	−4.8	1.9	1.9	−1.1	−0.6	1.1	1.7	1.6	2.4	1.5	1.5	−6.2	5.9	2.9
EU27	3.8	2	0.9	0.5	2.2	1.6	3.2	2.8	0.3	−4.6	2.1	2.1	−0.8	−0.3	1.3	2.1	1.8	2.7	1.9	1.7	−5.7	6.1	3.4

Source: Author's own elaboration based on the World Bank database

Note: AUT-Austraia, BEL-Belgium, BGR-Bulgaria, CYP-Cyprus, CZE-Czech Republic, DEU-Germany, DNK-Denmark, ESP-Espania,EST-Estonia, FIN-Finland, FRA-France, GRC-Greece, HRV-Croactia, HUN-Hungary,IRL-Irleand, ITA-Italy, LTU-Lithueania, LUX-Luxemburg, LVA-Latvia, MLT-Malta, NLD-Netherlands, POL-Poland, PRT-Portugal, ROU-Romania, SVK-Slovakia, SVN-Slovenia, SWE-Sweden

Table 2.3 Gini index – income inequality in EU countries

Country code	*2000*	*2001*	*2002*	*2003*	*2004*	*2005*	*2006*	*2007*	*2008*	*2009*	*2010*	*2011*	*2012*	*2013*	*2014*	*2015*	*2016*	*2017*	*2018*	*2019*	*2020*
AUT	29	N/A	N/A	29.5	29.8	28.7	29.6	30.6	30.4	31.5	30.3	30.8	30.5	30.8	30.5	30.5	30.8	29.7	30.8	30.2	29.8
BEL	33.1	N/A	N/A	28.1	30.5	29.3	28.1	29.2	28.4	28.6	28.4	28.1	27.5	27.7	28.1	27.7	27.6	27.4	27.2	27.2	26
BGR	N/A	N/A	N/A	N/A	N/A	N/A	35.7	36.1	33.6	33.8	35.7	34.3	36	36.6	37.4	38.6	40.6	40.4	41.3	40.3	40.5
CYP	N/A	N/A	N/A	N/A	30.1	30.3	31.1	31.1	31.7	32.1	31.5	32.6	34.3	37	35.6	34	32.9	31.4	32.7	31.2	31.7
CZE	N/A	N/A	26.6	N/A	27.5	26.9	26.7	26	26.3	26.2	26.6	26.4	26.1	26.5	25.9	25.9	25.4	24.9	25	25.3	26.2
DEU	28.8	29.9	29.9	29.9	30.2	31.6	31	31.1	30.9	30.5	30.3	30.7	31.1	31.5	30.9	31.4	31.4	31.9	31.8	31.7	N/A
DNK	23.8	N/A	N/A	25.6	24.9	25.2	25.9	26.2	25.2	26.7	27.2	27.3	27.8	28.5	28.4	28.2	28.2	28.7	28.2	27.7	27.5
ESP	34.1	N/A	N/A	31.8	33.3	32.4	33.5	34.1	34.2	34.9	35.2	35.7	35.4	36.2	36.1	36.2	35.8	34.7	34.7	34.3	34.9
EST	N/A	N/A	N/A	37.2	33.6	33.4	33.7	31.2	31.9	31.4	32	32.5	32.9	35.1	34.6	32.7	31.2	30.4	30.3	30.8	30.7
FIN	27.2	N/A	N/A	27.7	27.9	27.6	28	28.3	27.8	27.5	27.7	27.6	27.1	27.2	26.8	27.1	27.1	27.4	27.3	27.7	27.1
FRA	32.6	32.5	31.8	31.4	30.6	29.8	29.7	32.4	33	32.7	33.7	33.3	33.1	32.5	32.3	32.7	31.9	31.6	32.4	31.2	30.7
GRC	34.2	N/A	N/A	32.8	33.6	34.6	35.1	34	33.6	33.6	34.1	34.8	36.3	36.1	35.8	36	35	34.4	32.9	33.1	33.6
HRV	N/A	N/A	N/A	N/A	N/A	N/A	N/A	N/A	N/A	32.6	32.4	32.3	32.5	32	32.1	31.1	30.9	30.4	29.7	28.9	29.5
HUN	N/A	N/A	N/A	N/A	29.9	34.7	28.3	27.9	27.5	27	29.4	29.2	30.8	31.5	30.9	30.4	30.3	30.6	29.6	30	29.7
IRL	33	N/A	32.3	32.9	33.6	33.8	32.7	31.9	30.9	32.7	32.3	32.9	33.2	33.5	31.9	31.8	32.8	31.4	30.6	30.8	29.2
ITA	35.3	N/A	N/A	34.9	34.3	33.8	33.7	32.9	33.8	33.8	34.7	35.1	35.2	34.9	34.7	35.4	35.2	35.9	35.2	34.6	35.2
LTU	N/A	N/A	N/A	N/A	37	35.3	34.4	34.8	35.7	37.2	33.6	32.5	35.1	35.3	37.7	37.4	38.4	37.3	35.7	35.3	36
LUX	30.1	30.9	31	30.2	30.2	30.8	30.9	31.1	32.6	31.2	30.5	32.1	34.3	32	31.2	32.9	31.7	34.5	35.4	34.2	33.4
LVA	N/A	N/A	N/A	N/A	36.4	39	35.6	37.5	37.2	36	35	35.8	35.2	35.5	35.1	34.2	34.3	35.6	35.1	34.5	35.7
MLT	N/A	N/A	N/A	N/A	N/A	N/A	28	29.2	29	30.2	29	29.1	29.4	28.8	29	29.4	29.1	29.2	28.7	31	31.4
NLD	N/A	N/A	N/A	N/A	29.8	29	30	29.6	29.3	27.9	27.8	27.8	27.6	28.1	28.6	28.2	28.2	28.5	28.1	29.2	26
POL	N/A	N/A	N/A	N/A	38	35.8	34.7	34	33.5	33.4	33.2	33.2	33	33.1	32.8	31.8	31.2	29.7	30.2	28.8	N/A
PRT	N/A	N/A	N/A	38.8	38.9	38.5	38.1	36.8	36.6	34.9	35.8	36.3	36	36.2	35.6	35.5	35.2	33.8	33.5	32.8	34.7
ROU	N/A	N/A	N/A	N/A	N/A	N/A	39.6	37.5	36.4	35.6	35.5	35.9	36.5	36.9	36	35.9	34.4	36	35.8	34.8	34.6
SVK	N/A	N/A	N/A	N/A	27.1	29.3	25.8	24.7	26	27.2	27.3	26.5	26.1	28.1	26.1	26.5	25.2	23.2	25	23.2	N/A
SVN	N/A	N/A	N/A	N/A	24.8	24.6	24.4	24.4	23.7	24.8	24.9	24.9	25.6	26.2	25.7	25.4	24.8	24.2	24.6	24.4	24
SWE	27.2	N/A	25.8	25.3	26.1	26.8	26.4	27.1	28.1	27.3	27.7	27.6	27.6	28.8	28.4	29.2	29.6	28.8	30	29.3	28.9

Source: Author's own elaboration based on the World Bank database

Note: AUT-Austraia, BEL-Belgium, BGR-Bulgaria, CYP-Cyprus, CZE-Czech Republic, DEU-Germany, DNK-Denmark, ESP-Espania, EST-Estonia, FIN-Finland, FRA-France, GRC-Greece, HRV-Croactia, HUN-Hungary, IRL-Irleand, ITA-Italy, LTU-Lithueania, LUX-Luxemburg, LVA-Latvia, MLT-Malta, NLD-Netherlands, POL-Poland, PRT-Portugal, ROU-Romania, SVK-Slovakia, SVN-Slovenia, SWE-Sweden

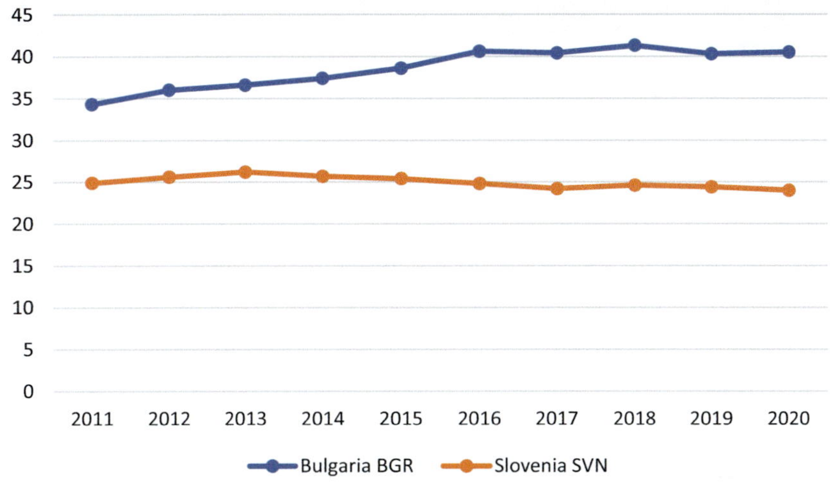

Figure 2.1 Level of income distribution as measured by the national Gini coefficient (%)

Source: Author's own elaboration based on World Bank database

Lithuania (35.8%), Latvia (35.7%), Italy (34.7%), Spain (34.6%) and Greece (34.4%). The average social stratification over the study period for all EU countries was 31.3%. It is worth noting here that all the results are subject to error, as many statistics for 2000 through 2002 were missing, and were therefore not taken into account. Between 2003 and 2008, and in 2020, some data was still missing.

Considering all the countries, the most disturbing trend is the upward trend in Bulgaria between 2011 and 2016, which remained at around 40% for subsequent years from 2017 to 2020. This can be observed in Figure 2.1. This chart also shows statistics for Slovenia, which, in contrast, had the least social stratification.

2.1.3 Poverty rate (% of population)

Figure 2.2 and Table 2.4 show the poverty rate as a percentage of the population living on 6.85 USD a day in EU countries from 2004 to 2020. Similar to other statistics, the most significant percentage of the population that did not earn an income of 6.85 USD a day resided in Bulgaria and Romania. The average for Romania was 28.15% and for Bulgaria 14.25%. These results were significantly higher than those of the next highest country, Latvia, where the average was 8.38%. Right behind Latvia were Lithuania (7.26%), Croatia (5.24%), Poland (4.88%), Hungary (4.65%) and Greece (4.29%). Every other country had a rate of less than 4%. It is comforting to note that the statistics for Bulgaria and Romania were decreasing year by year. At the beginning of the study period, i.e. in 2004, 42.2% of people had incomes lower than 6.85 USD per day, and in 2020 only 10% did so. The situation was similar in Bulgaria, which recorded 28.5% of people in 2004 and only 4.5% in 2020. By far, the best statistics were obtained by Cyprus and Finland (0.17% for both countries). The situation was also good in Slovenia, Germany, France,

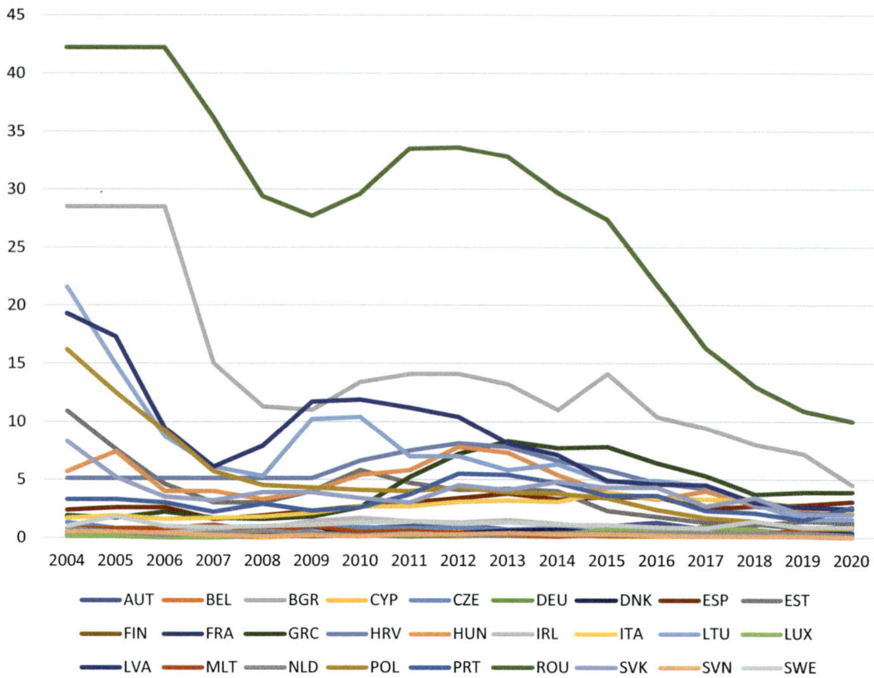

Figure 2.2 Poverty headcount ratio at 6.85 USD a day (2017 PPP) in EU countries (% of population)

Source: Author's own elaboration based on World Bank database

Luxembourg, Belgium, the Netherlands, Denmark, Malta, Czechia, Ireland and Austria. The values in these countries were below 1%.

2.1.4 Percentage of income that accrues to subgroups of the population indicated by deciles or quintiles

Tables 2.5–2.7 show the percentage of income per quintile and decile in 2004, 2012 and 2020, respectively. Regarding the situation in 2004, the most equal distribution of income was in countries such as Denmark, Slovenia, Finland, Czechia and Sweden. The highest income inequality was noted in Romania, Poland, Lithuania, Latvia and Portugal. It is worth mentioning that several of these countries, particularly in the third quintile, had a relatively rational distribution. This was the case in Lithuania, Latvia and Portugal, among others. In the third quintile, these countries had income levels similar to the top 20% – at 22.9%, 21.9% and 21%, respectively. The share of the 10% of countries with the highest and lowest incomes was similar to that for the highest and lowest quintiles. The highest inequality was seen in the same CEE countries and Portugal. The 2012 figures brought little change, though several countries were added to each category. Greece and Spain joined the countries with the most income inequality. On the other hand, among the countries

Table 2.4 Poverty headcount ratio at 6.85 USD a day (2017 PPP) in EU countries (% of population)

Country code	*2004*	*2005*	*2006*	*2007*	*2008*	*2009*	*2010*	*2011*	*2012*	*2013*	*2014*	*2015*	*2016*	*2017*	*2018*	*2019*	*2020*
AUT	0.4	0.5	0.5	0.8	1	1	0.8	1	1.1	0.7	0.7	1	1.3	0.7	1.2	0.8	1
BEL	0.4	0.5	0.4	0.4	0.3	0.3	0.5	0.6	0.5	0.5	0.3	0.2	0.3	0.4	0.2	0.2	0.3
BGR	28.5	28.5	28.5	15	11.3	11	13.4	14.1	14.1	13.2	11	14.1	10.4	9.4	8	7.2	4.5
CYP	0.3	0.1	0	0.1	0	0.2	0.2	0.2	0.1	0.3	0.4	0.1	0.1	0.1	0.2	0.3	0.2
CZE	1.3	0.8	0.8	0.7	0.5	0.8	0.9	0.8	0.9	0.7	0.8	0.4	0.7	0.5	0.2	0.3	0.4
DEU	0.2	0.2	0.2	0.2	0.2	0.2	0.2	0.2	0.2	0.2	0.2	0.2	0.2	1	0.2	0.2	0.2
DNK	0.4	0.5	0.3	0.6	0.8	1	0.2	0.6	0.4	0.6	0.7	0.4	0.5	0.3	0.3	0.4	0.4
ESP	2.4	2.6	2.6	1.6	1.9	2.3	2.7	3	3.4	3.8	3.3	3.5	3.5	2.5	2.7	2.8	3.1
EST	10.9	7.6	4.6	3	3	4	5.8	4.7	4.1	4.2	4	2.3	1.8	1.3	1.1	1.4	1.3
FIN	0.2	0.2	0.2	0.1	0.2	0.1	0.2	0.1	0.2	0.2	0.2	0.2	0.2	0.1	0.2	0.2	0.1
FRA	0.3	0.3	0.2	0.1	0.1	0.4	0.3	0.2	0.3	0.2	0.2	0.3	0.3	0.1	0.1	0.4	0.4
GRC	1.9	1.7	2.2	1.7	1.6	1.8	2.6	5.2	7.2	8.3	7.7	7.8	6.4	5.3	3.7	3.9	3.9
HRV	5.1	5.1	5.1	5.1	5.1	5.1	6.6	7.5	8.1	7.8	6.6	5.8	4.7	4.2	2.7	2.4	2.1
HUN	5.7	7.4	4	4	3.3	4	5.4	5.8	7.8	7.3	5.4	3.9	3.3	4	2.8	2.5	2.5
IRL	0.4	0.3	0.6	0.5	0.8	1.4	1.7	1.4	1.3	1.5	1.2	0.8	0.8	0.5	0.1	0.2	0.2
ITA	1.7	1.9	1.6	1.7	1.8	2.1	2.7	2.7	3.1	3.2	3.1	3.9	3.4	3.3	3.2	2.6	2.2
LTU	21.6	14.9	8.7	6.1	5.3	10.2	10.4	7	7	5.8	6.3	4.8	4.9	4.4	2.9	1.6	1.6
LUX	0.1	0.1	0	0	0.1	0.2	0.3	0.2	0.3	0.3	0.3	0.7	0.5	0.9	0.7	0.3	0
LVA	19.3	17.3	9.4	6.1	7.9	11.7	11.9	11.2	10.4	8.1	7.1	4.9	4.6	4.5	3	2.6	2.5
MLT	0.8	0.8	0.8	1.1	0.6	1	0.5	0.6	0.4	0.2	0.1	0.3	0.3	0.3	0.3	0.7	0.8
NLD	0.8	0.5	0.2	0.4	0.6	0.4	0.2	0.4	0.2	0.3	0.4	0.4	0.4	0.4	0.4	0.4	0.2
POL	16.2	12.5	9.2	5.7	4.5	4.3	4.1	4	4.3	3.9	3.8	3.4	2.4	1.7	1.4	0.8	0.8
PRT	3.3	3.3	3	2.2	2.9	2.3	2.6	3.7	5.5	5.4	4.7	3.6	3.6	2.3	2.1	1.5	2.6
ROU	42.2	42.2	42.2	36.2	29.4	27.7	29.6	33.5	33.6	32.8	29.7	27.4	21.8	16.3	13	10.9	10
SVK	8.3	5.2	3.5	3.2	3.9	3.9	3.4	3	4.5	4.1	4.8	4.3	4.3	2.7	3.4	2	2
SVN	0.5	0.5	0.4	0.2	0.1	0.2	0.1	0.3	0.3	0.4	0.3	0.3	0.2	0.1	0.1	0.1	0
SWE	1	1.8	1	0.9	1	1.1	1.3	1.4	1.2	1.3	1.1	1.1	0.9	0.8	1.4	0.9	0.9

Source: Author's own elaboration based on the World Bank database

Note: AUT-Austraia, BEL-Belgium, BGR-Bulgaria, CYP-Cyprus, CZE-Czech Republic, DEU-Germany, DNK-Denmark, ESP-Espania, EST-Estonia, FIN-Finland, FRA-France, GRC-Greece, HRV-Croactia, HUN-Hungary, IRL-Irleand, ITA-Italy, LTU-Lithueania, LUX-Luxemburg, LVA-Latvia, MLT-Malta, NLD-Netherlands, POL-Poland, PRT-Portugal, ROU-Romania, SVK-Slovakia, SVN-Slovenia, SWE-Sweden

Table 2.5 Percentage of income or consumption attributable to each quintile and top and bottom deciles in EU countries in 2004

Country code	*First quintile*	*Second quintile*	*Third quintile*	*Fourth quintile*	*Fifth quintile*	*Top ten %*	*Bottom ten %*
AUT	8.5	13.2	17.2	22.5	38.5	23.8	3.4
BEL	8.4	13.4	17.1	21.9	39.2	25.1	3.4
BGR	5.7	12.6	17.1	22.9	41.8	26.6	1.6
CYP	8.8	13.0	17.0	22.3	39.0	24.3	3.6
CZE	9.0	14.3	17.7	21.9	37.0	23.1	3.6
DEU	8.5	13.1	17.0	22.5	38.9	24	3.4
DNK	9.9	14.5	18.0	22.6	34.9	20.7	4
ESP	6.9	12.5	17.1	23.2	40.3	24.9	2.4
EST	7.1	12.8	16.4	22.4	41.2	25.9	2.5
FIN	9.4	13.8	17.2	22.2	37.4	23.2	3.9
FRA	8.4	12.9	17.0	22.4	39.2	24.5	3.4
GRC	7.1	12.3	16.9	23.0	40.8	25.5	2.6
HRV	6.9	12.7	17.3	23.3	39.7	24.3	2.5
HUN	8.3	13.5	17.5	22.3	38.4	24.2	3.3
IRL	7.6	12.4	16.4	22.3	41.4	26.6	3
ITA	6.8	12.3	16.9	22.6	41.3	26.3	2.4
LTU	5.8	11.9	16.4	22.2	43.7	27.9	2
LUX	8.3	13.2	17.2	22.6	38.7	23.7	3.3
LVA	6.5	12.3	15.9	21.9	43.5	28.5	2.2
MLT	8.6	13.8	17.9	23.0	36.7	22.1	3.4
NLD	8.4	13.4	17.3	22.6	38.3	23.7	3.2
POL	5.7	11.2	16.3	22.9	43.9	28.2	1.9
PRT	6.4	11.2	15.1	21.0	46.3	30.9	2.4
ROU	5.0	10.8	16.3	22.8	45.0	29	1.7
SVK	8.7	14.4	18.5	22.6	35.9	22.1	3.3
SVN	9.8	14.6	18.2	22.6	34.7	20.6	4
SWE	9.3	14.3	17.9	22.9	35.5	21.1	3.7

Source: Author's own elaboration based on the World Bank database

Note: AUT-Austraia, BEL-Belgium, BGR-Bulgaria, CYP-Cyprus, CZE-Czech Republic, DEU-Germany, DNK-Denmark, ESP-Espania, EST-Estonia, FIN-Finland, FRA-France, GRC-Greece, HRV-Croactia, HUN-Hungary, IRL-Irleand, ITA-Italy, LTU-Lithueania, LUX-Luxemburg, LVA-Latvia, MLT-Malta, NLD-Netherlands, POL-Poland, PRT-Portugal, ROU-Romania, SVK-Slovakia, SVN-Slovenia, SWE-Sweden

Table 2.6 Percentage of income or consumption attributable to each quintile and top and bottom decile in EU countries in 2012

Country code	*First quintile*	*Second quintile*	*Third quintile*	*Fourth quintile*	*Fifth quintile*	*Top 10%*	*Bottom 10%*
AUT	7.8	13.3	17.5	23	38.4	23.4	2.8
BEL	8.7	14.2	18	22.8	36.4	21.9	3.4
BGR	6.2	12.2	16.6	22.4	42.7	27.4	2
CYP	8	12.1	15.8	21.4	42.7	28	3.3
CZE	9.6	14.5	17.9	21.9	36.1	22.2	3.9
DEU	8.2	12.9	17	22.6	39.4	24.4	3.2

(*Continued*)

Table 2.6 (Continued)

Country code	*First quintile*	*Second quintile*	*Third quintile*	*Fourth quintile*	*Fifth quintile*	*Top 10%*	*Bottom 10%*
DNK	9.3	14	17.4	22.1	37.3	23.1	3.7
ESP	6.1	11.9	17	23.4	41.6	25.8	2
EST	7.3	12.9	16.5	22.6	40.7	25.2	2.6
FIN	9.4	14	17.4	22.5	36.7	22.3	3.9
FRA	7.8	12.6	16.5	21.8	41.3	26.9	3.1
GRC	5.8	11.7	17.2	23.2	42.1	26.6	1.9
HRV	6.9	12.7	17.3	23.7	39.5	23.9	2.5
HUN	7.6	13.3	17.6	22.8	38.6	23.9	2.9
IRL	7.5	12.5	16.6	22.3	41.1	25.9	3
ITA	6.3	12.3	16.9	22.8	41.7	26.4	2
LTU	6.5	12.2	16.6	22.6	42	26.8	2.4
LUX	7.3	11.8	16.5	22.7	41.7	26.4	3
LVA	6.5	12.2	16.5	22.5	42.3	26.6	2.3
MLT	8.4	13.5	17.6	22.5	38	23.4	3.4
NLD	9.1	13.9	17.6	22.4	37	22.5	3.7
POL	7.2	12.5	17	22.9	40.4	25.3	2.8
PRT	6.4	12.1	16.2	22.1	43.2	27.8	2.2
ROU	5.3	11.5	17.1	24.3	41.8	25.5	1.7
SVK	8.6	14.6	18.7	23.2	34.9	20.5	3.1
SVN	9.4	14.6	18.2	22.6	35.2	21.1	3.7
SWE	8.5	14.3	17.9	23	36.4	21.6	3

Source: Author's own elaboration based on the World Bank database

Note: AUT-Austraia, BEL-Belgium, BGR-Bulgaria, CYP-Cyprus, CZE-Czech Republic, DEU-Germany, DNK-Denmark, ESP-Espania,EST-Estonia, FIN-Finland, FRA-France, GRC-Greece, HRV-Croactia, HUN-Hungary,IRL-Irleand, ITA-Italy, LTU-Lithueania, LUX-Luxemburg, LVA-Latvia, MLT-Malta, NLD-Netherlands, POL-Poland, PRT-Portugal, ROU-Romania, SVK-Slovakia, SVN-Slovenia, SWE-Sweden

Table 2.7 Percentage of income or consumption attributable to each quintile and top and bottom deciles in EU countries in 2020

Country code	*First quintile*	*Second quintile*	*Third quintile*	*Fourth quintile*	*Fifth quintile*	*Top 10%*	*Bottom 10%*
AUT	7.9	13.5	17.8	23	37.8	23.1	2.8
BEL	9.4	14.5	18.1	22.6	35.5	21.4	3.7
BGR	6.1	10.9	14.9	20.7	47.4	32.6	2.1
CYP	8.5	12.8	16.5	21.6	40.6	26.3	3.5
CZE	9.8	14.4	17.6	21.7	36.5	22.5	4
DEU	7.9	13	17	22.3	39.8	25.2	3.1
DNK	9.4	14	17.5	22.1	37	22.9	3.7
ESP	6	12.1	17.2	23.7	41	25	1.9
EST	8.1	13	16.8	23.1	39	23.5	3
FIN	9.5	14	17.4	22.3	36.7	22.6	3.9
FRA	8	13.2	17.5	22.5	38.8	24.5	3.1
GRC	6.7	12.5	17.2	23	40.5	25.2	2.4
HRV	7.9	13.4	17.9	23.5	37.3	22.3	2.9

(*Continued*)

Table 2.7 (Continued)

Country code	*First quintile*	*Second quintile*	*Third quintile*	*Fourth quintile*	*Fifth quintile*	*Top 10%*	*Bottom 10%*
HUN	8.1	13.4	17.7	22.9	37.8	23.3	3.1
IRL	9	13.3	17	22.3	38.3	23.8	3.7
ITA	6.3	12.1	16.9	23.1	41.7	26.1	2.1
LTU	7.1	11.9	15.7	21.5	43.8	28.5	2.7
LUX	7.1	12.3	16.8	23.3	40.5	25	2.8
LVA	6.9	11.7	16.2	22.3	42.9	27.5	2.5
MLT	8	13	17	22.3	39.7	25.1	3.1
NLD	9.2	14.6	18.3	22.5	35.4	21.6	3.6
POL	8.6	13.7	17.6	22.5	37.6	23.1	3.4
PRT	6.9	12.4	16.4	22.2	42.1	26.9	2.4
ROU	5.6	12.3	17.8	24.3	40	24.2	1.7
SVK	9.5	15.4	19	23.2	32.8	18.8	3.6
SVN	10.3	14.8	18.2	22.4	34.4	20.5	4.2
SWE	8.2	13.8	17.7	23.1	37.2	22.4	3

Source: Author's own elaboration based on the World Bank database

Note: AUT-Austraia, BEL-Belgium, BGR-Bulgaria, CYP-Cyprus, CZE-Czech Republic, DEU-Germany, DNK-Denmark, ESP-Espania,EST-Estonia, FIN-Finland, FRA-France, GRC-Greece, HRV-Croactia, HUN-Hungary, IRL-Irleand, ITA-Italy, LTU-Lithueania, LUX-Luxemburg, LVA-Latvia, MLT-Malta, NLD-Netherlands, POL-Poland, PRT-Portugal, ROU-Romania, SVK-Slovakia, SVN-Slovenia, SWE-Sweden

with the lowest income inequality, Czechia came out on top, performing evenly in every quintile. Equal income distribution could also be seen in Finland, Slovenia, Denmark and the Netherlands. Similar to the previous years, 2020 did not bring significant changes in this indicator. It can be seen that the distribution of income in EU economies has remained at a similar level over the past two decades. Again, Slovenia, Czechia, Finland, Belgium, Denmark, the Netherlands and Slovakia achieved the most balanced income in quintiles, with Slovakia having a slightly elevated ratio of 23.2% in the fourth quintile. Countries with an uneven income distribution were joined by Italy, which recorded an uneven income distribution across all quintiles. Luxembourg, which recorded an uneven income distribution mainly in the second, third, fourth and fifth quintiles, also worsened. Conversely, Poland recorded significantly better, more balanced incomes, joining the countries in the middle. The countries with the most balanced incomes remained unchanged during the study period.

2.2 Regional Competitiveness Index

The European Union is on a dynamic development path, but not one without difficulties. In the literature, the term 'two-speed Europe' is becoming popular, reflecting the differences of individual Member States and regions. The EU is focussed on reducing regional inequality, which is why the EU presented the European Regional Competitiveness Report. In 2002, the European Commission established the Competitiveness Council (COMPET), which prepares regular competitive reports on the functioning of the economy of the European Union. In the EU, the issue of competitiveness has become critical in connection with the Lisbon strategy, whose primary goal is for the EU to be the most dynamic and competitive knowledge economy. The interest of the EU in the competitiveness of regions and cities has grown due to the identification of its critical factors and the development of policies that encourage and support these influencing factors (Kitson et al., 2004). The index provides comparable information on economic and social issues at the regional level. It measures regional competitiveness and enables comparisons with others of a similar nature, which can be helpful in creating long-term development plans.

The Regional Competitiveness Index (RCI) assesses 11 pillars grouped into three groups: Basic, Efficiency and Innovation. The Basic dimension includes institutions, macroeconomic stability, infrastructure, health and basic education – these measure continuous economic development and competitiveness. The measure of efficiency is an evaluation of higher education and lifelong learning as well as the efficiency and size of the labour market. The Innovation dimension reflects the level of innovation, technological readiness and business sophistication (Dijkstra et al., 2011). The index generally follows the methodology adopted in the first edition of 2010 (Annoni & Kozovska, 2010).

The RCI can be represented as follows (Benzaquen et al., 2010):

$$\mathrm{RCI} = \frac{\sum_{k=1}^{1} \mathrm{Pillar}_k}{l} \quad (1)$$

where RCI is the average of its constituent l pillars and each pillar (Pillar_k) is represented as the average of its constituent m factors.

The EU RCI provides a competitive assessment for each NUTS 2 region of the EU27 Member States. The RCI highlights critical challenges in less developed regions and innovative benefits in more developed regions. Pillars measure not only essential indicators for companies but also residents' quality of life. The index is used to monitor, evaluate and compare regions' development. The first RCI adopted the definition of competitiveness as the ability of a region to generate high, growing incomes and to improve the livelihoods of the people living there (Meyer-Stamer, 2008). In the last report, the definition of regional competitiveness was updated as the ability of a region to offer businesses and residents an attractive, sustainable environment in which to live and work (Annoni et al., 2017).

Currently, five editions of this RCI have already been released. The first was published in 2010. Each subsequent edition has been issued every three years (2010, 2013, 2016, 2019 and 2022). However, the 2022 edition contains some changes compared to the four previous editions. In brief, since 2010 the EU RCI has measured the most important competitiveness factors in all NUTS 2 regions across the European Union. The index measures the ability of a region to offer businesses and residents an attractive living and working environment with very different indicators. The indices published in 2013, 2016 and 2019 changed the methodology, as the pillar weights were modified. GDP per capita in the EU index was divided into five groups, while in 2013 the division was into three groups. This division existed only for the 2013, 2016 and 2019 indices. It is also worth noting that the latest version of the index, created in 2022, has changed the methodology and is therefore called the RCI 2.0. In 2022, the division that existed in 2010 was again returned, but the weights were modified. Due to the nature and availability of indicators, two pillars – 'Macroeconomic Stability' and 'Basic Education' – are measured at the country level. In contrast, the pillars 'Institutions' and 'Technological Readiness' include two sub-pillars, one at the national level and another at the regional level. Unlike previous editions, EU regions are divided into three stages of development based on their average GDP per capita, expressed in purchasing power standards (PPS). In the three previous versions of the RCI – 2013, 2016 and 2019 (Annoni & Dijkstra, 2013, 2019; Annoni et al., 2017) – EU regions were divided into five stages of development, similar to the Global Competitiveness Index (WEF-GCI). This remained unchanged until the 2017/2018 edition. Since then, WEF-GCI stopped using development stages. As a result, the RCI 2.0 returned to the original approach used in the 2010 version, which used three stages and adapted them to the thresholds currently used in the EU's Cohesion Policy. These development phases are recalculated for each edition and do not fully correspond to the regional category used in the Cohesion Policy. Moreover, the RCI 2.0 release comes with several interactive tools. It is worth noting that the main pillars remain the same as in previous editions (see Figure 2.3), while the weights of these pillars have changed due to the countries' degree of development (see Table 2.10). The individual weights and the distribution of countries by stage of development for the index in other years are shown in Tables 2.8 and 2.9.

The 2022 edition of the RCI 2.0 shows significant differences in EU regional competitiveness. As in previous editions, it is multi-centric, performing well in areas with large urban areas in the EU. However, the gap between the capitals and other regions varies from one EU Member State to another, and more competitive countries generally have a smaller gap between their capital and different regions

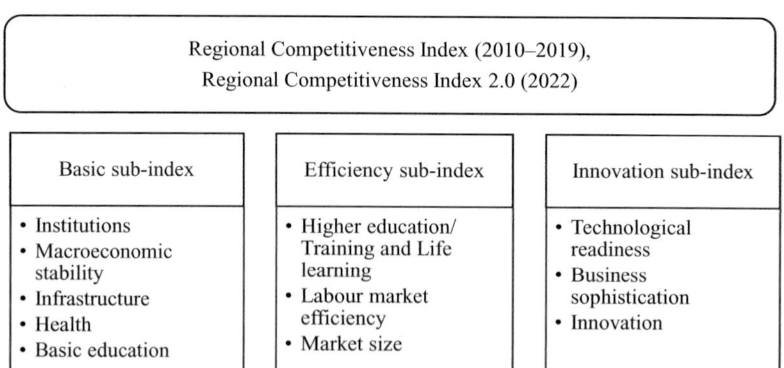

Figure 2.3 Pillars of EU RCI 2010–2019 and EU RCI 2.0 2022

Source: Based on Annoni and Kozovska (2010); Dijkstra et al. (2011); Annoni et al. (2017); Annoni and Dijkstra (2019)

Table 2.8 Weighting system for the three RCI sub-indices, broken down by the development stage (2010 RCI)

Stage of development	*Sub-index weights*		
	Basic (%)	*Efficiency (%)*	*Innovation (%)*
Stage 1: GDP index (GDP/head [PPS]) < 75, EU27 =1 00	40	50	10
Stage 2: GDP index (GDP/head [PPS]) ≤ 75 and < 100, EU27 = 100	30	50	20
Stage 3: GDP index (GDP/head [PPS]) ≥ 100, EU27 = 100	20	50	30

Source: Based on Annoni and Kozovska (2010); Dijkstra et al. (2011)

Table 2.9 Weighting system for the three RCI sub-indices, broken down by the development stage (2013–2019 RCI)

Stage of development	*Sub-index weights*		
	Basic (%)	*Efficiency (%)*	*Innovation (%)*
Stage 1: GDP index (GDP/head [PPS]) < 50, EU27 = 100	35	50	15
Stage 2: GDP index (GDP/head [PPS]) <50–75, EU27 = 100	31.25	50	18.75
Stage 3: GDP index (GDP/head [PPS]) < 75–90, EU27 = 100	27.50	50	22.50
Stage 2: GDP index (GDP/head [PPS]) < 90–110, EU27 = 100	23.75	50	26.25
Stage 3: GDP index (GDP/head [PPS]) > 110, EU27 = 100	20	50	30

Source: Based on Annoni et al. (2017); Annoni and Dijkstra (2019)

and a smaller internal gap. Between 2016 and 2022, regional competitiveness improved in less developed regions, while the performance of transition regions was more variable. The more developed regions still achieved the highest scores, but they came closer to the EU average.

The fifth edition of the RCI maintains the structure of previous editions, but uses an improved framework to facilitate comparisons over time. The RCI sub-indices are weighted according to different stages of development, as shown in Table 2.10.

The most successful region in the 2022 edition of the RCI was Utrecht (NL), followed by Zuid-Holland (NL) and the French capital region of Île-de-France (Table 2.11). All three scored at least 40 points above the EU average (EU27 = 100). In total, the top ten regions included five regions in the Netherlands (including the capital, Amsterdam, and its commuter zone), two regions in Belgium (including the capital region for Brussels and its commuter zone) and the three capitals of Denmark, France and Sweden. At the other end of the scale, 50 or more points behind the EU average were six regions in Romania, two in Greece and two in Bulgaria (Table 2.12). There were no metropolitan areas in the bottom ten regions

Table 2.10 Weighting system for the three RCI sub-indices, broken down by the development stage (2022 RCI)

Stage of development	*Sub-index weights*		
	Basic (%)	*Efficiency (%)*	*Innovation (%)*
Stage 1: GDP index (GDP/head [PPS]) < 75, EU27 = 100	30	50	20
Stage 2: GDP index (GDP/head [PPS]) <75–100, EU27 = 100	25	50	25
Stage 3: GDP index (GDP/head [PPS]) > 100, EU27 = 100	20	50	30

Source: Based on Dijkstra et al. (2023)

Table 2.11 Top ten EU regions in the 2022 RCI 2.0

Member state	*Region code*	*Region name*	*2022 RCI 2.0 (EU27 = 100)*	*Rank*
The Netherlands	NL31	Utrecht	151.1	1
The Netherlands	NL33	Zuid-Holland	142.5	2
France	FR10	Ile-de-France	142.0	3
The Netherlands	NL41	Noord-Brabant	140.6	4
The Netherlands	NL_C	Amsterdam and its commuting zone	140.6	4
Sweden	SE11	Stockholm	138.9	6
Denmark	DK01	Hovedstaden	137.7	7
Belgium	BE_C	Brussels and its commuting zone	136.3	8
The Netherlands	NL22	Gelderland	135.7	9
Belgium	BE23	Oost-Vlaanderen	134.6	10

Source: Based on Dijkstra et al. (2023)

Note: An equal ranking was assigned if the regions have the same score at the one-digit level

Table 2.12 Bottom ten EU regions in the 2022 RCI 2.0

Member state	*Region code*	*Region name*	*2022 RCI 2.0 (EU27 = 100)*	*Rank*
Greece	EL51	Anatoliki Makedonia, Thraki	56.2	225
Romania	RO11	Nord-Vest	56.0	226
Bulgaria	BG34	Yugoiztochen	53.4	227
Greece	EL64	Sterea Elláda	53.2	228
Romania	RO12	Centru	52.5	229
Romania	RO31	Sud-Muntenia	52.1	230
Romania	RO41	Sud-Vest Oltenia	50.2	231
Bulgaria	BG31	Severozapaden	49.0	232
Romania	RO21	Nord-Est	47.0	233
Romania	RO22	Sud-Est	46.0	234

Source: Based on Dijkstra et al. (2023)

Note: An equal ranking was assigned if the regions have the same score at the one-digit level

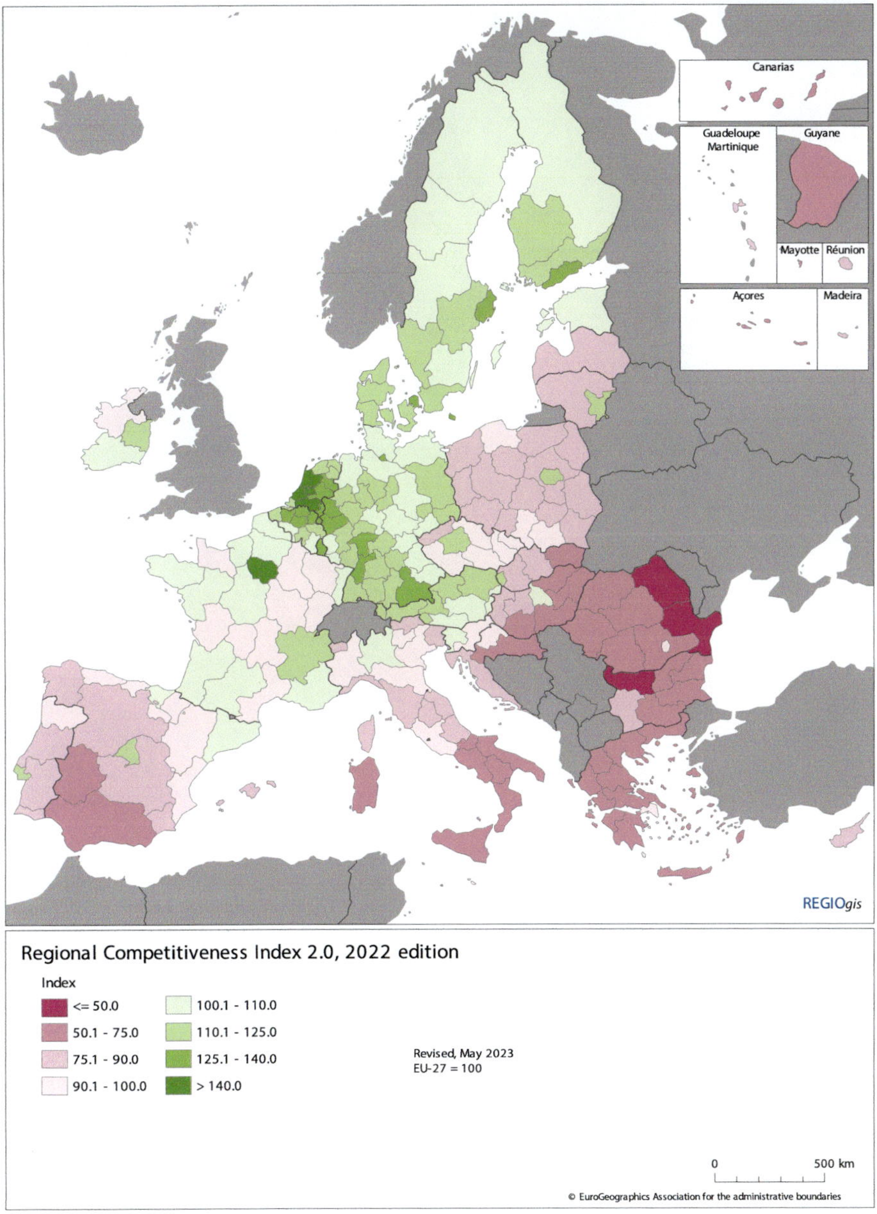

Figure 2.4 EU Regional Competitiveness Index 2.0

Source: European Commission (2023)

Figures 2.4–2.7 show the EU Regional Competitiveness Index 2.0 and the regional distribution of the Basic, Efficiency and Innovation sub-indices. According to previous publications, the main sub-index has the most minor fluctuations within the country, while the Efficiency and especially the Innovation sub-indices vary more.

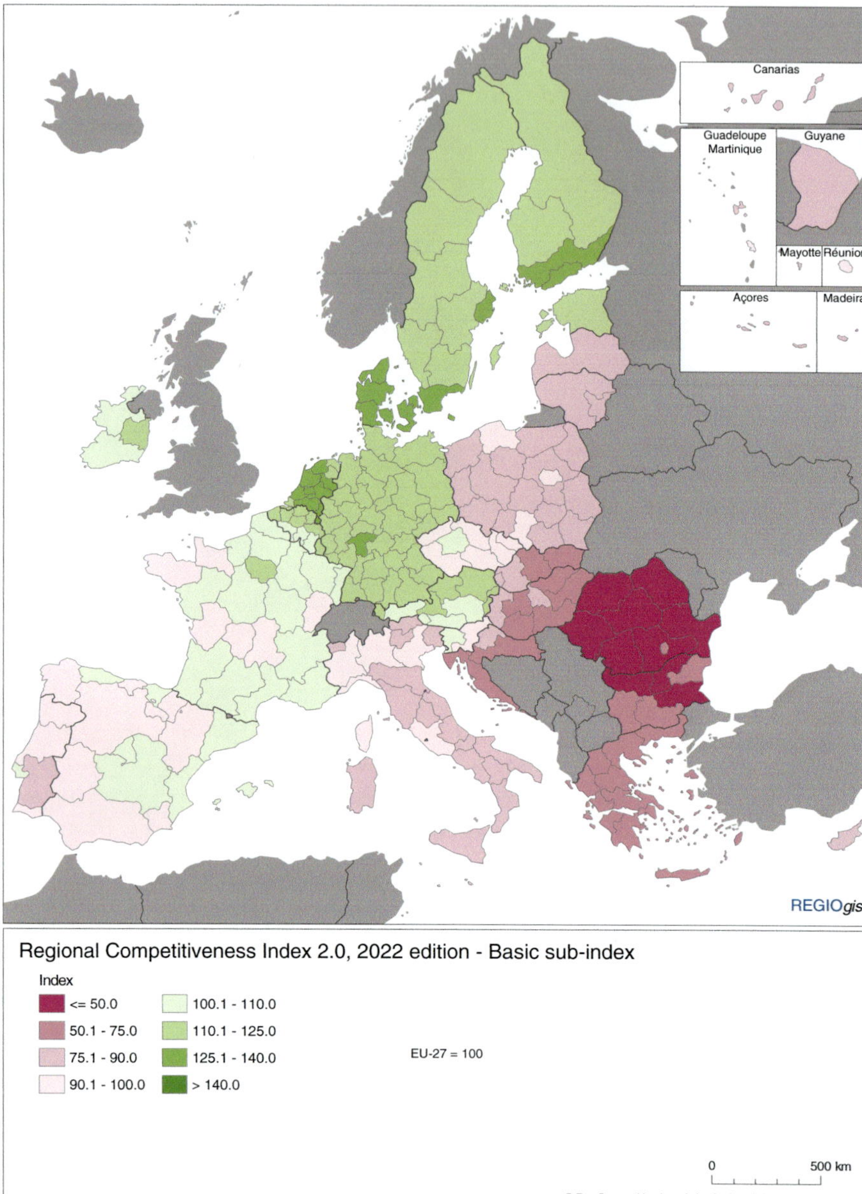

Figure 2.5 EU Regional Competitiveness Index 2.0 – Basic sub-index

Source: European Commission (2023)

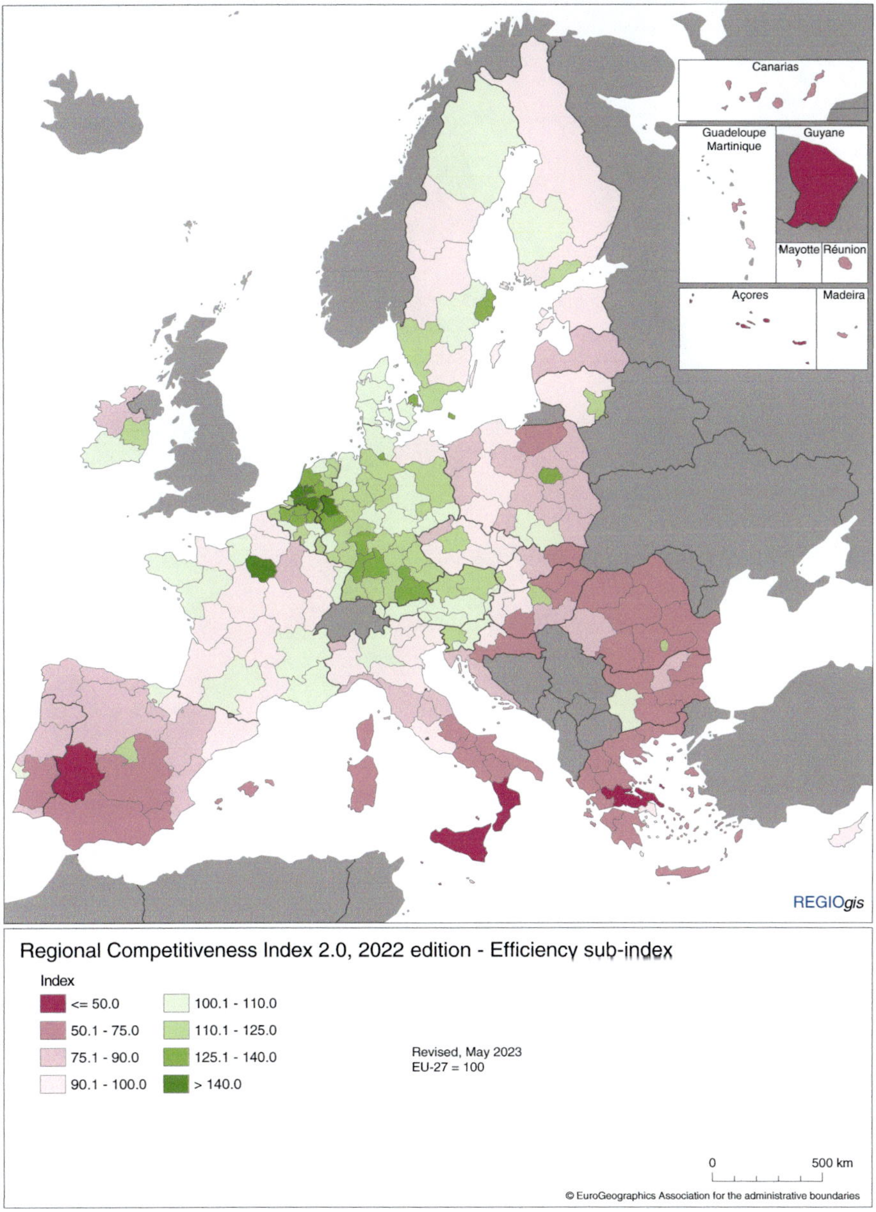

Figure 2.6 EU Regional Competitiveness Index 2.0 – Efficiency sub-index

Source: European Commission (2023)

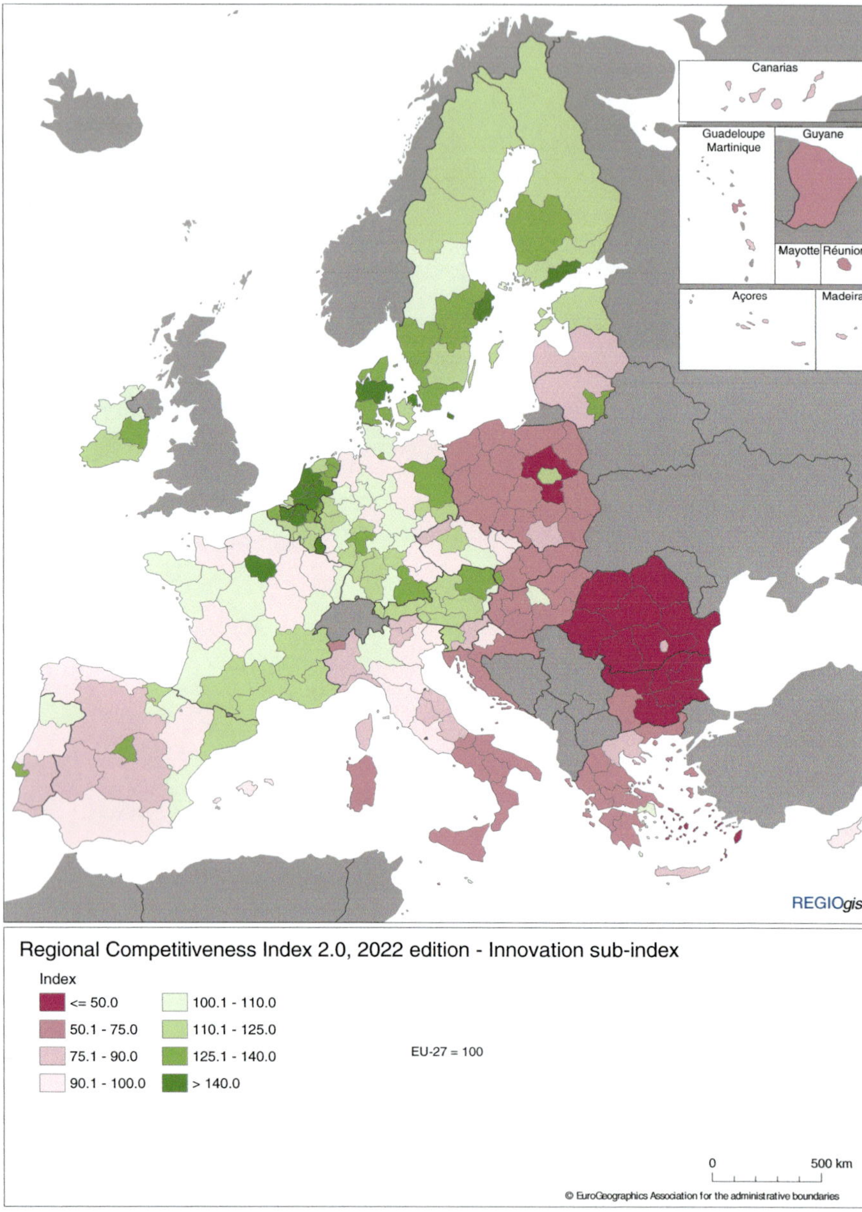

Figure 2.7 EU Regional Competitiveness Index 2.0 – Innovation sub-index

Source: European Commission (2023)

The variation in score increases from the 'core' index to the Innovation sub-index between countries, and even more within countries. Domestic variability and the gap between the capital and other regions of the country are more significant in the more developed components of competitiveness, i.e. the Efficiency and Innovation sub-indices.

The best results were mainly observed in Germany, Austria, the Benelux countries (the Netherlands, Belgium and Luxembourg) and the Scandinavian countries (Denmark, Sweden and Finland). Very different results were observed in Ireland, where three regions (IE06, IE05 and IE04) were marked with three different colours. The IE06 region was rated very well, while IE04 was rated the weakest. This shows that there were significant differences between regions in this country. A similar situation can be observed in the decidedly larger country of Italy. The best-performing area was Lombardy, located in the north of the country (ITC4). Farther to the south, worse statistics were reported.

It is worth noting that in many countries, the best values were assigned to regions where the capital is located. This can be seen in France (FR10), Poland (PL91), Spain (ES30), Ireland (IE06), Sweden (SE11), Lithuania (LT01), Portugal (PT17), Czechia (CZ01), Austria (AT13), Finland (FI1B), Romania (RO32) and others.

Regions belonging to Central and Eastern Europe, in particular those in Bulgaria, Romania and Greece, performed the weakest in the 2022 RCI. Regions in countries such as Croatia, Poland and Spain also recorded poor performance in the 2022 RCI. This can be seen in Figure 2.4.

The performance of the regions in the Basic sub-index was similar to the main 2022 RCI index, with the best results being posted in Benelux, Scandinavia, Germany and Austria. It is noteworthy that the statistics in Spain, France and Ireland improved. The results between regions in these countries were less varied than in the 2022 RCI. In Italy, there was less variation between regions in the north versus the south. Lombardy was not among the high-index regions in this edition, but the country looked better overall. The worst statistics were observed in the same countries as before, i.e. the CEE countries. Unfortunately, the performance of Bulgaria's regions, and especially Romania's, was very poor. In addition, it is worth noting that the disparity between the regions in which the countries' capitals lie had decreased in many countries. This can be seen in Figure 2.5.

The performance of the regions in the Efficiency sub-index differed from the previously discussed indices, the Basic sub-index and the overall 2022 RCI. In the Efficiency index, the variation of the regions within the EU27 countries was most apparent. Quite large regional inequalities were noted in Sweden and Finland, where they had previously been aligned and had performed very well. Again, the best performance in this index can be seen in the regions of Belgium, the Netherlands, Luxembourg, Denmark and Austria. Furthermore, the regions of Ireland were characterised by a wide disparity in performance. Italy and France again recorded more significant variation between regions. Similarly, the worst statistics were observed in Bulgaria, Romania, Greece and Croatia. It is also worth noting that the disparity between the regions in which the capital is located had increased in many countries. This can be observed in Figure 2.6.

The best performance in the Innovation sub-index was recorded by regions in Benelux, Scandinavia, Ireland and Austria. Again, the difference between regions within countries was noticeable. Interestingly, earlier sub-indices did not show a differentiation in German regions, but here they did. As in all previous statistics, the weakest performing regions were those from Central and Eastern Europe. In particular, this includes the regions of Bulgaria, Romania, Greece and Croatia.

It is worth noting that the disparity between the regions where a country's capital is located had increased in many countries. This can be seen in Figure 2.7.

Comparing the RCI over time has always been complicated because each edition of the index contains minor modifications. There are many reasons for this: new indicators may become available at the regional level, while others are no longer available, and changes in NUTS 2 boundaries cause breaks in the series. Thanks to the 2022 edition, for the first time we were able to provide an enhanced temporal comparison between 2016, 2019 and 2022. Starting with the original data, the results were recalculated using a new methodology and were labelled 'RCI 2.0, 2016' and 'RCI 2.0, 2019'. Throughout the period, i.e. between the 2016 and 2019 editions, we mainly observed a catching-up process in the eastern regions of the EU Member States, coupled with improvements in the southern regions of the EU Member States (Spain, Greece, Italy and Portugal) as they recovered from the financial crisis. The catching-up process took place in the context of the RCI, which improved steadily at the EU level over the same period (Dijkstra et al., 2023).

Between the 2019 edition of the RCI and the 2022 edition, regional competitiveness improved by 10 index points or more. While the 2022 edition continued to show a clear spatial pattern in the EU, with the most competitive regions mainly being concentrated in the Austrian, Benelux, German and Nordic regions, there was a clear process of catching-up by regions throughout the eastern/southern EU Member States. A more differentiated spatial pattern emerged between 2019 and 2022. Regions in the eastern EU Member States continued to catch up in the Baltics, Croatia, Hungary, Poland and Slovenia. Regions in Czechia, Romania, Slovakia and parts of Bulgaria, however, moved away from the EU average. In the southern EU Member States, regions in Greece, Portugal and Spain continued to improve their performance relative to the EU average, but those in Italy did not (with the exception of the regions of Lombardy, Marche and the autonomous region of Valle D'Aosta) (Dijkstra et al., 2023).

There are large regional differences in 2022 RCI 2.0 in the EU. The lowest values were concentrated in the regions of the eastern EU, followed by the southern regions. In these areas, there were only a few regions with the capital or a large city that scored above the EU average. Austria, the Benelux countries, Germany and the three Nordic countries achieved above average index values in all regions, while France and Ireland showed more variation, with regions below and above the EU average. The capital city region was usually the most competitive in a country, with a few exceptions (Germany, Italy and the Netherlands). However, the difference between the capital region and the rest varied, with substantial differences being observed in France, Romania and Slovakia. The usual rule of thumb is that the difference between the capital and the other regions was minor in more competitive countries. More competitive countries also showed more minor differences between all regions. This indicates that the performance of all regions matters to a country's overall competitiveness. Therefore, public policy should aim to promote a convergence process that will help the less competitive regions catch up and keep the most competitive regions moving forward. In the period 2016–2022, regional competitiveness improved in less developed areas, while the performance in transition areas was more variable. More advanced regions still received the highest marks, but approached the EU average (Dijkstra et al., 2023).

2.3 Studies about inequity in Europe

The issue of socio-economic inequality is currently one of the most important economic topics. Economic inequality may result from various forces: geography, technology, globalisation of finance and trade, changes in labour market regulations and redistributive policies. Reducing regional inequalities within the community is one of the primary goals of the EU. This challenge became more difficult to meet with the subsequent EU enlargements including new countries that significantly differed in their level of development from the old EU15. This greatly impacted the distribution of regional results and, consequently, the adaptation of the EU programmes and the Cohesion Policy. Inequalities in the EU are a frequent topic of scientific publications.

As mentioned in Chapter 1, the literature provides extensive research on the convergence of European regions. In studies about convergence, the results depend on the selected research methods, the selected regions and the study period. Beta convergence, which is the process of poor regions growing faster than rich ones, was confirmed for European regions by numerous studies, but at quite a slow pace of 2% or less yearly (e.g. Barro & Sala-i-Martin, 1991; Cuadrado-Roura, 2001; López-Bazo, 2003; Le Pen, 2011; Dauderstädt, 2018; Alcidi, 2019). Other studies found diminishing beta convergence or no evidence of convergence (Fagerberg & Verspagen, 1996; Martin, 2001; Hegerty, 2016). U-shaped convergence with the minimum falling at the beginning of the 1980s was confirmed by Yin et al. (2003), Niebuhr and Schlitte (2004) and Geppert et al. (2005). Sigma convergence, which refers to a reduction in the distribution of income levels between economies/regions, was confirmed by Boldrin and Canova (2001) and Yin et al. (2003), but rejected by Neven and Goymte (1995), Barrios and Strobl (2005) and Cappelen et al. (2003). Other studies focussed on the identification of convergence clubs. Canova (2004) identified four homogeneous clubs with different convergence rates and steady-state values that highlighted North–South or poor–rich dimensions. Badinger et al. (2004) indicated that regions tend to cluster according to their growth performance, and that regions with high economic growth are often surrounded by regions with above-average growth.

The literature on the subject also contains extensive research on the level of inequality, identifying the most backward regions. It highlights the main trends in inequality in the EU. Firstly, a socio-economic imbalance exists both between and within EU countries. Even countries with high economic and social standards have the same patterns of spatial disparities as their neighbours who are lagging behind. Moreover, the structural origins of inequalities vary significantly across Europe. Regarding socio-economic variables, Spain, Romania and Bulgaria are among the most disparate groups of countries compared to the rest of the EU. Some countries are characterised by low levels of inequality, such as Czechia, the Netherlands and Finland (Szymańska, 2021).

Secondly, there are greater differences in income between regions than between Member States (Carrera et al., 2021, Hacker, 2021). There are inequalities at the regional level, and the gap between them is widening. This applies to both the geography of production and the geography of income. Inequalities persist and create a kind of path dependence correlated with proximity in space. In some countries, significant growth may be limited to a few regions, usually including the capital. Moreover, countries characterised by greater spatial inequalities at the regional level are also characterised by greater social inequalities. According to the Organisation for Economic Co-operation and Development (OECD) (2017) report, the most equal European countries are the Nordic countries and the CEE countries (Slovenia, Czechia and Slovakia). Western European countries such as France, Germany and the Netherlands rank close to the European average, while income inequality is above average in all southern European countries. In turn, the highest level of income inequality in Europe is found in the Baltic countries.

Thirdly, inequality within countries has shown a tendency to increase (Rodriguez-Pose & Gill 2006; Arabia et al., 2010; Szymańska, 2021). The EU27 has made progress in reducing inequalities between countries, but income inequality within countries persists or has even widened. Disparities between countries are evident between Spain, Bulgaria and Romania and the rest of the EU countries. A further division into Western and Eastern countries and the 'old' and 'new' EU can also be observed (Szymańska, 2021). Although inequality within countries is still lower on average in the EU than in other developed regions, most EU17 countries in south-central and eastern Europe have levels of inequality above the OECD average. The increase in inequality within countries is due to the relative increase in labour incomes at the top of the distribution, while low-income households lag behind (Inchauste & Karver, 2017).

Fourthly, economic activities are concentrated in growth centres, which perform much better than the peripheral regions (Dauderstädt, 2018). Cities and hubs of economic activity are the most unequal areas. In the EU, metropolitan areas are the most developed; in many cases, they are the capitals of countries with an average income of 17% higher than the national average. However, metropolitan areas are more unequal than countries as a whole, and inequality increases with size (Boulant et al., 2016). Carrera et al. (2021) confirm the relationship between agglomerations, growing economies of scale in production and growth in regional inequality. Capital regions are getting closer to Western standards, while industrial and peripheral regions are lagging behind (Meliciani, 2016).

The literature also contains publications that point to the main factors influencing income inequality in the EU. Szymańska (2021) emphasises that the Cohesion Policy is insufficient and requires additional actions to help eliminate disproportions. Potential directions for policy changes include considering mainly demographic changes, since one factor that leads to higher inequality is the ageing of the population, which applies to all EU countries. Appropriate social policy could effectively support the Cohesion Policy and contribute to a more lasting reduction in inequalities. Allmendinger and von den Driesch (2014) state that there is an increasing risk in the EU that various forms of education, employment and financial inequalities will deepen over time. European social policy should address the disparities resulting from the growing pluralisation of lifestyles and social security models. Meliciani (2016) points to the increasing importance of innovation and human capital in explaining inequalities in income and employment among old EU Member States, especially after the 2008 financial crisis. Regional differences in the new Member States are fundamentally linked to socio-economic factors (Cohen & Ladaique, 2018). The direct factor behind the increase in inequality is the more significant disparity in wages and salaries. This is not surprising, since earnings account for three quarters of total household income among the working-age population. Muštra and Škrabić (2014) pay attention to institutions in reducing inequality. Institutions shape regional inequalities indirectly through political channels. More significant investments in infrastructure, education, training and industrial innovation will reduce regional disparities. Moreover, social and institutional proximity interdependence indicates the need to combine various institutional factors for harmonious regional development. Georgiev (2017) points out that overcoming inequalities between Member States is only possible through a targeted reform of EU economic policies. The EU should reform the resources system by introducing progressivity, whereby Member States' contributions will be increased or decreased according to a coefficient reflecting deviations from the EU averages in gross national income (GNI) per capita, employment and trade balance for each Member State. Similarly, changes may be applied to the rules of financing and co-financing the Cohesion Policy and other policies causing redistributive effects.

References

Aiginger, K. (2006). Competitiveness: From a dangerous obsession to a welfare creating ability with positive externalities. *Journal of Industry, Competition and Trade*, *6*(2), 161–177.

Alcidi, C. (2019). Economic integration and income convergence in the EU. *Intereconomics*, *54*(1), 5–11. https://doi.org/10.1007/s10272-019-0783-6

Allmendinger, J., & von den Driesch, E. (2014). *Social inequalities in Europe: Facing the challenge* [WZB Discussion Paper, No. P 2014–005, Wissenschaftszentrum Berlin für Sozialforschung].

Annoni, P., & Dijkstra, L. (2013). *EU regional competitiveness index: RCI 2013* [Joint Research Centre Scientific and Policy Report]. Retrieved December 20, 2023 from https://ec.europa.eu/regional_policy/information-sources/publications/studies/2013/eu-regional-competitiveness-index-rci-2013_en

Annoni, P., & Dijkstra, L. (2019). *EU regional competitiveness index 2019, DG regional and urban policy*. Retrieved December 20, 2023 from https://ec.europa.eu/regional_policy/information-sources/publications/working-papers/2019/the-european-regional-competitiveness-index-2019_en

Annoni, P., Dijkstra, L., & Gargano, N. (2017). *EU regional competitiveness index 2016, DG regional and urban policy*. Retrieved December 20, 2023 from https://ec.europa.eu/regional_policy/information-sources/publications/working-papers/2017/the-eu-regional-competitiveness-index-2016_en

Annoni, P., Kozovska, K. (2010). *EU regional competitiveness index (RCI) 2010. EUR 24346 EN*. Publications Office of the European Union. Retrieved December 20, 2023 from https://publications.jrc.ec.europa.eu/repository/handle/JRC58169

Arbia, G., Battisti, M., & Di Vaio, G. (2010). Institutions and geography: Empirical test of spatial growth models for European regions. *Economic Modelling*, *27*(1), 12–21. doi:10.1016/j.econmod.2009.07.004

Badinger, H., Müller, W., & Tondl, G. (2004). Regional convergence in the European Union, 1985–1999: A spatial dynamic panel analysis. *Regional Studies*, *38*(3), 241–253. doi:10.1080/003434042000211105

Barrios, S., & Strobl, E. (2005). The dynamics of regional inequalities. *Economic Papers of the European Commission*, No. 229.

Barro, R. J., & Sala-i-Martin, X. (1991). Convergence across states and regions. *Brookings Papers on Economic Activity*, 22(1), 107. doi:10.2307/2534639

Benzaquen, J., Carpio, L., Zegarra, L., & Valdivia, C. (2010). A competitiveness index for the regionsof a country. *Cepal Review*, 102, 67–84.

Boldrin, L., & Canova, F. (2001). Inequality and convergence in Europe's regions: Reconsidering European regional policies. *Economic Policy*, *16*(32), 207–253.

Boulant, J., Brezzi, M., & Veneri, P. (2016). Income levels and inequality in metropolitan areas: A comparative approach in OECD countries. *OECD Regional Development Working Papers*, No. 2016/06. http://dx.doi.org/10.1787/5jlwj02zz4mren

Canova, F. (2004). Testing for convergence clubs in income per capita: A predictive density approach. *International Economic Review*, *45*(1), 49–77.

Cappelen, A., Castellacci, F., Fagerberg, J. & Verspagen, B. (2003). Regional disparities in income and unemployment in Europe. In B. Fingleton (Ed.), *European regional growth* (pp. 323–350). Springer.

Carrera, E. J. S., Rombaldoni, R., & Pozzi, R. (2021). Socioeconomic inequalities in Europe. *Economic Analysis and Policy*, *71*, 307–320. doi:10.1016/j.eap.2021.05.007

Cohen, G., & Ladaique, M. (2018). Drivers of growing income inequalities in OECD and European countries. In R. M. Carmo, C. Rio, & M. Medgyesi (Eds.), *Reducing inequalities: A challenge for the European Union?* (pp. 31–43). Cham, Switzerland: Palgrave Macmillan.

Cuadrado-Roura, J. (2001). Regional convergence in the European Union: From hypothesis to the actual trends. *The Annals of Regional Science 35*, 333–356. https://doi.org/10.1007/s001680100054

Dauderstädt, M. (2018). Inequality, cohesion and crisis in Europe. In R. M. Carmo, C. Rio, & M. Medgyesi (Eds.), *Reducing inequalities: A challenge for the European Union?* Cham, Switzerland: Palgrave Macmillan.

Dijkstra, L., Annoni, P., & Kozovska, K. (2011). *A new regional competitiveness index: theory, methods and findings. DG Regional and Urban Policy Working Paper*, No. 2. Retrieved December 10, 2023 from https://ec.europa.eu/regional_policy/information-sources/publications/working-papers/2011/a-new-regional-competitiveness-index-theory-methods-and-findings_en

Dijkstra L., Papadimitriou E., Martinez B.C., Dominicis L. & Kovacic M. (2023). *EU Regional Competitiveness Index 2.0 2022 edition*. Retrieved May 28, 2024 from https://ec.europa.eu/regional_policy/sources/work/rci_2022/eu-rci2_0-2022_en.pdf

Fagerberg, J., & Verspagen, B. (1996). Heading for divergence? Regional growth in Europe reconsidered. *Journal of Common Market Studies*, *34*(3), 431–448.

Georgiev, D. (2017). Inequalities and the future of the European Union. In *The EU beyond 2020: In search of identity, sustainability and growth* [Bulgarian European Studies Association Annual conference, October 26, 2017] (pp. 70–79).

Geppert, K., Happich, M., & Stephan, A. (2005). Regional disparities in the European Union: Convergence and agglomeration. *DIW Working Paper*, No. 525. https://www.diw.de/documents/publikationen/73/diw_01.c.43804.de/dp525.pdf

Hacker, B. (2021). *Unequal Europe: Tackling regional disparities in the EU*. Friedrich-Ebert-Stiftung/Foundation for European Progressive Studies.

Hegerty, S. W. (2016). Regional convergence and growth clusters in Central and Eastern Europe: An examination of sectoral-level data. *Eastern European Business and Economics Journal*, *2*(2), 95–110.

Inchauste, G., & Karver, J. (2017). *Understanding changes in inequality in the EU: background to "Growing united: Upgrading Europe's convergence machine."* World Bank Group Retrieved December 12, 2023 from https://www.worldbank.org/en/region/eca/publication/europe-growing-united

Kitson, M., Martin, R., & Tyler, P. (2004). Regional competitiveness: An elusive yet key concept? *Regional Studies*, *38*(9), 991–999.

Le Pen, Y. (2011). A pair-wise approach to output convergence between European regions. *Economic Modelling*, *28*(3), 955–964. doi:10.1016/j.econmod.2010.11.00

López-Bazo, E. (2003) Growth and convergence across economies: The experience of the European regions. In B. Fingleton, A. Eraydin, & R. Paci (Eds.), *Regional economic growth, SMEs and the wider Europe* (pp. 49–74), Routledge.

Martin, R. (2001). EMU versus the regions? Regional convergence and divergence in Euroland. *Journal of Economic Geography*, *1*(1), 51–80.

Meliciani, V. (2016). *Regional disparities in the enlarged European Union: Geography, innovation and structural change*. London: Routledge.

Meyer-Stamer, J. (2008). Systemic competitiveness and local economic development. In S. Bodhanya (Ed.), *Large scale systemic change: Theories, modelling and practices*. Duisburg: Mesopartner.

Muštra, V., & Škrabić, B. (2014). Regional inequalities in the European Union and the role of institutions. *Review of Urban & Regional Development Studies*, *26*(1), 20–39. doi:10.1111/rurd.12017

Neven, D., & Goymte, C. (1995). Regional convergence in the European Community. *Journal of Common Market Studies*, *33*(1), 47–65. doi:10.1111/j.1468-5965.1995.tb00516.x

Niebuhr, A., & Schlitte, F. (2004). Convergence, trade and factor mobility in the European Union: Implications for enlargement and regional policy. *Intereconomics*, *39*(3), 167–176.

OECD. (2017). *Understanding the socio-economic divide in Europe*. http://oe.cd/cope-divide-europe-2017

Rodríguez-Pose, A., & Gill, N. (2006). How does trade affect regional disparities? *World Development*, *34*(7), 1201–1222. doi:10.1016/j.worlddev.2005.12.0

Szymańska, A. (2021). Reducing socioeconomic inequalities in the European Union in the context of the 2030 Agenda for Sustainable Development. *Sustainability*, *13*, 7409. https://doi.org/10.3390/su13137409

Yin, L., Zestos, G. K., & Michelis, L. (2003). Economic convergence in the European Union. *Journal of Economic Integration*, *18*(1), 188–213.

3 EU policy for reducing inequalities

3.1 European Union's regional policy

The positive economic effects of European integration cannot be disputed. However, huge disparities still exist in the EU between countries and regions. Recognising the importance of regional policy, the Treaty on the Functioning of the European Union (European Union, 2012) dedicates Articles 174–178 to 'economic, social and territorial cohesion'. 'In order to promote its overall harmonious development, the Union shall develop and pursue its actions leading to the strengthening of its economic, social and territorial cohesion. In particular, the Union shall aim to reduce disparities between the development levels of the various regions and the backwardness of the least favoured regions'.

Regional policy is one of the fundamental policies of the EU, which aims to reduce the economic and social disparities between the EU regions. The genesis of its regional policy dates back to the establishment of the European Communities. Historically, when the Customs Union was being formed, the need to implement a uniform regional policy was less significant than it is today due to the minor variance in the development of the member nations (Hall, 2016). The original Treaty of Rome of 1957, signed by six founding countries to establish the European Economic Community (EEC), stated in the preamble that the Member States were 'anxious to strengthen the unity of their economies and to ensure their harmonious development by reducing the differences existing between the various regions and the backwardness of the less-favoured regions'. In the 1960s, actions towards creating a common regional policy were rather postulates than specific undertakings. In 1958, two funds were established to support the development of the Community's regions: the European Social Fund and the European Agricultural Guidance and Guarantee Fund. At the beginning of the 1970s, the Cohesion Policy began to play a greater role due to the troubles of European economies related to the oil crisis of the 1970s and the enlargement of the Union with Denmark, the UK and Ireland exacerbating regional disparities. In 1975, the European Regional Development Fund was established, whose main objective was to support poorer areas. Regional policy became a Community responsibility and social and economic cohesion a Community goal with the signing of the Single European Act (SEA) by the member states. (1986): 'In order to promote its overall harmonious

DOI: 10.4324/9781032615516-4

development, the Community shall develop and pursue its actions, strengthening its economic and social cohesion. In particular, the Community shall aim to reduce disparities between the development levels of the various regions and the backwardness of the least-favoured regions, including rural areas' (Art. 130a). An important breakthrough in the history of the EU's regional policy was the signing of the Maastricht Treaty in 1992. It provided the basis for creating an economic and monetary union. To alleviate the problems of poorer regions in adapting to financial discipline, the European Cohesion Fund was created to support investments in economically underdeveloped areas and to facilitate the implementation of the Maastricht convergence criteria (Brunazzo, 2016). Plans to extend integration to include new Central and Eastern European countries were associated with the creation of a new concept of regional policy. The admission to the Community of many countries that significantly differed economically from the EU15 countries required many modifications.

The objectives of the regional policy are divided into regional, under which assistance is provided to selected regions that meet the eligibility criteria, and horizontal, for which funds can be applied throughout the territory of the Community. The objectives, tasks and instruments of the EU's regional policy were shaped along with the progress of the European integration process. The list of regional policy priorities has changed over the years. An evaluation of the EU's regional policy objectives in six programming periods between 1989 and 2027 is presented in Table 3.1.

The list of tasks for levelling inequalities between regions has changed over the years. The first set of objectives was defined for the period 1989–1993, in which five priorities were distinguished. Objectives 1, 2 and 5b were important for regional policy, as they concerned regional interventions in problem areas of the Community. The second set for the period 1994–1999 included a sixth objective: 'Development and adaptation of particularly sparsely populated areas'. In the second programming period, numerous adjustments and new components were introduced to the specific objectives of regional policy formulated during the 1988

Table 3.1 EU regional policy objectives, 1989–2027

1989–1993	
1	Promoting the development and adjustment of regions whose development is lagging behind
2	Converting the regions, frontier regions or parts of regions (including employment areas and urban communities) seriously affected by industrial decline
3	Combating long-term unemployment (above the age of 25 and unemployed for more than 12 months)
4	Facilitating the occupational integration of young people (job-seekers below the age of 25)
5a	Reforming the Common Agricultural Policy by adapting production, processing and marketing structures in agriculture and forestry
5b	Reforming the Common Agricultural Policy by promoting the development of rural areas

(Continued)

Table 3.1 (Continued)

1994–1999	
1	Promoting the development and adjustment of regions whose development is lagging behind
2	Converting the regions, frontier regions or parts of regions (including employment areas and urban communities) seriously affected by industrial decline
3	Combating long-term unemployment (above the age of 25 and unemployed for more than 12 months)
4	Facilitating the occupational integration of young people (job-seekers below the age of 25)
5a	Reforming the Common Agricultural Policy by adapting production, processing and marketing structures in agriculture and forestry
5b	Reforming the Common Agricultural Policy by promoting the development of rural areas
6	Encouraging development and structural adjustment in regions with low population density
2000–2006	
1	Promoting the development and structural adjustment of regions whose development is lagging behind
2	Supporting the economic and social conversion of areas experiencing structural difficulties
3	Supporting the adaptation and modernisation of education, training and employment policies and systems in regions not eligible under Objective 1
2007–2013	
1	Convergence
2	Regional competitiveness and employment
3	European territorial cooperation
2014–2020	
1	Strengthening research, technological development and innovation
2	Enhancing access to, and the use and quality of, information and communication technologies
3	Enhancing the competitiveness of SMEs
4	Supporting the shift towards the low-carbon economy
5	Promoting climate change adaptation, risk prevention and management
6	Preserving and protecting the environment and promoting resource efficiency
7	Promoting sustainable transport and improving network infrastructures
8	Promoting sustainable and quality employment and supporting labour mobility
9	Promoting social inclusion and combating poverty and any discrimination
10	Investing in education, training and lifelong learning
11	Improving the efficiency of public administration
2021–2027	
1	A more competitive and smarter Europe
2	A greener, low-carbon transition towards a net-zero-carbon economy
3	A more connected Europe by enhancing mobility
4	A more social and inclusive Europe
5	Europe closer to citizens by fostering the sustainable and integrated development of all types of territories

Source: Author's own elaboration based on the European Commission (2023a)

reform. The budget of the first programming period accounted for 0.40% of the EU's GDP (Leonardi, 2005). In the second programme, it was increased to 0.51% of GDP, but the programming period was extended by one year (Martin, 1998). In the 1997 Amsterdam Treaty, cohesion was transformed into one of the basic defining principles of the European Union.

The objectives for the third programming period were modified due to the planned enlargement of the EU in 2004, which was to strengthen its competitive position by extending economic and political links. However, the basic problem of the new Member States was major structural problems, requiring huge financial outlays so that they could actively participate in the single European market. The number of priority objectives was reduced to three in order to strengthen the effectiveness of the actions taken and to facilitate the proper assessment of their results. As in the previous programming period, Objective 1 covered the same activities as the old Objective 1, but also included regions with low population density (former Objective 6) and peripheral regions. The new Objective 2 combined the former Objectives 2 and 5b, but it was defined slightly differently, as it was used to restructure not only regions of crisis industry (previous Objective 2) and rural areas (previous Objective 5b) but also other regions with structural difficulties. Between 2000 and 2006, expenditure supporting regional and rural development accounted for approximately 42% of the European Union's budget expenditure, which was 0.46% of the total EU GDP (Szlachta, 2004).

Three more specific regional objectives were pursued in the 2007–2013 programming period. Among them, the most important for the regions left behind was the first objective, i.e. convergence, which was aimed at accelerating development and equalising the opportunities of the poorest regions by improving the conditions for growth and employment. Areas of action included human and material capital, innovation, a knowledge-based society, adaptability to change, environmental protection and increasing administrative efficiency. The second objective, i.e. competitiveness of regions and employment, was addressed in more developed areas. The task of financial support under this objective was to enable anticipation of economic and social changes, promotion of innovation, entrepreneurship, environmental protection and development of labour markets conducive to social integration. Objective 3, 'European territorial cooperation', was intended to promote common solutions for neighbouring regional authorities. The total budget of the European Structural and Investment Funds (ESIFs) allocated to regional policy was 35.7% of the EU budget and 0.38% of the total EU GDP in the period 2007–2013.

The assumptions of the EU's regional policy in the period 2014–2020 were significantly influenced by the EU's actions to counteract the negative effects of the economic crisis and to implement the 'Europe 2020' strategy, which was adopted in 2010. The aim of the strategy was to correct the shortcomings of the European economic growth model and to create the conditions that would make sustainable economic development conducive to social inclusion. In order to achieve these objectives, three new economic policy objectives were established. An important role in the implementation of the Europe 2020 strategy has been assigned to the regions, which are responsible for implementing effective measures to achieve the goals of the strategy. The 11 objectives set for the 2014–2020 programme are horizontal. In this way, the previous method of defining regional policy objectives was abandoned. It was considered sufficient to correlate the assumptions of the EU's regional policy with the priorities of the 'Europe 2020' strategy. The distribution of financial resources was based on gross domestic product (GDP). The regions were divided into three groups: less developed regions (GDP per capita less than 75% of the average GDP in the EU), regions in transition (GDP per capita 75%–90% of the average GDP in the EU for the programming period 2014–2020 and 75%–100% for the programming period 2021–2027) and more developed regions (GDP per capita exceeding 90% of the average GDP in the EU for the 2014–2020 allocation and exceeding 100% for the 2021–2027 allocation). This scheme for the objectives of the EU's regional policy made it possible to cover all EU member regions with support from Structural Funds.

The programme for the period 2021–2027 supports competitiveness, sustainable research and innovation, digital transformation, the goals of the European Green Deal and Europe's pillar of social rights. It is one of the most cross-cutting policies, contributing to most of the Sustainable Development Goals. With the changes to the regulatory framework, the EU has prioritised supporting national health care systems and tapping into the potential of culture and tourism, as the pandemic hit these sectors hardest. The new law provides greater flexibility by establishing a mechanism to deal with future crises, allowing Member States and the region to mobilise EU resources more quickly to respond to the challenges of unpredictable events (Cavalli et al., 2023). For the 2021–2027 period, the planned Cohesion Policy budget is estimated as an annual average of 0.2% of the EU's GDP (European Commission, 2023b).

As pointed out by Huggins and Williams (2011), regional policymakers are pressurised by short-term outputs, which force them towards short-term policy goals. While regional policies contain many positive elements, there is still a need for more long-term policy. The European Commission is currently working on the future of the Cohesion Policy. For this purpose, it has established a group of specialists who aim to formulate strategic conclusions and recommendations that will maximise the effectiveness of the Cohesion Policy to face numerous challenges, ranging from the innovation gap to demographic changes. This document will also guide policies in supporting a just digital and ecological transition, economic renewal and regional growth. The expert group's work took place in 2023 during nine meetings in Brussels. The group will publish its strategic conclusions and recommendations in early 2024. The meetings concerned, among others, Cohesion Policy actions to support sustainable economic development and to correct internal disparities through investments in general public goods, innovation, digitisation, human capital, environment and climate, social integration and transport. The group's work was also aimed at strengthening the region's resilience to emerging challenges identified in the '8th Cohesion Report', such as demographic changes and increased (skills) shortages in the labour market, climate transformation, technological changes and globalisation. The issue of tailoring support to specific development needs was also raised, considering the diversity of starting positions and the uneven impact of ongoing changes and current and future external shocks. Meeting asymmetric development challenges requires a differentiated approach and place-based policies, complementing national structural policies. The issue of developing more country-specific links between investments in the Cohesion Policy programmes and relevant reforms, in addition to other policies and instruments, was also discussed (European Commission, 2023a).

During the past 25 years, regional policy has had a significant impact on EU countries and societies. Key achievements for each programming period are listed in Table 3.2. The areas targeted in each programming period are job creation and support for enterprises, which in turn translates into an increase in GDP per capita and a reduction in the differences between EU regions. The policy also results in thousands of kilometres of newly built or modernised roads and railways. In recent years, emphasis has also been placed on achieving goals related to research and innovation, the digital economy, the low-carbon economy, environmental and climate action, network infrastructure, social inclusion and human capital.

Table 3.2 Key achievements of the EU's regional policy

Programming period	*Key achievements of the EU's regional policy*
1989–1993	Regions closed the GDP per head gap compared to the EU average by 3%. 600,000 jobs were created through Structural Funds in Greece, Ireland, Portugal and Spain; the average GDP per head of those countries increased from 68.3% to 74.5% of the EU average. 917,000 individuals were trained through the ESF. 470,000 small and medium-sized enterprises received assistance in Objective 2 regions.
1994–1999	GDP growth was estimated at an additional 4.7% in Portugal, 3.9% in the East German Lander, 2.8% in Ireland, 2.2% in Greece, 1.4% in Spain and 1.3% in Northern Ireland. In Objective 1 regions, 700,000 net jobs were created, adding almost 4% to employment in Portugal, 2.5% in Greece and between 1% and 2% in the new German Lander, the south of Italy and Spain. 800,000 small and medium-sized enterprises, including 500,000 in Objective 1 regions, received direct investment aids. 4,104 km of motorways were built or upgraded, as well as around 31,844 km of other roads; investments were made in rail infrastructure. In Objective 2 regions, an estimated 567,000 additional jobs were created, and unemployment rates fell from 11.3% to 8.7%.
2000–2006	An additional 570,000 jobs in Objective 1 regions were created, of which 160,000 were in new Member States. In Spain, the Structural Funds invested around 4 billion EUR in research, technological development, innovation and information technologies for over 13,000 research projects. For Objective 2 regions 730,000 jobs were created.

(*Continued*)

Table 3.2 (Continued)

Programming period	*Key achievements of the EU's regional policy*
2007–2013	Income increased in the poorest EU regions, with GDP per capita growing in these areas from 60.5% of the EU average in 2007 to 62.7% in 2010. 1.3 million new jobs were created. 2.4 million participants in ESF actions supporting access to employment found a job within 6 months (2007–2010). 356,800 projects were implemented by SMEs receiving direct investment aid. 141,052 start-ups were supported. 125,668 research projects were supported and 45,371 co-operation projects were supported. 70,900 new long-term research jobs were created. 20.6 million more EU citizens were covered by broadband connectivity. 15 million citizens benefited from water supply system modernisation and 19.7 million citizens were served by wastewater projects. 1,650 km^2 of area was rehabilitated. 5,309 MW of additional capacity of renewable energy production was added. 6,700 km of roads were built and 41,189 km of roads reconstructed; 475 km of railways were built and 7,500 km reconstructed.
2014–2020	1.8 million enterprises (mainly SMEs) were supported. Over 360,000 new jobs were created in various EU regions, mainly in SMEs. 180,000 new enterprises were supported to start and grow their business. 85,000 researchers were given access to improved research infrastructure facilities. 12 million households had access to broadband of at least 30 Mbps. 6,700 MW of additional capacity of renewable energy production was added. 15 million people gained access to a new or improved water supply, and 21 million people benefited from new or improved wastewater treatment. 5,800 km of new, reconstructed or upgraded rail track and 14,900 km of roads were built across Europe. 17.9 million students had access to improved childcare or education infrastructure. 66.4 million people benefitted from improved health services.

Source: Author's own elaboration based on the European Commission (2023a, 2023c, 2023d)

There are many arguments for the European Union to pursue a regional policy. Armstrong (2011) lists several of them. He draws attention to the vested interest argument, by which the economic well-being of citizens of one Member State depends on the prosperity of the economies of other Member States; therefore, there is a vested interest in ensuring that the regional problems are reduced. Moreover, the EU can draw resources from the more prosperous parts of the EU and can ensure that they are allocated to the most disadvantaged regions, which is impossible if regional policy is done at the national level only (financial targeting argument). A third argument that can be made in support of the EU's regional policy concerns the merits of a coordinated approach. The EU has great potential to improve effectiveness by acting as a supranational coordinating body. The effect of integration argument suggests that EU involvement in regional policy is necessary to overcome the negative regional effects of the integration process. If economic integration is left to its own devices, it can cause regional disparity. The EU, not the Member States, is best placed to deal with the regional problems that arise as integration progresses. Another argument often put forward supporting the EU regional policy is the need to help mitigate the negative regional effects of other EU policies, i.e. Value Added Tax (VAT) or the Common Agricultural Policy.

3.2 Instruments and funding

The EU is focussed on decreasing the regional disparities in economic development and on eliminating the economic deficits observed in the least-privileged regions. Regions compete on the basis of absolute advantages and therefore need solid instruments and policy tools to enhance their competitiveness (Camagni & Capello, 2010). The European Structural and Investment Funds (ESIFs) are financial instruments of regional policy. The ESIFs consist of five funds: the European Regional Development Fund, the European Social Fund, the Cohesion Fund, the European Agricultural Fund for Rural Development and the European Maritime, Fisheries and Aquaculture Fund. They all play a fundamental role in the development of regions within the European Union.

The European Regional Development Fund (ERDF) is the most important structural fund, established in 1975. It is designed to strengthen the European Union's economic, social and territorial cohesion by 'correcting imbalances between regions enabling investments in a smarter, greener, more connected and more social Europe closer to its citizens' (European Commission, 2023e). The ERDF supports regional development, economic change, enhanced competitiveness and territorial cooperation throughout the EU. The ERDF funds programmes under the joint responsibility of the European Commission and the national and regional authorities of the Member States. Local authorities are responsible for selecting the projects to be financed and continually managing their implementation. The funding priorities for the ERDF for the last two programming periods, i.e. 2014–2020 and 2021–2027, are presented in Table 3.3. The fund involves financing investments to modernise economic structure, support small and medium-sized enterprises (SMEs), help companies and create new jobs. They also concentrate on environmental protection, social inclusion and local sustainable development.

Most ERDF resources will be concentrated on Objectives 1 and 2 (i.e. smart and green economy). To increase flexibility, thematic concentration criteria will apply at the national level, with some scope for adjustment at the individual programme level. All regions and Member States will concentrate at least 30% of their allocation to Objective 2. More developed regions or Member States will dedicate at least

Table 3.3 EU ERDF funding priorities

Funding priorities 2014–2020	*Funding priorities 2021–2027*
1 Innovation and research 2 The digital agenda 3 Support for SMEs 4 The low-carbon economy	1 More competitive and smarter, through innovation and support to SMEs, as well as through digitisation and digital connectivity 2 Greener, low-carbon and resilient 3 More connected, by enhancing mobility 4 More social, by supporting employment, education, skills, social inclusion and equal access to health care, as well as by enhancing the role of culture and sustainable tourism 5 Closer to citizens, supporting locally led development and sustainable urban development across the EU

Source: Based on the European Commission (2023c)

85% of their allocation to Objectives 1 and 2, transition regions or Member States will budget at least 40% to Objective 1 and less developed regions or Member States at least 25% to Objective 1 (European Parliament, 2021).

The European Social Fund (ESF) is the oldest regional policy instrument, introduced in 1960. It was established to counteract unemployment and develop human resources potential. It aims to improve job opportunities across the EU, raise living standards, help people acquire better skills and improve their employment prospects. It promotes equal opportunities for women and men and people at risk of social exclusion. It helps with consulting and organising vocational training and entrepreneurship development. In 2021, the ESF was transformed into the ESF+, which integrates the former ESF, the Youth Employment Initiative (YEI), the Fund for European Aid to the Most Deprived (FEAD) and the EU Programme for Employment and Social Innovation (EaSI), allowing funding to be used as efficiently as possible. The European Social Fund Plus (ESF+) is the main instrument of the EU to invest in people and support the implementation of the European Pillar of Social Rights. ESF+ priorities for the period 2021–2027, with a budget of almost 99 billion EUR, include support for young people who have been particularly affected by the COVID-19 crisis, actions to combat child poverty and support for the most vulnerable in society suffering from job losses and income reductions. ESF+ will also invest in reskilling and upskilling people to transition to a green and digital economy, support social partners and civil society organisations and promote transnational cooperation for promoting social innovation across the EU (European Commission, 2023f). The fund's assistance takes the form of support for individuals, not businesses, and includes education, training and grants. A wide range of financial instruments supported by the ESF can be implemented: loans, microcredit, guarantees and equity. Financial instruments may also be offered with grants and other forms of assistance (European Commission, 2015).

The Cohesion Fund (CF), established in 1993, is intended for poorer countries whose gross national product per capita is below 90% of the EU average, in order to strengthen the EU's economic, social and territorial cohesion. The CF is not a typical structural fund. It does not support the development programmes of individual regions, but finances individual projects for the Member States' economies. The main goal of the Cohesion Fund is to support investment in the environment and the Trans-European transport infrastructure (TEN-T). For the programming period, 37% of the budget will contribute to achieving the climate goals. The Member States that apply income criteria are Bulgaria, Czechia, Estonia, Greece, Croatia, Cyprus, Latvia, Lithuania, Hungary, Malta, Poland, Portugal, Romania, Slovakia and Slovenia. The CF programmes are under the joint responsibility of the European Commission and the national and regional authorities of the Member States (European Commission, 2023g, 2023h).

The European Agricultural Fund for Rural Development (EAFRD) is another structural fund established to fund EU contributions to rural development programmes (RDPs). Rural development is a crucial policy area that affects more than 50% of the EU population and almost 90% of EU land. The EAFRD budget in the RDP is used to achieve various rural development goals, including improving the competitiveness of agriculture, promoting sustainable management of natural resources and climate action and achieving the balanced territorial development of the rural economy and communities. Programmes are prepared on a national or regional level and should be geared towards specific objectives related to the EU's rural development goals. The EAFRD budget for 2021–2027 amounts to 95.5 billion EUR, which includes an injection of 8.1 billion EUR from the next-generation EU recovery instrument to help address the challenges posed by the COVID-19 pandemic. Through financial instruments, the EAFRD acts as a source for loans, microcredit, guarantees and equity, available to recipients in agriculture, forestry and rural areas undertaking financially viable projects that support the EAFRD's priorities (European Commission, 2023i, 2023j).

The European Maritime, Fisheries and Aquaculture Fund (EMFAF), previously known as the European Maritime and Fisheries Fund (EMFF), is the financial instrument for funding the structural policy pillar of the Common Fisheries Policy of the European Union. The EMFAF was established to support waterside regions that profit from fishing. Funding under this fund is provided for the renewal and modernisation of fishing vessels, adapting the fishing industry to the current requirements and protecting marine resources, among other goals. The fund helps achieve sustainable fisheries and conserve marine biological resources, leading to food security through the supply of seafood products, the growth of a sustainable blue economy and healthy, safe and sustainably managed seas and oceans. Through the Financial Instrument for Fisheries Guidance (FIFG), port equipment and support for processing and other activities in the sector are financed. The EMFAF has an overall budget of over 6 billion EUR for the period 2021–2027 (European Investment Bank, 2023; European Commission, 2023k).

The ERDF, ESF+ and CF are subject to the Cohesion Policy. All EU regions are eligible for ERDF and ESF funding, but only the less developed ones can receive support from the Cohesion Fund. Two other funds, which are the EAFRD (under the Common Agricultural Policy) and the EMFAF (under the Common Fisheries

Policy), are specifically designed to meet the needs of agricultural and maritime regions, respectively.

The ESIFs are tools to promote economic and social cohesion, but they do not operate in isolation. They are tightly integrated into a broader, multi-level governance system involving many actors and organisations (Hooghe & Marks, 2001). The planning and implementation of Structural Funds is carried out through Operational Programmes. Documents are prepared by Member States and adopted by the European Commission within the National Strategic Reference Frameworks. The areas covered by the ESIFs and the number of Operational Programmes vary from country to country. Small countries may have two or three programme goals, while larger countries may have a dozen or more.

The methodology for allocating funds was introduced in the 2000–2006 programming period and has not changed significantly since then. The main criterion for granting EU funds to Member States and regions is their level of wealth. Regions are divided into three groups: less developed regions (average GDP per capita under 75% of the EU average), transition regions (average GDP per capita 75%–100% of the EU average) and more developed regions (average GDP per capita above the EU average). Other measures are used in the allocation process to reflect policy priorities, but those criteria are much less important. In the 2014–2020 programming period, criteria related to the labour market and education were used; in turn, for 2021–2027, the Commission introduced migration flows and greenhouse gas emissions as additional criteria (see Table 3.4). The Commission uses Eurostat data as the basis for its allocations, so the data are comparable and reliable for all regions. The allocations to Member States resulting from the processes set out above are subject to further adjustments in order to mitigate significant variation in amounts across Member States. These adjustments include ceilings that limit the maximum receivables and safeguards that guarantee a minimum level of financing. Final decisions regarding the allocation of funds are made in a highly political context, as the distribution of funds must be approved unanimously by the European Parliament and all Member States. The final allocation of funds represents a political compromise (European Court of Auditors, 2019).

The Cohesion Policy is one of the most frequently discussed and evaluated EU policies. As spending on regional policy is the largest part of the EU budget, it is crucial to control its effectiveness. Assessing whether the indicated programme activities contribute to competitiveness, productivity and employment in the

Table 3.4 Financial weighting of the allocation criteria

Criterion	*2014–2020*	*2021–2027*
Prosperity (GDP/GNI)	86%	81%
Labour market, education, demographics	14%	15%
Climate	0%	1%
Migration	0%	3%
Total	100%	100%

Source: European Court of Auditors (2019)

regions verifies whether it is advisable to conduct a given programme at the EU level. Measuring the impact of EU programmes is important to meet the growing demands for accountability to budget authorities and European taxpayers. While some Member States are net beneficiaries of the policy, others are net contributors, and the policy is constantly scrutinised for its use of funds and ability to deliver results. During the 1990s, the evaluation of Structural Fund programmes was developed and improved, leading to greater transparency and accountability in fund management. The scope of the audit was expanded to focus on results achieved through actual spending. Although all Member States carry out periodic reviews of the use of funds at various stages of the programming cycle, the way reviews are organised and carried out varies between Member States. On the other hand, the EU's Cohesion Policy has contributed to networking between European regional and local authorities to exchange experiences and generate ideas for new policy initiatives (Mairate, 2006).

3.3 Implementation of regional policy

National and regional authorities implement regional policy in partnership with the European Commission. The programming period is set at seven years. The implementation of the EU's regional policy takes place in several stages. Firstly, the policy's budget and the rules for its use are established jointly by the European Council and the European Parliament based on a proposal from the Commission. The principles and priorities of the Cohesion Policy are set in a consultation process between the Commission and the EU countries. Each Member State presents a 'Partnership Agreement', which describes the country's strategy, indicates the priorities of a given country/region and proposes a list of programmes. The Commission negotiates the final content of the partnership agreement and each programme with the national authorities. All workers, employers and civil society bodies can participate in the programming and management of the programmes. Member States and their regions implement the programmes. In each country/region, managing authorities select, monitor and evaluate hundreds of thousands of projects. The Commission allocates funds to enable countries to start spending on their programmes. The Commission pays the certified expenditure to each country and monitors each programme along with the country concerned. The Commission and the Member States are responsible for reporting and evaluation throughout the programming period (European Commission, 2023l).

A comparison of the Cohesion Policy budget for the programming periods 2021–2027 and 2014–2020 is presented in Table 3.5. The 2021–2027 policy continues to play the vital role of implementing a third of the European Union's long-term budget under the Multiannual Financial Framework. In 2021–2027, a total planned support of 367 billion EUR from the EU is expected to lead to investments of 530 billion EUR, once national co-financing of 163 billion EUR is taken into account. The planned budget for the 2014–2020 programming period was slightly higher, amounting to 533 billion EUR, with 405 billion EUR coming from EU funds and the remaining 128 billion EUR from national co-financing. It is worth underscoring

Table 3.5 Planned Cohesion Policy budget by funding source and funds

	2021–2027	*2014–2020*
Total budget	530 bn EUR	533 bn EUR
EU	367 bn EUR	405 bn EUR
National	163 bn EUR	128 bn EUR
ERDF	59.0%	57.9%
ESF+	26.8%	26.5%
CF	9.3%	13.6%
JTF (2021–2027)/YEI (2014–2020)	4.9%	2.0%

Source: European Commission (2023m)

that the budget for the 2021–2027 programming period was for only 27 Member States, while 2014–2020 was for 28 countries, including the UK, which exited the EU in 2020. Moreover, in the 2014–2020 period, EU countries benefited from the additional flexibility provided by investment initiatives in response to the coronavirus pandemic (CRII and CRII+), as well as from additional funds made available under the NextGenerationEU recovery package, including the Recovery and Enhancing Resilience Plan and REACT-EU. The biggest beneficiaries of the Cohesion Policy budget are the ERDF and ESF+ funds. In the new 2021–2027 programming period, the share of CF decreased in favour of the two largest funds and the Just Transition Fund (JTF). The JTF replaced the Youth Employment Initiative (YEI) fund as a result of the revised regional policy goals. The JTF supports the economic diversification and reconversion of the territories expected to be the most negatively impacted by the transition towards climate neutrality.

In the 2014–2020 programming period, Cohesion Policy funding constituted almost 14% of total government investment in the EU and 52% in the cohesion countries. The Cohesion Policy set 11 thematic objectives supporting growth for the period 2014–2020. Investment from the ERDF supported all 11 objectives, but Objectives 1–4 were the main priorities for investment. The main priorities for the ESF were 8–11, though the Fund also supported Objectives 1–4. The Cohesion Fund supported Objectives 4–7.

The EU Cohesion Policy budget by theme for 2014–2020 is presented in Figure 3.1. The first three thematic goals in the 2014–2020 period are called smart growth. In the area of research and innovation, EU support has enabled more than 60,000 companies to partner with research institutions (94% of the target), and around 30,000 companies have introduced new products to the market (95% of the target). In addition, the ESIFs significantly contributed to the digital transformation by improving IT infrastructure and empowering people and enterprises with next-generation technologies and skills. Over 6.3 million households benefited from improved access to broadband thanks to selected ERDF projects. More than 5.1 million rural residents benefited from improved infrastructure or IT services. The ESIFs provide vital support for companies to grow and become more productive and competitive and for businesses to introduce innovative solutions. Overall, 124 billion EUR (17% of the total budget) was earmarked for enhancing

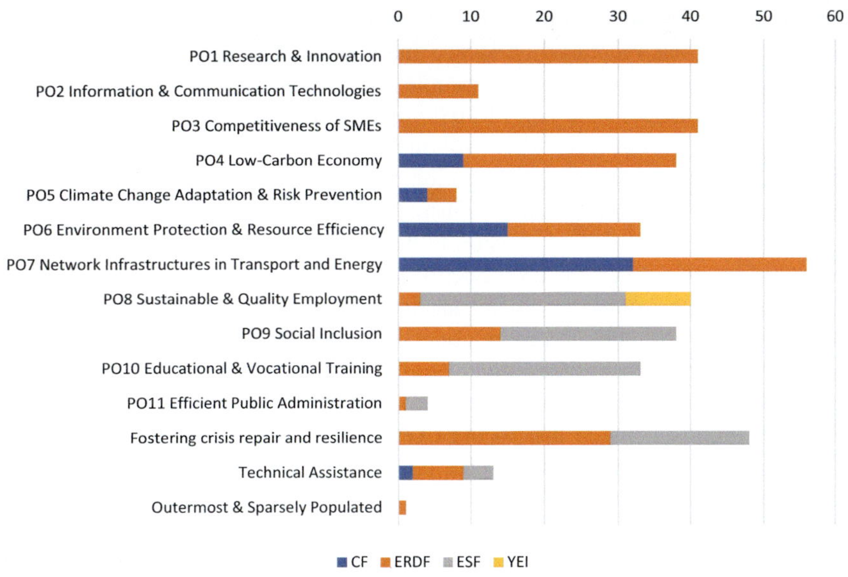

Figure 3.1 EU Cohesion Policy budget by theme for 2014–2020, in bn EUR

Source: European Commission (2023m)

the competitiveness of European SMEs, constituting the single most considerable objective in the budget. Two million SMEs benefitted from EU support (European Commission, 2023n).

Programming Objectives 4–7 are grouped together as sustainable growth. By providing climate-neutral, clean and circular-economy support to investments that involve adaptation to environmental and climate change, the ESIFs make an essential contribution to the goals of the European Green Deal. The COVID-19 crisis temporarily slowed the implementation of projects contributing to low-carbon and climate goals. Unspent funds were redirected to emergency measures in the health care and business sectors. However, this situation was reversed by the addition of 50.6 billion EUR of REACT-EU funds to existing Cohesion Policy programmes in June 2021 to help them bridge the gap between emergency measures and long-term recovery by providing new resources to Member States to restart green projects. European funds have been the primary EU public finance support for clean energy; they have financed energy efficiency through building renovation and renewables and developing the energy network. Investments in inclusive growth make up about 24% of the total funding and cover three objectives: quality, sustainable employment; social inclusion; and educational and vocational training (European Commission, 2023n).

The ESF fosters social services, retention of employment and support to vulnerable groups and others. In terms of social inclusion, 3.6 million participants with disabilities, 8 million migrants, participants with a foreign or minority background and 10.3 million other disadvantaged people received assistance to improve their employability and to develop skills appropriate to their needs. EU support from the ERDF has increased childcare and education infrastructure capacity for 19.7 million people, and 53 million people now benefit from improved health services across the EU. By the end of 2021, thanks to support from the ESF and the Youth Employment Initiative, 25.9 million people with low qualifications received support, 8.8 million obtained qualifications and 2.6 million were in education and training (European Commission, 2023n).

The objectives of the EU Cohesion Policy for 2021–2027 features a shorter list of five policy objectives for a competitive, future-proof Europe. The funds will be invested in jobs, growth and European regional cooperation to create a more competitive, smarter, greener, more connected, more social and inclusive Europe. A total of 379 new Cohesion Policy programmes will help EU regions achieve these goals. Programming took place in an unstable environment and the negotiations were greatly delayed due to the COVID-19 crisis and the war in Ukraine; therefore, in the new programming period, adjustments may be made due to new challenges and emerging needs.

The EU Cohesion Policy budget by objective for 2021–2027 is presented in Figure 3.2. The ERDF supports five cohesion policy goals, with the highest impact being on Smarter Europe and Greener Europe. The ESF+ focusses only on the Social Europe goal, while the CF supports the Greener Europe and Connected Europe goals related to transport and the environment. The largest allocation under PO1 will be the development and strengthening of research and innovation potential (help for 148,000 enterprises and 83,000 researchers) and support for the creation and competitiveness of over 450,000 SMEs. The ERDF and the CF finance PO2 and aim to transform the energy sector and achieve the EU's medium- and long-term

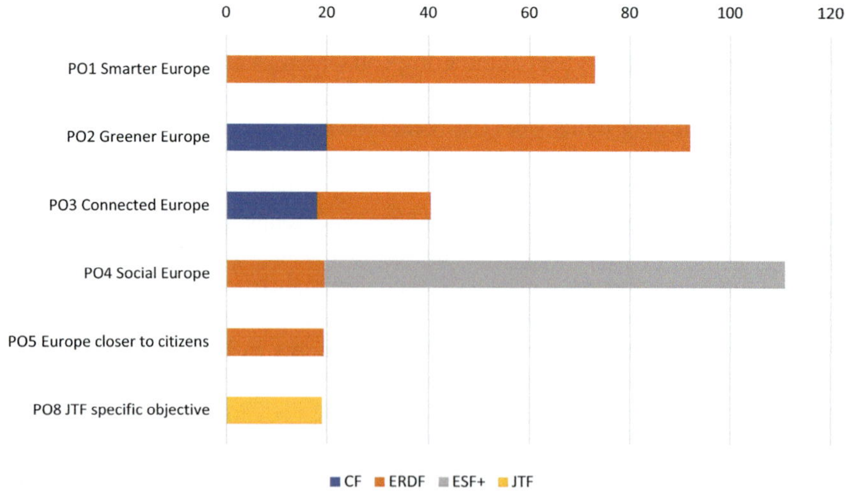

Figure 3.2 EU Cohesion Policy budget by theme for 2021–2027, in bn EUR

Source: European Commission (2023o)

energy and climate goals by investing in renewable energy, sustainable urban mobility, clean water and improved wastewater infrastructure. PO3 is financed by the ERDF and the CF, which will finance the construction, modernisation or reconstruction of 3,900 km of TEN-T railway lines. PO4, funded by the ESF+ in close coordination with the ERDF, aims to support just over 37 million people by the end of the decade in areas ranging from education and training to health, long-term care and the inclusion of vulnerable groups. The ESF+ aims to support at least 6.5 million unemployed people and almost 1.3 million economically inactive people. The ERDF finances PO5 and aims to invest in the support of integrated and inclusive social, economic and environmental development, as well as culture, natural heritage, sustainable tourism and security in urban and non-urban areas. In addition, under the JTF, a specific objective was created to address the social, employment, economic and environmental impacts of the transition towards climate neutrality. The geographical scope of the FST includes territories dependent on the extraction or production of hard coal, lignite, peat or oil shale and carbon-intensive industries such as steel, cement or chemicals. Under PO11, more than 3,000 projects targeting national, regional or local public administrations or public services have been supported by the ESF (European Commission, 2023o).

The Cohesion Policy for 2021–2027 will impact all European regions by focussing on the green and digital transformations while striving to leave no-one behind. It will help the EU and its Member States achieve the three headline targets for 2030 agreed at the Porto Summit in 2022: increasing quality employment to 78%, encouraging at least 60% of adults to participate in training every year and reducing poverty levels by 15 million people, including at least 5 million children. In addition, the Cohesion Policy for 2021–2027 will aim to mitigate the effects of the shrinking working-age population; eliminate imperfections in the labour market, education, training and adult learning systems; improve results in the field of innovation, public management and the business environment; and increase the level of services and access to them. By the end of the implementation period, this policy is expected to increase EU GDP by 0.5% and support the creation of 1.3 million additional jobs while supporting nearly 850,000 enterprises (European Commission, 2023o).

The distribution of funds from the cohesion budget for individual countries in programming periods 2014–2020 and 2021–2027 is presented in Figure 3.3. A comparison of the 2014–2020 and 2021–2027 allocations for individual Member States reveals different patterns. The change in funding varied from a reduction of 24% to an increase of 8%. The largest beneficiary of the EU Cohesion Policy budget is Poland, which received almost 79 billion EUR in the 2014–2020 programming period and 76 billion EUR in 2021–2027. Poland receives the most funds from the ERDF. In 2014–2020, Poland also received the most from the CF of all countries, which was related to large investments in Trans-European transport networks and environmental aspects of transport. The other main beneficiaries of the Cohesion Policy were Italy, Spain, Romania and Portugal. In most of these countries, the most funds were obtained from the ERDF, followed by the ESF/ESF+. Compared to the 2014–2020 programming period, these countries – apart

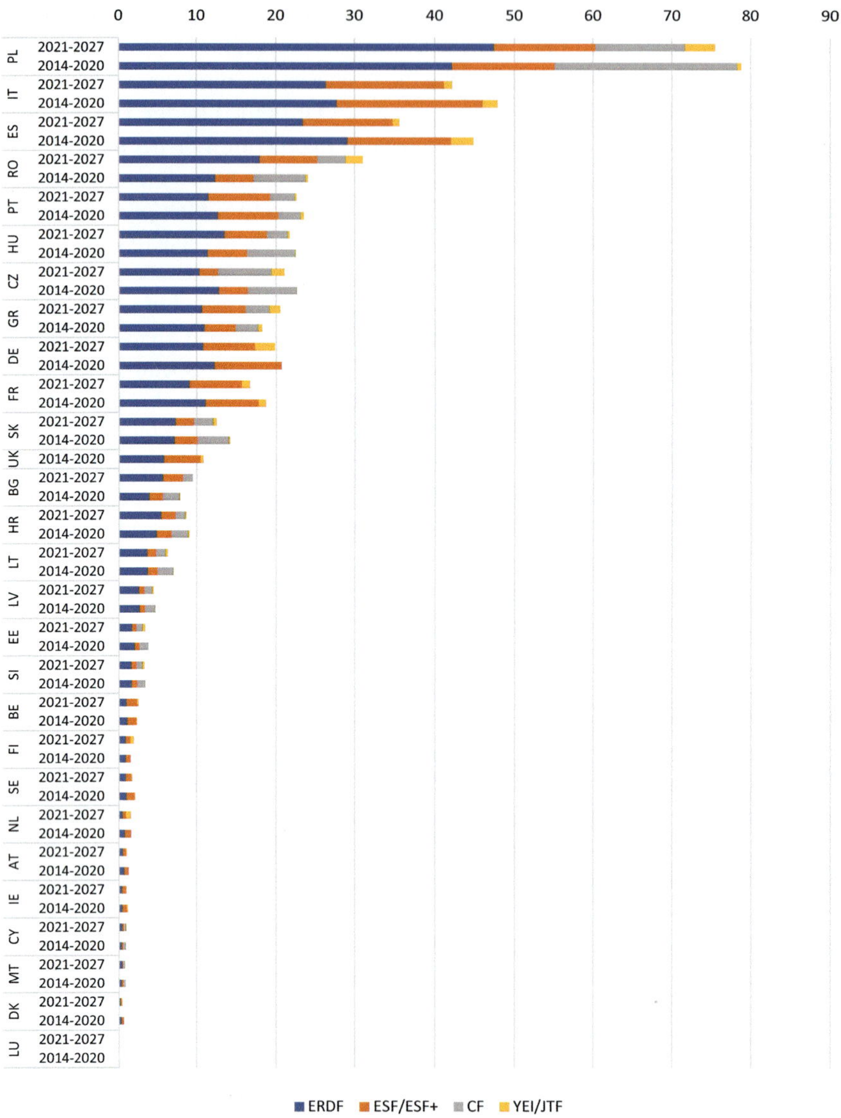

Figure 3.3 EU Cohesion Policy budgets for 2014–2020 and 2021–2027 by country, in bn EUR

Source: European Commission (2023k)

from Romania – received less funding in the new 2021–2027 programming period. The countries that benefited the least from the EU Cohesion Policy budget were Luxembourg, Denmark, Malta, Cyprus and Ireland. In addition, the CF in the period 2021–2027 supports 15 cohesive countries in the fields of environment and Trans-European Transport Networks.

The European Union uses the NUTS classification for regional comparisons. The NUTS classification ensures that comparable regions appear at the same NUTS level. With the population size being defined in the NUTS Regulation as a critical indicator for comparability, each level inevitably contains regions that differ significantly in terms of area, economic weight or administrative powers. The current NUTS nomenclature, applicable from 1 January 2018, changed the number of NUTS 2 regions for Poland, Germany and France. For example, the Mazovian Voivodeship was split into two NUTS units in Poland. The country's capital and adjacent districts have been classified as NUTS 2, while the remaining part of the Masovian Voivodeship is separate NUTS 2 (European Union, 2019).

Funds from the ERDF and the ESF+ are allocated in three categories of regions (less developed, more developed or transition); some countries benefit from the CF, while all countries benefit from the JTF. The least developed regions benefit the most: they are allocated 70% of the funds from the ERDF and the ESF+. The change in the prosperity of many regions led to a reclassification of their status, which can be seen in Figure 3.4. Estonia, Lithuania and some regions of Czechia, Poland and Bulgaria changed from less developed regions to transition regions. The reverse trend occurred in Greece and Spain, where the number of less developed regions increased significantly. This was also the case with Italy and Portugal, but to a lesser extent. Due to the change in the upper criteria for transition regions from 90% to 100% of the EU average, some regions of Finland, France, Germany, the Netherlands, Slovenia, Austria, Belgium, Italy, Spain, Greece, Cyprus and Ireland were reclassified from developed regions to transition regions.

The Cohesion Policy is designed to reduce the gap between poor and rich European regions. Under this policy, the main principle underlying allocation is to direct resources to the poorest countries and regions. However, more prosperous regions are not excluded from cohesion funding, as challenges related to globalisation and the transition to a low-carbon economy affect many regions across the EU, including more developed ones. The Commission proposes that for 2021–2027, transition regions are those where the GDP per capita is between 75% and 100% of the EU average, while for the period 2014–2020, it was 75%–90% of the EU average; thus, many of the previous more developed regions are now categorised as transition regions. This change significantly expanded the population this category covers, from less than 15% to more than 25% of the EU population. Moving from more developed to transition status means that the regions in question receive more cohesion funding. Member States with a GNI per capita below 90% of the EU average are eligible for the CF. For 2021–2027, the Commission has proposed a 45% reduction to the CF compared to the previous period. However, higher ERDF and ESF+ allocations to poorer regions compensate for this reduction in CF funding, so the overall relative allocation of Cohesion Policy funds to poorer regions remains unchanged. Table 3.6 compares the result of the allocation methodology by region type in 2014–2020 with the proposal for 2021–2027. Despite the reduction in the CF, the overall relative allocation of Cohesion Policy funds to less developed regions in the 2021–2027 proposal remains constant at three quarters of the available funding (European Court of Auditors, 2019).

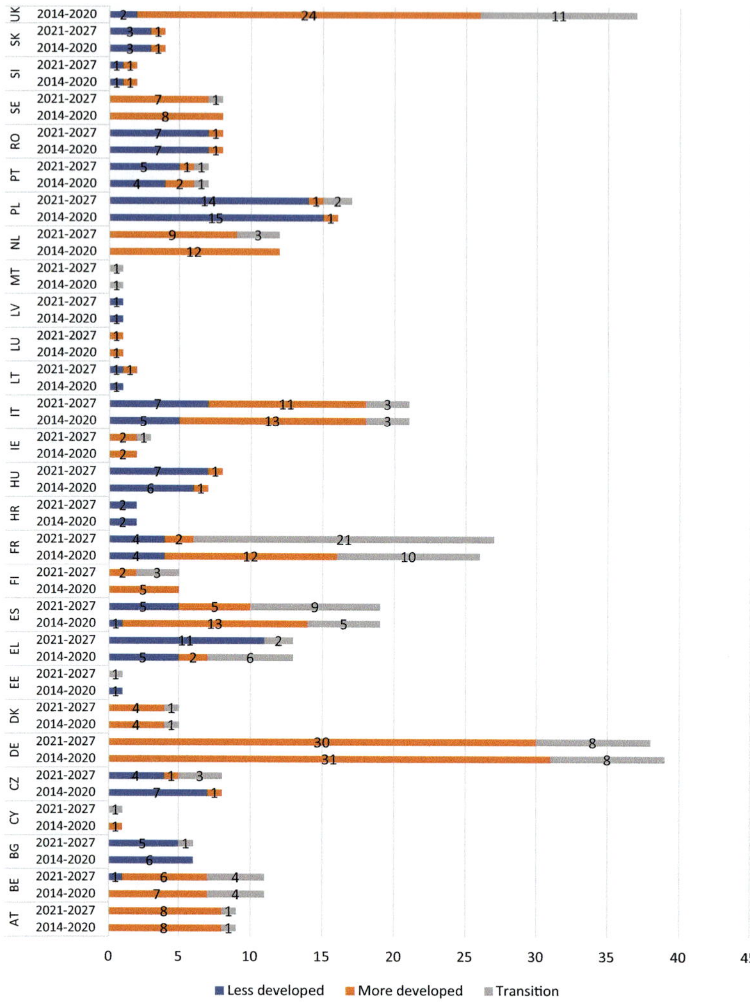

Figure 3.4 Category of NUTS 2 regions by country for the 2014–2020 and 2021–2027 programming periods

Source: European Commission (2023m)

Table 3.6 Allocation by type and region

Fund (type of region)	*2021–2027*	*2014–2020*
CF	13%	22%
ERDF/ESF+ (less developed)	62%	53%
ERDF/ESF+ (transition)	14%	10%
ERDF/ESF+ (more developed)	11%	15%
Total	100%	100%
CF+ERD/ESF+ (less developed)	75%	75%

Source: European Court of Auditors (2019)

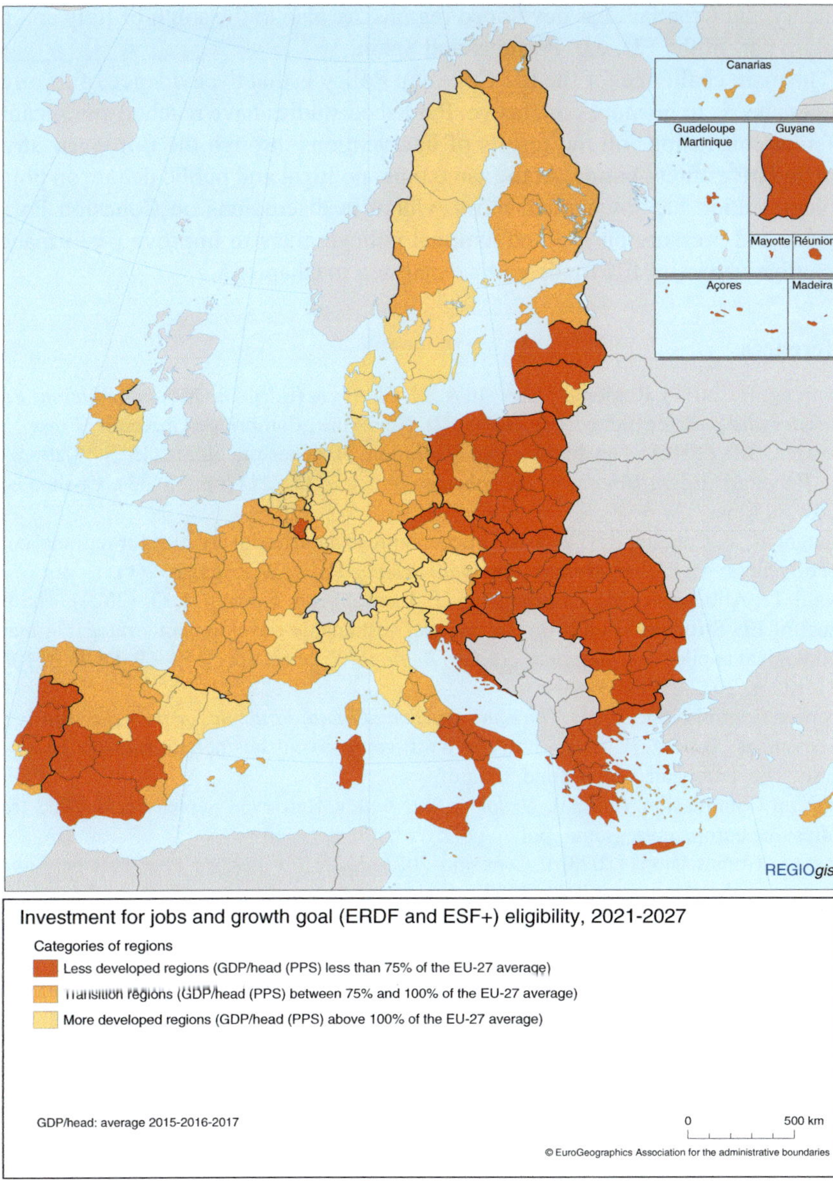

Figure 3.5 Category of NUTS 2 regions by country for the 2021–2027 programming period

Source: European Commission (2023p)

A map with 240 NUTS 2 regions in the EU divided into less developed, transition and more developed for the 2021–2027 programming period is presented in Figure 3.5. Most areas covered by ERDF and ESF+ support are in the eastern part of the EU, mainly in Poland, Romania, Bulgaria, Latvia, Lithuania, Slovakia,

Hungary and Croatia. Less developed regions are also in the south of Italy and the western part of the EU, e.g. Portugal and Spain.

The main challenge for the EU Cohesion Policy is that the evidence of its effectiveness needs to be more conclusive. Published studies have reached significantly different conclusions on the results of interventions through the European Structural and Investment Funds. At the same time, political and public debate on policy implementation has intensified, most evident in discussions on Cohesion Policy reforms and pressure on EU and national policymakers to improve performance. The effectiveness of EU funds will be analysed in Chapter 5.

References

Amstrong, H. (2011). Regional policy. In A. M. El-Agraa (Ed.), *The European Union: Economics and policies* (9th ed.; pp. 348–362). New York: Cambridge University Press.

Brunazzo, M. (2016). The history and evolution of cohesion policy. In S. Piattoni & L. Polverari (Eds.), *Handbook on cohesion policy in the EU* (pp. 13–33). Cheltenham: Edward Elgar.

Camagni, R., & Capello, R. (2010) Macroeconomic and territorial policies for regional competitiveness: An EU perspective. *Regional Science Policy & Practice*, *2*(1), 1–19.

Cavalli, L., Alibegovic, M., Cruickshank, E., Farnia, L., & Romani, I. G. (2023). The impact of EU Structural Funds on the national sustainable development strategy: A methodological application. *Regional Studies, Regional Science*, *10*(1), 52–69. DOI: 10.1080/21681376.2022.2160655

European Commission. (2015). *The European Social Fund: Financial instruments*. Retrieved September 6, 2023 from https://www.fi-compass.eu/sites/default/files/publications/ESF_The_european_social_fund_EN.pdf

European Commission. (2023a). *History of the policy*. Retrieved September 6, 2023 from https://ec.europa.eu/regional_policy/policy/what/history_en

European Commission. (2023b). *Cohesion 2021–2027: Forging an ever stronger union. Report on the outcome of 2021–2027 cohesion policy programming*. Retrieved September 6, 2023 from https://ec.europa.eu/regional_policy/sources/reports/2021-2027-programming-outcome/report-outcome-2021-2027-cohesion-policy-programming-part1.pdf

European Commission. (2023c). *Key achievements of Regional Policy 2007–2013*. Retrieved September 6, 2023 from https://ec.europa.eu/regional_policy/policy/what/key-achievements/2007-2013_en

European Commission. (2023d). *Key achievements of Regional Policy 2014–2020*. Retrieved September 6, 2023 from https://ec.europa.eu/regional_policy/policy/what/key-achievements_en

European Commission. (2023e). *European regional development fund*. Retrieved September 6, 2023 from https://ec.europa.eu/regional_policy/funding/erdf_en

European Commission. (2023f). *A new, stronger European Social Fund Plus*. Retrieved September 6, 2023 from https://ec.europa.eu/esf/main.jsp?catId=62&langId=en

European Commission. (2023g). *Cohesion fund*. Retrieved September 6, 2023 from https://ec.europa.eu/regional_policy/funding/cohesion-fund_en

European Commission. (2023h). *The future of cohesion policy*. Retrieved September 6, 2023 from https://ec.europa.eu/regional_policy/policy/how/future-cohesion-policy_en

European Commission. (2023i). *Rural development*. Retrieved September 6, 2023 from https://agriculture.ec.europa.eu/common-agricultural-policy/rural-development_en

European Commission. (2023j). *European Agricultural Fund for Rural Development (EAFRD)*. Retrieved September 6, 2023 from https://commission.europa.eu/funding-tenders/find-funding/eu-funding-programmes/european-agricultural-fund-rural-development-eafrd_en

European Commission. (2023k). *European maritime, fisheries and aquaculture fund*. Retrieved September 6, 2023 from https://cinea.ec.europa.eu/programmes/european-maritime-fisheries-and-aquaculture-fund_en

European Commission. (2023l). *Programming and implementation*. Retrieved September 6, 2023 from https://ec.europa.eu/regional_policy/policy/how/programming-and-implementation_en

European Commission. (2023m). *Cohesion open data platform*. Retrieved September 26, 2023 from https://cohesiondata.ec.europa.eu/cohesion_overview

European Commission. (2023n). *European structural and investment funds 2022: Summary report of the programme annual implementation reports covering implementation in 2014–2020*. Retrieved September 30, 2023 from https://ec.europa.eu/regional_policy/sources/reports/annual_2022/2022_annual_summary_report.pdf

European Commission. (2023o). *EU cohesion policy: 2021–2027 programmes expected to create 1.3 million jobs in the EU*. Retrieved September 30, 2023 from https://ec.europa.eu/regional_policy/information-sources/publications/reports/2023/report-on-the-outcome-of-2021–2027-cohesion-policy-programming_en

European Commission. (2023p). *Maps*. Retrieved October 11, 2023 from https://ec.europa.eu/regional_policy/information-sources/maps_en

European Court of Auditors. (2019). *Rapid case review: Allocation of cohesion policy funding to member states for 2021–2027*. Retrieved September 6, 2023 from https://www.eca.europa.eu/lists/ecadocuments/rcr_cohesion/rcr_cohesion_en.pdf

European Investment Bank. (2023). *The European maritime, fisheries and aquaculture fund*. Retrieved October 11, 2023 from https://www.fi-compass.eu/funds/emfaf

European Parliament. (2021). *European regional development fund and cohesion fund 2021–2027*. Retrieved September 6, 2023 from https://www.europarl.europa.eu/RegData/etudes/BRIE/2018/625141/EPRS_BRI(2018)625141_EN.pdf

European Union. (2012). *Consolidated version of the treaty on the functioning of the European Union* [October 26, 2012, OJ L. 326/47–326/390]. Retrieved September 1, 2023 from https://eur-lex.europa.eu/LexUriServ/LexUriServ.do?uri=CELEX:12012E/TXT:en:PDF

European Union. (2019). *Methodological manual on territorial typologies 2018 edition*. Retrieved September 6, 2023 from https://ec.europa.eu/eurostat/documents/3859598/9507230/KS-GQ-18-008-EN-N.pdf/a275fd66-b56b-4ace-8666-f39754ede66b?t=1573550953000

Hall, R. (2016). The development of regional policy in the process of European integration: An overview. In G. Bischof (Ed.), *Regional economic development compared: EU-Europe and the American South* (pp. 13–33). Innsbruck: Innsbruck University Press.

Hooghe, L., & Marks, G. (2001). *Multi-Level governance and European integration*. Lanham, MD: Rowman-Littlefield.

Huggins, R., & Williams, N. (2011). Entrepreneurship and regional competitiveness: The role and progression of policy. *Entrepreneurship & Regional Development*, *23*(9–10), 907–932.

Leonardi, R. (2005). *Cohesion policy in the European Union: The building of Europe*. London: Palgrave Macmillan London. https://doi.org/10.1057/9780230503861

Mairate, A. (2006). The “added value” of European Union cohesion policy. *Regional Studies*, *40*(2), 167–177. doi:10.1080/00343400600600496

Martin, R. (1998) Financing EU cohesion policy in Central and Eastern Europe. *Intereconomics 33*, 103–111. https://doi.org/10.1007/BF02926817

Single European Act (1986). Official journal of the European Communitie, No L 169/1. https://eur-lex.europa.eu/resource.html?uri=cellar:a519205f-924a-4978-96a2-b9af8a598b85.0004.02/DOC_1&format=PDF

Szlachta, J. (2004). The role of the structural funds and cohesion fund in the stimulation of sustained economic growth in Poland. *TIGER Working Paper Series*, No. 69. Warsaw: Transformation, Integration and Globalization Economic Research.

4 Left-behind places in the EU – shift-share labour productivity analysis

4.1 Literature review

As presented in Chapter 3, the European Union consists of 27 very diverse countries. This diversity deepened with subsequent EU enlargements in 2004, 2007 and 2013. The goal of the EU Cohesion Policy is the convergence of regions left behind. However, distributing benefits between rural and urban areas remains a fundamental challenge. The problem for decision-makers at the national and EU levels is to select the most effective actions to increase productivity. One way is to invest in left-behind areas and human capital to increase productivity and growth and reduce the gap to the EU average. Investments in less developed regions can enable access to their untapped potential and can mobilise the resources needed to exploit it towards more resilient growth trajectories (Carrascal-Incera et al., 2020). Another option is investments in skills, housing and transport to make it easier for people to move to successful agglomerations. Odendahl et al. (2019) point out that high-productivity levels in some regions are related to the fact that they contain or are geographically close to successful cities. The movement of resources to successful agglomerations could lead to the greatest productivity gains, but would risk deepening European political divisions.

Research on the productivity of EU regions mainly analyses productivity convergence (e.g. Cuadrado Roura et al., 2000; Martin, 2001; Cuadrado-Roura, 2001; Tondl, 2001; Corrado et al., 2005; Gardiner et al., 2006; Le Gallo & Dall'erba, 2008; Villaverde & Maza, 2008; Enflo & Hjertstrand, 2009; O'Leary & Webber, 2014; Hegerty, 2016). Gardiner et al. (2006) confirm the low rate of productivity convergence, which was little more than 1% per year for EU regions. Much of the convergence took place during the boom in the second half of the 1980s; there has been very little, if any, convergence. Moreover, there is no visible convergence within the Member States. There has been no discernible reduction in productivity, and the slight decline in overall regional dispersion over this period was entirely due to reduced differences between states.

Moreover, in many regions of the EU progress in productivity – mainly occurring through industrial rationalisation, labour shock effects and capital substitution – has ranged from increasing technological efficiency, advances, higher value products and so on. Enflo and Hjertstrand (2009) report that capital accumulation and

DOI: 10.4324/9781032615516-5

expanded technical capabilities mainly explain the increase in labour productivity. Although these two forces are equally important in increasing the average labour productivity distribution, technological change has created relatively large opportunities to catch up in initially low-productivity regions. However, these opportunities have yet to be exploited, leaving low-productivity regions lagging behind in relative productivity. Cuadrado-Roura et al. (2000) stress that a 'catching-up' effect is visible for EU regions; however, different equilibrium trends exist in the long run. EU regions exhibit heterogeneous behaviour inside conventional groups like central, industrialised, lagging and peripheral regions. Therefore, there are no territorially defined patterns of productivity growth. Sondermann (2012) found no convergence at the aggregate level, only in selected service sectors and manufacturing sub-industries.

The literature on the subject also focusses on the key factors that lead to regional productivity growth. Kutan and Yigit (2009) and Bronzini and Piselli (2009) indicate human capital as the dominant factor in labour productivity growth. Kutan and Yigit (2009) report that foreign direct investments (FDIs) and exports improve productivity, but that imports have a negative impact. Villaverde and Maza (2008) draw attention to the relationship between the aggregate productivity of each region and its geographical location. Generally, most productive areas tend to be spatially concentrated. Skorupinska and Torrent-Sellens (2015) confirm in their research that productivity is significantly influenced by information and communication technology capital. In their analysis, Stojcic et al. (2019) highlight the strength of spatial connections between core regions and peripheries. Sondermann (2012) highlights investment in research and development and highly skilled employees as critical factors in improving productivity, whereas regulations constitute a burden. Radosevic (2017) emphasises the importance of modernising technology to enhance productivity, but for developing countries, production capacity is the key, not innovation itself. Friesenbichler and Peneder (2016) point out the positive impact of competition on productivity. In their research, Habib et al. (2019) confirm a significant contribution to increasing the productivity of human capital, intellectual property rights and research and development expenses. According to the results obtained by Stojcic et al. (2018), trade liberalisation also affects structural transformation and increased productivity. De Noni et al. (2018) also underscore the importance of the ability of local innovative organisations to activate collaborative inventors' networks. Rosés and Wolf (2021) recognise the fundamental role that institutions and geography play in productivity convergence.

The relationship between economic structure and productivity growth is an important topic. Over the years, many researchers have confirmed that changes in the economic structure lead to changes in productivity growth and, consequently, economic growth (Lewis, 1954; Kuznets, 1967; Feder, 1986; Dowrick, 1989; Fagerberg, 2000; McMillan et al., 2014). The speed of structural changes is one of the key factors that determine the competitiveness of an economy or region. Currently, most developed economies can diversify their activities from agriculture and other traditional products and can focus mainly on high-tech production and specialised services, which increases wages and positively impacts economic growth. Duarte and Restuccia (2010) state that the economic structure of a country is closely related to its level of development. The poorest countries have a much higher share of labour in agriculture than rich countries. A faster pace of labour reallocation characterises countries that start the process of structural transformation later. Moreover, differences in labour productivity between rich and poor countries are significant in agriculture and services but smaller in industry. As countries progress through structural transformation, relative aggregate labour productivity may initially increase, stagnate or decline. Fagerberg (2000) states that advanced technologies play an essential role in generating structural changes by increasing productivity rapidly, but without a significant increase in the share of total employment. The relationships between growth in production, productivity and employment need to be clearly defined. The leading technologies and industries most affected changeover time, as do the associated rewards. Focussing on technologically leading industries can have significant potential economic growth benefits, but their size could be more stable. McMillan et al. (2014) point out substantial differences in labour productivity between the traditional and modern parts of the economy. Still, these disproportions can be an essential driver of economic growth in developing countries. Through structural change, when labour and other productive resources move from less productive to more productive activities, the economy grows even if there is no increase in productivity in particular sectors. The flow of labour from low-productivity to high-productivity activities is a key development factor. The speed of structural changes determines the country's economic success. However, structural change, like economic growth itself, is not an automatic process and requires a push in the right direction, especially when a country has a strong comparative advantage in natural resources.

Research on economic structure and its impact on productivity for EU countries and regions has been conducted, for example, by Ezcurra and Pascual (2007), Villaverde and Maza (2008), Marrocu et al. (2012), Bah and Brada (2009), Kutan and Yigit (2009), Havlik (2015), Naveed and Ahmad (2016), Stojcic et al. (2019), Dobrzański (2019), Dobrzański and Olszewski (2019), Dobrzański and Grabowski (2019) and Rosés and Wolf (2021). A study by Ezcurra and Pascual (2007) considered the causes of differences in regional productivity and pointed out that the influence of economic structure is very small. Similarly, Villaverde and Maza (2008) state that the increase in total productivity in the EU results solely from the increase in productivity in the entire country. The so-called structural change brings a negative, although quantitatively insignificant contribution to total productivity growth. In sectoral terms, this effect is positive in half of the cases and negative in the other half. Bah and Brada (2009) emphasise that transition economies are not homogeneous groups because they have huge differences in total factor productivity. The new EU countries were characterised by a decline in employment in agriculture and industry and the highest employment rate in services. However, the increase in employment in more profitable sectors did not translate into an increase in productivity. Marrocu et al. (2012) divide the EU countries into Old and New Europe. Old Europe is in an advanced phase of industrial restructuring, service expansion and reorientation: traditional production districts are being liquidated or transformed, which implies a process of delocalisation, which is often directed to the regions of New Europe. As a result, Old Europe focusses on knowledge-based services and activities with high added value, exploiting both types of agglomeration externalities: specialisation and diversity. However, the newly acceded countries are still in the initial phase of development and use the full range of typical externalities, such as the provision of specific goods and services, the availability of adequate labour, the reduction of transport costs and the transfer of specialised knowledge, which affect production mainly in traditional, low-technology industries. The results of O'Leary and Webber (2014) suggest that the impact of the cross-sectoral component is not negligible and is significantly stronger for the regions towards the higher deciles of the distribution. Moreover, it seems to particularly affect growth, improving when a region is either 'high and improving' or 'low and deteriorating'. In addition to physical capital resources and research and development expenditures, which are key factors in the growth of intra-sector productivity, factors related to structure changes, such as labour mobility between sectors, can also play a role in increasing overall productivity. These results confirm the significant importance of structural changes for economic growth and convergence. Naveed and Ahmad (2016) draw attention to the fact that in European Union countries in recent years, there have been many structural changes, concerning not only the share of employment by sector but also changes in the demand for goods due to technology and trade. Their study shows that conditional convergence occurs at national, regional and industry levels, but convergence speed varies at different levels of aggregation. The pace of convergence at the regional level is faster than at the national and industry levels. Moreover, failure to consider structural changes may result in the convergence rate being overestimated or underestimated.

This literature review covers the topic of productivity, its main determinants and relationships with structural changes. The rest of this chapter examines the productivity of EU regions and identifies the EU regions with the lowest productivity. A more detailed analysis is carried out for left-behind regions, combining productivity changes with structural changes using the shift-share methodology. The study will be carried out for data from the last 20 years available, i.e. from 2000 to 2020. Productivity changes will be divided into three sub-indices: pure productivity growth, structural productivity growth and dynamic external effect.

4.2 Methodology

Labour productivity is one of the basic indicators for describing the regions' performance; it can be calculated as the gross value added (GVA) per employee. This indicator informs how much gross value is added on average by each employee in the economy. Apart from the analysis of basic productivity indicators, the shift-share methodology is used to make a more detailed analysis of the productivity of the EU regions that perform the worst in this respect. Shift-share analysis is a method that deconstructs aggregate change into components. In the basic shift-share equation, the first component concerns changes in the composition of the aggregate, while the second component concerns changes within individual units included in the aggregate (Fagerberg, 2000).

Shift-share was first used by Fabricant (1942) to measure the relationship between productivity and the movement of labour. Since then, the methodology has been reviewed and modified, and numerous extensions have been created. Esteban-Marquillas (1972) applied homothetic employment in a sector and region, leading to the identification of an additional allocation effect. Arcelus (1984) further developed Esteban-Marquillas's model. The model also assumes that the concept of homothetic employment represents the degree of specialisation of the region. Still, Arcelus's model also allows for an approximate estimation of the impact of local and export markets, while Esteban-Marquillas's formula does not assume a local market. However, Keil (1992) and Loveridge and Selting (1998) demonstrated some empirical deficiencies of the homothetic idea.

Static shift-share models capture only the static structural change components to measure the reallocation effect, and they do not consider the differences in productivity growth rates across sectors. Therefore, Barff and Knight (1988) developed dynamic shift-share models that implement continuous changes in the regional industrial mix and the size of the employment base. Nazara and Hewings (2004) introduced spatial structure recognition into shift-share analysis, emphasising that the location of a given region is an essential element of the growth calculation. Over the years, many variants of dynamic shift-share analysis were applied to understand structural changes and their impacts on productivity growth. The main difference in those variants is the base year or weighting.

In this book, the shift-share model introduced by Timmer and Szirmai (2000) is used. This model breaks productivity growth down into three elements. As in many other shift-share models, an increase in labour productivity can be achieved by either improving production processes (pure labour productivity) or transferring labour from low-productivity sectors to high-productivity sectors (structural labour productivity). In addition to these two static measures, a third element is introduced here: the dynamic effect (D). This is the combined effect of changes in the employment share and changes in sector productivity levels.

In Timmer and Szirmai's shift-share model, the growth rate of labour productivity is the sum of the endogenous effect (W), the static external effect (S) and the dynamic external effect (D), as presented in Equation 1.

$$\frac{\Delta y_t}{y_{t-k}} = \sum_j (w_{j,t-k}\ \tilde{y}_{j,t-k} g_{j,t}) + \sum_j \left(\tilde{y}_{j,t-k}\ \Delta w_{j,t}\right) + \sum_j \left(\tilde{y}_{j,t-k} g_{j,t} \Delta w_{j,t}\right) = W + S + D \tag{1}$$

In the equation, $\frac{\Delta y_t}{y_{t-k}}$. is the growth rate of labour productivity in the national economy between period t and t-k. $\tilde{y}_{j,t-k}$ is the relative labour productivity, which is calculated as the quotient of labour productivity in sector *j* in period *t-k* and labour productivity in the national economy in period *t-k*. $w_{j,t}$ is the share of employment in sector *j* out of total employment at time *t* and $g_{j,t}$ is the growth rate of labour productivity in sector *j* at time *t*.

The endogenous effect (*W*) is the average increase in labour productivity in the sectors of the national economy, assuming a constant initial employment structure, weighted by relative labour efficiency. It determines what part of the labour productivity growth in the national economy is due to technological progress. The static external effect (*S*) represents labour reallocation between sectors, weighted by relative labour productivity. If changes in employment share are positively correlated with productivity levels, this term will be positive, and structural change will increase economy-wide productivity growth. In contrast, a negative value of *S* indicates that labour was reallocated to less productive sectors, negatively impacting overall productivity. *D* measures the shifting of labour between sectors with different rates of labour productivity growth, weighted by relative labour productivity. If it has a positive value, the labour force has moved to sectors with relatively dynamic labour productivity. However, a negative value of *D* indicates an increased share of employment in sectors with relatively low labour productivity dynamics.

Although the shift-share methodology has some limitations, it helps to understand structural change patterns and their repercussions on growth. One of the most significant advantages of the shift-share methodology is that its procedure is technically simple, which makes the analysis fast and reasonably accurate (Stevens & Moore, 1980). Moreover, it only requires detailed data, though these are sometimes not readily available (Barff & Knight, 1988). The main limitation of shift-share analysis is its static nature, as it is mainly applied only over a certain period, to examine changes between a starting date and an ending date. This method also has limited predictive capabilities (Knudsen, 2000). Criticism of the shift-share model also concerns the neglect of increasing returns to scale described in Verdoorn's law (2002). As Kaldor (1966) states, if economies of scale vary across sectors and inputs shift to sectors with higher rates of return, the impact of structural change on productivity growth is more significant than conventional shift-share analysis would indicate. Therefore, a modified shift-share analysis was used in the calculation, which considers the Verdoorn effects. This allows us to better assess the importance of structural changes for aggregate productivity growth.

4.3 Data and empirical analysis

Eurostat data was used in the empirical analysis. The database covers 27 EU countries: Austria, Belgium, Bulgaria, Czechia, Denmark, Germany, Estonia, Ireland, Greece, Spain, France, Croatia, Italy, Cyprus, Latvia, Lithuania, Luxembourg, Hungary, Malta, the Netherlands, Poland, Portugal, Romania, Slovenia, Slovakia, Finland and Sweden. NUTS 2 regions are often large territorial units, so further analysis was reduced to NUTS 3 regions. Data was analysed for 1,166

NUTS 3 regions. The following ten sectors are based on a statistical classification of economic activities in the European Community (NACE Rev. 2): agriculture, forestry and fishing (A); industry (except construction) (B–E); construction (F); wholesale and retail trade, transport, accommodation and food service activities (G–I); information and communication (J); financial and insurance activities (K); real estate activities (L); professional, scientific and technical activities and administrative and support service activities (M+N); public administration, defence, education, human health and social work activities (O–Q); and arts, entertainment and recreation, other service activities and activities of household and extraterritorial organisations and bodies (R–U).

To calculate productivity, I used Eurostat data for GVA and employment for 2000–2020, as data for 2021 were only available for some of the NUTS 3 regions. Table 4.1 contains statistics on the level of productivity in the 1,166 NUTS 3 regions surveyed. Δ2020–2000 for productivity per employee is the growth rate calculated as the difference between the 2020 and 2000 values divided by the 2000 value. Average productivity per employee increased from 36,210 EUR to 54,440 EUR per employee from 2000 to 2020. Minimum productivity increased sevenfold from 1.21 to 8.66. In 2000 the worst-performing region was in Romania (RO216), while in 2020, it was in Bulgaria (BG325). The maximum value increased almost threefold, from 98.44 to 283.25. In 2000, the best-performing region was in Germany (DE21H), while in 2020, it was in Ireland (IE053). During the 20-year study period, a decline was noted in 21 of Greece's regions. The highest increase of over 800% during 2000–2020 was indicated in Romania's regions; however, in 2020, they were still below 50% of the EU average.

The distribution of productivity levels for NUTS 3 regions is presented in Table 4.2. In the 20-year study period, a slow process of equalising productivity

Table 4.1 Descriptive statistics for NUTS 3 productivity in EU27 countries

	Average		*Minimum*		*Maximum*		*%Δ 2020/2000*	
	2000	*2020*	*2000*	*2020*	*2000*	*2020*	*Min*	*Max*
Productivity	36.21	54.44	1.21	8.66	98.44	283.25	−47%	885%

Source: Author's own elaboration based on the Eurostat database

Table 4.2 Distribution of productivity level in NUTS 3 regions (% of EU average)

Percent of EU average		*0–25*	*26–50*	*51–75*	*76–100*	*101–125*	*126–150*	*151–175*	*>176*
Number of NUTS 3 regions	2000	143	105	52	167	407	228	43	21
	2020	31	191	97	265	438	106	23	15
Percent of NUTS 3 regions	2000	12	9	4	14	35	20	4	2
	2020	3	16	8	23	38	9	2	1

Source: Author's own elaboration based on the Eurostat database

levels between NUTS 3 regions can be observed. A reduction in the number of outlier regions may evidence this. The number of regions with productivity below 50% of the EU average decreased from 248 in 2000 to 222 in 2020, while those with productivity below 25% of the EU average decreased from 143 to 31. The number of regions leading in terms of productivity index, with productivity more than 150% of the EU average, fell from 64 in 2000 to 38 in 2020. In 2000, 49% of EU regions achieved a productivity level between 76% and 125% of the EU average, while in 2020, the proportion increased to 61%.

Sectoral statistics for the EU27 average are presented in Table 4.3. This data will be used as a benchmark for the results of left-behind regions. Employment share by sector is calculated as the number of employees in a given sector divided by the number of all employees. GVA share by sector is calculated similarly. Δ2020–2000 is the difference between the values for 2020 and 2000. %Δ2020–2000 for productivity per employee is the growth rate, calculated as the difference between the 2020 and 2000 values divided by the 2000 value.

Employment share in the study period decreased the most in agriculture, forestry and fishing (A) and the industry sector (B–E). A slight decrease was noted in the construction sector (F) and the financial and insurance sector (K). Between 2000 and 2020, the most significant increase in employment occurred in industry (B–E) and professional, scientific and technical activities and administrative and support service (M–N). Wholesale and retail trade, transport, accommodation and food service activities (G–I) and public administration, defence, education, human health and social work activities (O–Q) had the largest share of employment in the EU27: almost 24% each. The most significant shares in GVA production were held by industry (B–E), wholesale and retail trade, transport, accommodation and food service activities (G–I) and public administration, defence, education, human health and social work activities (O–Q), but this mostly related to high employment in these sectors. We can assess the effectiveness of each sector by dividing GVA shares by employment share. Four of the ten sectors were effective in 2020. Real estate activities (L) was the recordholder in this field, with a value over 10. Other effective sectors were industry (B–E), information and communication (J) and financial and insurance (K). The agriculture sector (A) was inefficient despite a twofold increase during the period under study. Productivity per employee, measured in EUR, increased between 2000 and 2020 in most sectors. A record increase was noted for agriculture (A) (118.8%), but its productivity value was the lowest among all sectors. The lowest growth occurred in arts, entertainment and recreation, other service activities and activities of household and extraterritorial organisations and bodies (R–U).

The calculations identified left-behind regions in terms of productivity from the 1,166 NUTS 3 regions. In the period 2000–2020, valuable productivity growth occurred in most of the NUTS 3 regions, but the growth rate and take-off level varied greatly. A significant decline in productivity between 2000 and 2020 occurred in only 21 regions in Greece. In the further analysis, I focus firstly on regions with the worst level of productivity in 2020. A detailed analysis was also carried out for regions that recorded a decline in productivity during the period under study. The

Table 4.3 Employment, GVA and productivity per employee by sector for the EU27 average

	Employment share by sector (%)			*GVA share by sector (%)*			*GVA share/ employment share*		*Productivity per employee (thousands of EUR per employee)*		
Sector	*2000*	*2020*	*Δ2020–2000*	*2000*	*2020*	*Δ2020–2000*	*2000*	*2020*	*2000*	*2020*	*%Δ2020–2000*
A	8.59	4.53	−4.06	2.47	1.83	−0.64	0.29	0.40	10.80	23.63	118.81
B–E	19.94	15.99	−3.95	22.59	19.64	−2.94	1.13	1.23	42.63	71.95	68.79
F	6.89	6.54	−0.35	5.73	5.46	−0.27	0.83	0.83	31.32	48.89	56.08
G–I	23.06	24.08	1.02	19.35	17.74	−1.61	0.84	0.74	31.59	43.16	36.62
J	2.33	3.04	0.71	4.55	5.42	0.87	1.95	1.78	73.40	104.44	42.28
K	2.54	2.33	−0.21	4.80	4.63	−0.17	1.89	1.99	71.28	116.53	63.48
L	0.96	1.04	0.08	9.69	11.25	1.56	10.08	10.78	379.22	631.59	66.55
M–N	8.51	12.48	3.97	9.69	11.29	1.60	1.14	0.90	42.87	53.02	23.67
O–Q	21.77	23.97	2.20	17.74	19.72	1.98	0.82	0.82	30.68	48.20	57.14
R–U	5.42	5.99	0.58	3.40	3.02	−0.37	0.63	0.50	23.59	29.55	25.22
Total	100.00	100.00		100.00	100.00				37.64	58.59	55.66

Source: Author's own elaboration based on the Euros at database

Note: A: agriculture, forestry and fishing; B–E: industry (except construction); F: construction; G–I: wholesale and retail trade, transport, accommodation and food service activities; J: information and communication; K: financial and insurance activities; L: real estate activities; M+N: professional, scientific and technical activities and administrative and support service activities; O–Q: public administration, defence, education, human health and social work activities; R–U: arts, entertainment and recreation; other service activities; and activities of household and extraterritorial organisations and bodies

downward trend over the 20-year period may indicate severe problems in these regions and pose a threat of further decline in productivity in future. A productivity analysis was performed for selected left-behind regions, including a shift-share analysis for 10 NACE Rev. 2 sectors.

Regarding productivity levels in 2020, 25 Bulgarian and 5 Romanian regions were among the 30 least productive regions. For Bulgaria, 25 out of 28 NUTS 3 regions were indicated as being left-behind in terms of productivity. Only Sofia city (the country's capital), Sofia Province (the agglomeration surrounding the capital city) and Vratsa Province had much better productivity levels. In the case of Romania, all five NUTS 3 regions are located in one NUTS 2 region, RO21 Nord-Est, in the north-east of the country. Figure 4.1 shows changes in productivity levels for selected regions between 2000 and 2020. Detailed data for all 30 regions can be found in the Appendix. 1 As can be seen in the chart, an overall upward trend dominated in all regions over the 20 years under study. Selected regions increased productivity levels, from 1,000–4,000 EUR per employee in 2000 to 8,000–14,000 EUR in 2020; this was 2%–7% of the EU average in 2000 and 15%–24% of the EU average in 2020. Despite this increase, the level of productivity per employee was still low. Romania's regions had better growth than Bulgaria's because they started from a much lower level in 2000.

Table 4.4 consists of descriptive statistics for productivity levels of the 30 left-behind regions. These regions are very diverse in terms of employment structure. It is difficult to point to a single employment structure pattern common to all 30 regions. In Romania, all five regions had a very high share of employment in sector A. This sector posted the most significant decline in employment share, from

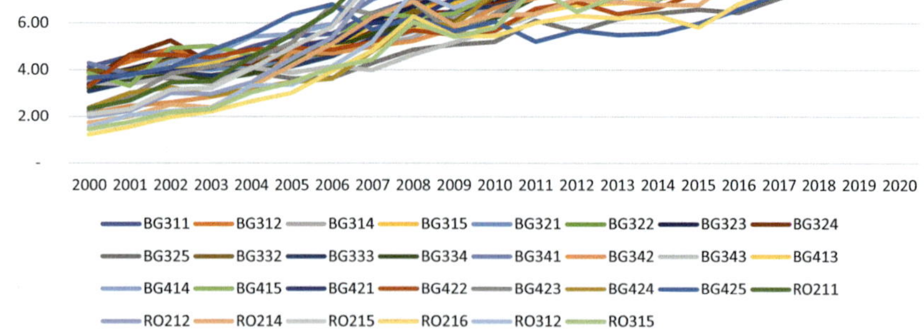

Figure 4.1 Productivity level for 30 left-behind NUTS 3 regions, in thousands of EUR per employee

Source: Author's own elaboration based on the Eurostat database

Table 4.4 Employment, GVA and productivity per employee by sector for 30 regions left behind in terms of productivity

		Sector	A	B–E	F	G–I	J	K	L	M–N	O–Q	R–U
BG311	Employment share by sector (%)	2000	21.14	21.01	2.47	19.67	1.81	1.11	0.17	2.22	28.73	1.67%
		2020	32.45	12.71	3.45	19.58	0.50	0.54	0.30	4.19	21.76	4.49
		Δ	11.31	−8.30	0.98	−0.09	−1.30	−0.58	0.13	1.97	−6.97	2.82
	GVA share by sector (%)	2000	20.34	7.36	2.01	20.17	3.56	1.66	18.38	2.60	22.61	1.30
		2020	15.84	10.71	1.22	15.12	0.78	1.11	23.73	2.22	27.96	1.31
		Δ	−4.51	3.35	−0.80	−5.05	−2.79	−0.55	5.35	−0.38	5.35	0.00
	Productivity per employee	2000	3.96	1.44	3.35	4.21	8.11	6.15	453.17	4.81	3.24	3.22
		2020	5.27	9.09	3.81	8.33	16.67	22.38	848.44	5.73	13.86	3.14
		%Δ	33.12	531.20	13.66	97.73	105.57	263.82	87.23	19.02	328.53	−2.33
BG312	Employment share by sector (%)	2000	19.59	28.26	3.74	16.62	1.63	0.98	0.14	2.19	24.64	2.19
		2020	28.23	22.89	4.24	17.56	0.80	1.13	0.31	2.80	20.28	1.79
		Δ	8.64	−5.37	0.50	0.94	−0.83	0.15	0.17	0.62	−4.36	−0.39
	GVA share by sector (%)	2000	23.66	11.28	2.50	15.14	3.50	1.44	18.14	3.22	19.70	1.41
		2020	14.79	23.19	2.13	17.48	0.70	0.81	16.81	1.16	22.19	0.76
		Δ	−8.87	11.91	−0.38	2.33	−2.80	−0.63	−1.33	−2.06	2.49	−0.65
	Productivity per employee	2000	4.66	1.54	2.58	3.52	8.27	5.66	508.14	5.68	3.09	2.49
		2020	6.18	11.95	5.91	11.74	10.23	8.42	641.6	4.88	12.9	4.98
		%Δ	32.52%	575.04%	128.80%	233.72%	23.78%	48.73%	26.26%	−14.24%	318.01%	100.16%
BG314	Employment share by sector (%)	2000	24.25	26.57	3.68	19.01	1.49	0.48	0.25	2.99	19.58	1.69
		2020	26.28	20.42	4.04	19.80	0.69	0.87	0.73	4.16	21.04	1.98
		Δ	2.02	−6.15	0.35	0.79	−0.80	0.39	0.48	1.17	1.46	0.29
	GVA share by sector (%)	2000	20.35	18.03	3.90	17.83	2.64	0.84	14.52	3.09	17.18	1.62
		2020	8.34	18.72	6.35	16.66	0.54	1.71	15.40	2.43	29.12	0.75
		Δ	−12.02	0.69	2.45	−1.18	−2.10	0.88	0.88	−0.66	11.93	−0.87
	Productivity per employee	2000	3.1	2.5	3.91	3.46	6.52	6.4	210.5	3.81	3.24	3.53
		2020	3.47	10.04	17.23	9.21	8.48	21.56	229.45	6.39	15.15	4.14
		%Δ	12.18%	300.83%	340.71%	166.05%	29.94%	237.07%	9.00%	67.73%	367.89%	17.42%

(*Continued*)

Table 4.4 (Continued)

		Sector	*A*	*B–E*	*F*	*G–I*	*J*	*K*	*L*	*M–N*	*O–Q*	*R–U*
BG315	Employment share by sector (%)	2000	28.85	30.48	2.29	14.39	1.17	0.75	0.11	1.61	19.06	1.29
		2020	24.53	27.95	2.76	19.15	0.46	1.27	0.22	2.43	19.38	1.83
		Δ	−4.32	−2.53	0.47	4.75	−0.71	0.52	0.11	0.82	0.33	0.54
	GVA share by sector (%)	2000	16.50	22.56	2.86	15.36	2.81	1.48	14.85	2.48	19.89	1.21
		2020	9.18	29.72	1.15	12.66	0.85	1.17	16.23	1.84	26.39	0.81
		Δ	−7.33	7.16	−1.72	−2.70	−1.95	−0.31	1.39	−0.64	6.50	−0.40
	Productivity per employee	2000	1.83	2.37	4.01	3.42	7.71	6.31	428.5	4.94	3.34	3.01
		2020	4.49	12.76	4.99	7.94	22.39	11.05	891.09	9.1	16.34	5.3
		%Δ	144.98%	438.08%	24.45%	132.16%	190.26%	74.94%	107.96%	84.19%	388.64%	76.18%
BG321	Employment share by sector (%)	2000	27.20	25.98	3.07	19.61	1.56	0.91	0.16	2.22	17.69	1.62
		2020	22.15	22.20	5.82	22.46	0.86	0.65	0.37	2.81	19.22	3.46
		Δ	−5.05	−3.77	2.75	2.85	−0.70	−0.26	0.21	0.59	1.53	1.85
	GVA share by sector (%)	2000	15.16	20.13	4.19	18.05	3.10	1.81	14.43	2.62	18.89	1.61
		2020	7.03	29.72	1.15	12.66	0.85	1.17	16.23	1.84	26.39	0.81
		Δ	−8.13	9.59	−3.04	−5.38	−2.25	−0.64	1.80	−0.78	7.50	−0.81
	Productivity per employee	2000	1.78	2.48	4.36	2.94	6.36	6.34	292.68	3.77	3.41	3.19
		2020	3.6	10.63	12.88	11.24	27.02	43.18	447.79	11.18	11.73	4.52
		%Δ	102.03%	329.60%	195.21%	282.28%	324.77%	581.45%	52.99%	196.67%	243.69%	41.83%
BG322	Employment share by sector (%)	2000	13.55	42.13	3.35	19.39	1.46	0.67	0.14	1.88	15.67	1.77
		2020	11.66	44.07	3.19	18.45	0.48	0.35	0.29	2.36	15.82	3.33
		Δ	−1.89	1.95	−0.16	−0.94	−0.97	−0.32	0.15	0.48	0.15	1.55
	GVA share by sector (%)	2000	11.66	29.82	3.89	17.12	2.64	1.33	13.07	2.22	16.13	2.13
		2020	4.79	39.01	2.85	16.32	1.69	0.72	12.20	2.22	18.39	1.80
		Δ	−6.87	9.20	−1.04	−0.80	−0.95	−0.61	−0.87	0.01	2.26	−0.33
	Productivity per employee	2000	2.87	2.36	3.88	2.95	6.06	6.64	319.56	3.94	3.44	4.01
		2020	5.54	11.92	12.04	11.91	47.16	27.78	566.4	12.69	15.66	7.3
		%Δ	92.65%	404.56%	210.55%	304.09%	677.90%	318.57%	77.25%	222.41%	355.67%	82.17%

BG323	Employment share by sector (%)	2000	20.33	29.25	3.64	22.58	1.75	0.66	0.21	2.56	17.59	1.44
		2020	20.17	27.46	4.18	23.33	0.83	1.25	0.70	4.44	14.92	2.74
		Δ	−0.17	−1.78	0.54	0.75	−0.92	0.59	0.49	1.88	−2.68	1.30
	GVA share by sector (%)	2000	13.41	22.80	3.76	21.92	2.83	1.34	13.39	2.80	15.57	2.19
		2020	6.02	27.78	4.29	20.16	1.90	1.24	11.11	4.18	22.29	1.03
		Δ	−7.39	4.98	0.53	−1.76	−0.93	−0.09	−2.27	1.38	6.72	−1.16
	Productivity per employee	2000	2.41	2.86	3.79	3.56	5.9	7.44	234.19	4.01	3.24	5.58
		2020	3.62	12.28	12.46	10.49	27.76	12.12	192.21	11.43	18.14	4.55
		%Δ	49.98%	330.15%	228.93%	194.99%	370.27%	62.90%	−17.93%	185.30%	459.83%	−18.36%
BG324	Employment share by sector (%)	2000	32.32	21.99	3.09	14.72	1.08	0.57	0.12	1.85	22.70	1.58
		2020	37.40	16.89	4.38	17.39	0.12	0.44	0.14	3.78	16.29	3.22
		Δ	5.08	−5.10	1.30	2.67	−0.96	−0.13	0.02	1.93	−6.41	1.64
	GVA share by sector (%)	2000	25.96	18.04	2.23	13.69	2.67	0.99	14.39	2.55	18.10	1.37
		2020	14.56	25.12	3.69	14.95	0.15	1.27	12.49	2.95	16.70	8.11
		Δ	−11.40	7.07	1.46	1.26	−2.52	0.28	−1.91	0.40	−1.40	6.75
	Productivity per employee	2000	2.86	2.93	2.58	3.32	8.85	6.18	421.33	4.92	2.84	3.08
		2020	4.05	15.48	8.77	8.95	13	30	927.71	8.11	10.67	26.2
		%Δ	41.47	428.86	240.13	169.75	46.91	385.55	120.19	64.65	275.26	751.46
BG325	Employment share by sector (%)	2000	41.32%	18.01%	2.53%	13.76%	1.01%	0.95%	0.08%	1.74%	18.85%	1.78%
		2020	41.74	13.80	3.80	19.16	0.20	0.62	0.15	2.57	16.37	1.64
		Δ	0.42	−4.20	1.28	5.39	−0.81	−0.33	0.08	0.83	−2.49	−0.14
	GVA share by sector (%)	2000	33.34	8.54	3.53	14.50	2.93	1.50	13.12	3.09	18.36	1.09
		2020	19.63	13.84	5.35	19.58	0.40	1.32	16.40	1.45	21.53	0.50
		Δ	−13.72	5.30	1.82	5.09	−2.53	−0.17	3.27	−1.64	3.17	−0.59
	Productivity per employee	2000	2.69	1.58	4.66	3.52	9.73	5.27	554.75	5.93	3.25	2.06
		2020	4.07	8.68	12.19	8.85	17.44	18.5	917	4.88	11.39	2.65
		%Δ	51.17%	448.38%	161.28%	151.73%	79.37%	250.99%	65.30%	−17.74%	250.45%	28.85%

(*Continued*)

Table 4.4 (Continued)

		Sector	*A*	*B–E*	*F*	*G–I*	*J*	*K*	*L*	*M–N*	*O–Q*	*R–U*
BG331	Employment share by sector (%)	2000	16.88	18.67	5.97	30.82	2.16	1.01	0.36	3.75	18.66	1.70
		2020	10.94	14.04	9.17	31.11	1.97	1.40	1.28	7.63	18.34	4.12
		Δ	−5.94	−4.64	3.20	0.29	−0.19	0.38	0.93	3.88	−0.33	2.42
	GVA share by sector (%)	2000	7.79	19.55	5.57	32.12	2.18	1.79	10.94	3.24	14.84	1.97
		2020	2.61	18.36	7.42	24.43	4.86	3.47	11.11	8.21	17.09	2.45
		Δ	−5.19	−1.20	1.86	−7.70	2.68	1.68	0.17	4.97	2.25	0.47
	Productivity per employee	2000	2	4.54	4.05	4.52	4.37	7.65	133.25	3.75	3.45	5.03
		2020	3.67	20.13	12.46	12.09	37.85	38.25	133.29	16.57	14.35	9.13
		%Δ	83.34%	343.46%	208.02%	167.49%	766.82%	399.68%	0.04%	342.05%	316.26%	81.71%
BG332	Employment share by sector (%)	2000	37.64	17.94	2.76	16.97	1.11	1.10	0.20	2.47	18.36	1.48
		2020	40.85	15.12	2.89	19.22	0.42	0.38	0.40	3.93	14.59	2.20
		Δ	3.21	−2.83	0.13	2.25	−0.69	−0.72	0.21	1.46	−3.77	0.72
	GVA share by sector (%)	2000	30.35	8.78	4.43	20.80	2.38	1.79	11.78	3.89	14.27	1.53
		2020	13.70	21.42	3.40	16.48	0.83	0.66	15.14	2.62	24.90	0.86
		Δ	−16.64	12.64	−1.02	−4.32	−1.55	−1.13	3.36	−1.27	10.63	−0.68
	Productivity per employee	2000	3.2	1.94	6.36	4.86	8.51	6.49	237.06	6.23	3.08	4.11
		2020	3.56	15.05	12.52	9.1	21.16	18.64	399.1	7.06	18.12	4.13
		%Δ	11.48%	675.67%	96.82%	87.41%	148.63%	187.06%	68.35%	13.33%	488.22%	0.48%
BG333	Employment share by sector (%)	2000	33.26	20.86	3.82	16.11	1.20	0.71	0.18	2.36	19.97	1.55
		2020	30.65	20.56	4.96	18.76	0.27	0.68	0.63	4.98	16.55	1.96
		Δ	−2.61%	−0.30%	1.14%	2.65%	−0.94%	−0.03%	0.45%	2.62%	−3.42%	0.41%
	GVA share by sector (%)	2000	21.90	12.23	6.19	16.69	3.05	1.50	14.66	3.35	18.84	1.59
		2020	11.05	21.42	3.40	16.48	0.83	0.66	15.14	2.62	24.90	0.86
		Δ	−10.85	9.19	−2.79	−0.21	−2.22	−0.84	0.48	−0.73	6.06	−0.74
	Productivity per employee	2000	2.02	1.8	4.97	3.18	7.78	6.52	254	4.37	2.9	3.16
		2020	3.46	12.78	8.45	7.01	20.32	45.89	196.12	6.24	13.45	2.45
		%Δ	71.12%	609.52%	69.90%	120.22%	161.19%	604.11%	−22.79%	42.77%	364.12%	−22.55%

BG334	Employment share by sector (%)	2000	34.43	22.47	2.79	13.16	1.16	0.61	0.14	2.18	21.43	1.63
		2020	37.97	19.03	5.66	17.98	0.09	0.38	0.17	3.26	13.37	2.09
		Δ	3.55	−3.43	2.87	4.82	−1.07	−0.23	0.03	1.08	−8.06	0.46
	GVA share by sector (%)	2000	26.00	13.04	2.50	14.99	3.01	1.14	15.31	2.82	19.87	1.31
		2020	11.97	20.34	12.94	19.49	0.27	1.74	12.82	1.80	17.71	0.90
		Δ	−14.03	7.30	10.44	4.50	−2.73	0.60	−2.48	−1.01	−2.16	−0.41
	Productivity per employee	2000	2.44	1.87	2.89	3.67	8.35	6.03	346.29	4.17	2.99	2.6
		2020	3.18	10.79	23.1	10.95	29	46.7	762.89	5.58	13.38	4.36
		%Δ	30.70%	476.60%	699.28%	197.96%	247.27%	674.03%	120.31%	33.82%	347.16%	67.71%
BG341	Employment share by sector (%)	2000	36.11	18.61	3.66	20.21	1.55	0.89	0.19	2.50	14.78	1.49
		2020	19.07	15.57	7.06	31.66	0.59	0.56	1.20	5.16	15.78	3.37
		Δ	−17.04	−3.05	3.40	11.45	−0.96	−0.34	1.01	2.65	1.00	1.88
	GVA share by sector (%)	2000	9.44	36.73	4.05	22.03	1.80	1.46	8.72	2.22	11.84	1.70
		2020	4.70	11.95	5.29	29.90	1.85	1.50	17.31	4.75	20.26	2.48
		Δ	−4.74	−24.78	1.24	7.86	0.05	0.05	8.60	2.53	8.42	0.78
	Productivity per employee	2000	1.12	8.43	4.72	4.66	4.98	6.98	195.35	3.79	3.42	4.88
		2020	2.75	8.57	8.36	10.54	35.06	30.2	161.22	10.29	14.33	8.22
		%Δ	146.36%	1.61%	77.06%	126.34%	603.92%	332.56%	−17.47%	171.52%	318.49%	68.39%
BG342	Employment share by sector (%)	2000	59.49	12.47	1.47	9.38	0.80	0.70	0.14	1.75	12.62	1.20
		2020	33.60	20.90	3.72	18.34	0.17	0.58	0.36	3.20	16.60	2.52
		Δ	−25.90	8.44	2.25	8.96	−0.64	−0.12	0.22	1.45	3.98	1.33
	GVA share by sector (%)	2000	30.27	8.86	3.07	16.02	2.56	1.78	14.43	3.52	17.62	1.87
		2020	8.93	23.27	4.31	18.58	0.59	1.87	17.19	2.90	21.27	1.07
		Δ	−21.34	14.41	1.25	2.56	−1.98	0.09	2.75	−0.62	3.65	−0.79
	Productivity per employee	2000	1.08	1.5	4.41	3.61	6.76	5.38	223.38	4.25	2.95	3.3
		2020	2.52	10.54	10.97	9.59	33.5	30.45	450.92	8.58	12.12	4.03
		%Δ	133.88%	601.09%	148.68%	165.37%	395.91%	466.23%	101.87%	101.61%	310.67%	22.04%

(Continued)

Table 4.4 (Continued)

		Sector	*A*	*B–E*	*F*	*G–I*	*J*	*K*	*L*	*M–N*	*O–Q*	*R–U*
BG343	Employment share by sector (%)	2000	37.73	17.72	3.04	14.42	1.09	0.95	0.13	1.91	21.79	1.26
		2020	32.81	20.95	4.63	18.39	0.31	1.22	0.44	2.72	15.71	2.87
		Δ	−4.92	3.23	1.59	3.97	−0.78	0.27	0.31	0.81	−6.08	1.61
	GVA share by sector (%)	2000	28.20	9.19	4.52	14.92	3.06	1.75	15.62	3.76	17.63	1.35
		2020	11.39	21.78	3.93	21.76	0.63	6.41	14.46	1.72	17.32	0.60
		Δ	−16.81	12.60	−0.59	6.85	−2.43	4.66	−1.16	−2.04	−0.31	−0.75
	Productivity per employee	2000	2.57	1.78	5.12	3.56	9.67	6.3	401.86	6.77	2.78	3.7
		2020	3.63	10.87	8.87	12.38	21.38	54.75	343.48	6.61	11.53	2.19
		%Δ	41.26%	509.63%	73.22%	247.76%	121.12%	769.05%	−14.53%	−2.43%	314.17%	−40.67%
BG344	Employment share by sector (%)	2000	26.12	32.63	4.37	15.54	1.21	0.64	0.22	2.45	15.74	1.08
		2020	18.73	35.82	4.57	17.73	0.61	0.69	0.49	4.28	14.82	2.27
		Δ	−7.39	3.19	0.21	2.20	−0.60	0.04	0.26	1.83	−0.91	1.19
	GVA share by sector (%)	2000	11.73%	41.54%	4.74%	13.96%	1.89%	1.01%	9.47%	2.40%	12.03%	1.23%
		2020	4.11%	49.49%	4.32%	13.26%	0.83%	1.78%	9.08%	3.43%	12.10%	1.60%
		Δ	−7.62	7.95	−0.42	−0.69	−1.06	0.77	−0.39	1.03	0.07	0.37
	Productivity per employee	2000	1.84	5.21	4.45	3.68	6.4	6.42	172.3	4.01	3.13	4.67
		2020	3.39	21.36	14.61	11.56	21.15	39.98	287.34	12.4	12.62	10.91
		%Δ	84.60%	309.99%	228.58%	214.54%	230.59%	523.22%	66.77%	208.86%	303.34%	133.74%
BG413	Employment share by sector (%)	2000	21.13	36.76	3.05	13.45	1.16	0.68	0.08	1.46	20.52	1.71
		2020	21.12	23.82	6.41	24.48	0.47	0.45	0.48	3.31	16.27	3.19
		Δ	−0.01	−12.95	3.36	11.03	−0.69	−0.23	0.39	1.85	−4.26	1.49
	GVA share by sector (%)	2000	15.44%	28.77%	3.18%	14.11%	2.26%	1.22%	11.58%	1.85%	19.87%	1.70%
		2020	8.10%	18.64%	5.96%	24.73%	2.17%	2.40%	12.46%	3.50%	18.82%	3.22%
		Δ	−7.34	−10.14	2.78	10.62	−0.10	1.18	0.88	1.65	−1.04	1.52
	Productivity per employee	2000	2.52	2.69	3.58	3.61	6.72	6.19	474.3	4.36	3.33	3.43
		2020	3.74	7.62	9.05	9.84	44.84	51.94	254.25	10.29	11.27	9.83
		%Δ	59.01%	104.99%	70.43%	75.40%	99.38%	135.77%	0.11%	54.08%	101.50%	83.34%

BG414	Employment share by sector (%)	2000	17.51	34.87	5.78	15.42	1.43	0.92	0.27	2.80	19.47	1.51
		2020	18.31	22.30	7.24	22.75	0.51	0.56	0.56	5.23	20.44	2.08
		Δ	0.80	−12.57	1.46	7.34	−0.92	−0.36	0.28	2.43	0.97	0.57
	GVA share by sector (%)	2000	18.25	16.92	5.27	14.58	2.87	1.44	18.64	2.77	17.77	1.50
		2020	5.44	23.80	5.92	20.21	0.66	1.16	19.05	3.46	18.54	1.76
		Δ	−12.81	6.88	0.65	5.62	−2.20	−0.28	0.40	0.69	0.77	0.26
	Productivity per employee	2000	3.65	1.7	3.19	3.32	7.03	5.47	238.21	3.47	3.2	3.48
		2020	3.78	13.58	10.41	11.3	16.65	26.45	433.91	8.43	11.54	10.76
		%Δ	3.60%	698.81%	226.02%	240.94%	136.93%	383.80%	82.15%	142.96%	260.88%	209.04%
BG415	Employment share by sector (%)	2000	21.14	33.27	3.81	16.82	1.22	0.87	0.14	1.72	19.72	1.31
		2020	18.41	25.46	5.38	26.39	0.14	0.39	0.30	3.48	17.25	2.81
		Δ	−2.73	−7.81	1.57	9.57	−1.08	−0.47	0.16	1.76	−2.47	1.50
	GVA share by sector (%)	2000	16.18	29.15	3.90	14.64	2.02	1.42	13.57	2.21	15.80	1.10
		2020	9.20	23.07	4.02	18.62	0.27	0.70	18.41	2.01	22.08	1.60
		Δ	−6.98	−6.08	0.12	3.98	−1.75	−0.72	4.84	−0.20	6.28	0.50
	Productivity per employee	2000	2.94	3.37	3.94	3.34	6.39	6.29	367	4.94	3.08	3.23
		2020	5.96	10.81	8.92	8.41	23	21.24	728.46	6.9	15.26	6.82
		%Δ	102.61%	220.96%	126.24%	151.59%	259.96%	237.56%	98.49%	39.80%	395.73%	111.16%
BG421	Employment share by sector (%)	2000	22.70	27.01	4.19	21.11	1.42	0.76	0.30	2.97	18.32	1.21
		2020	16.56	28.51	5.18	24.39	1.56	0.75	0.61	4.73	15.10	2.62
		Δ	−6.14	1.50	0.99	3.28	0.14	−0.01	0.31	1.75	−3.23	1.41
	GVA share by sector (%)	2000	14.76	19.34	5.34	20.73	3.11	1.67	12.29	3.54	17.36	1.87
		2020	3.39	31.40	4.34	16.08	5.90	1.78	10.35	4.42	20.67	1.66
		Δ	−11.37	12.06	−1.00	−4.64	2.80	0.11	−1.93	0.88	3.30	−0.21
	Productivity per employee	2000	2.19	2.42	4.3	3.31	7.4	7.42	138.11	4.01	3.2	5.22
		2020	2.61	14.07	10.72	8.42	48.48	30.33	216.65	11.94	17.48	8.07
		%Δ	19.10%	481.91%	149.18%	154.14%	555.56%	308.58%	56.87%	197.42%	446.58%	54.80%

(*Continued*)

Table 4.4 (Continued)

		Sector	*A*	*B–E*	*F*	*G–I*	*J*	*K*	*L*	*M–N*	*O–Q*	*R–U*
BG422	Employment share by sector (%)	2000	30.76	24.35	3.57	15.65	1.24	0.78	0.14	1.81	20.51	1.18
		2020	26.27	20.88	4.78	25.44	0.43	0.95	0.26	2.98	14.16	3.88
		Δ	−4.50	−3.47	1.20	9.79	−0.82	0.16	0.12	1.17	−6.35	2.70
	GVA share by sector (%)	2000	18.83	19.46	4.41	16.65	2.88	1.57	14.52	2.35	18.20	1.14
		2020	9.60	31.40	4.34	16.08	5.90	1.78	10.35	4.42	20.67	1.66
		Δ	−9.23	11.94	−0.07	−0.56	3.03	0.22	−4.17	2.07	2.46	0.52
	Productivity per employee	2000	2.03	2.65	4.09	3.52	7.67	6.62	345.93	4.3	2.94	3.18
		2020	3.55	10.1	8.31	7.67	25.73	16.65	607.13	6.26	14.18	8.15
		%Δ	75.15%	281.72%	103.25%	117.69%	235.31%	151.53%	75.51%	45.61%	382.23%	155.83%
BG423	Employment share by sector (%)	2000	51.29	18.27	1.83	12.59	0.83	0.58	0.10	1.37	12.38	0.77
		2020	29.50	23.58	4.23	20.91	0.32	1.28	0.54	2.31	14.90	2.45
		Δ	−21.79	5.31	2.40	8.32	−0.51	0.69	0.44	0.94	2.52	1.68
	GVA share by sector (%)	2000	20.30	20.45	2.67	18.38	2.63	1.45	13.38	2.43	17.31	0.99
		2020	7.41	39.02	2.69	15.81	0.87	0.94	12.42	1.53	18.10	1.22
		Δ	−12.89	18.57	0.01	−2.57	−1.76	−0.51	−0.96	−0.90	0.79	0.23
	Productivity per employee	2000	0.88	2.48	3.24	3.24	7.02	5.52	294.93	3.94	3.1	2.86
		2020	2.78	18.31	7.03	8.37	29.64	8.13	254.63	7.3	13.44	5.5
		%Δ	216.58%	637.06%	117.23%	158.21%	322.44%	47.43%	−13.66%	85.44%	333.23%	92.33%
BG424	Employment share by sector (%)	2000	38.24	17.86	3.49	16.14	0.96	0.67	0.26	2.48	18.89	1.02
		2020	20.39	31.65	4.39	19.37	0.15	0.25	0.15	3.75	16.63	3.31
		Δ	−17.85	13.79	0.90	3.23	−0.81	−0.42	−0.10	1.26	−2.26	2.29
	GVA share by sector (%)	2000	17.19	12.03	6.79	17.51	3.15	1.71	14.09	2.78	23.33	1.41
		2020	7.79	30.70	8.19	13.48	0.34	0.46	14.02	2.88	19.79	2.36
		Δ	−9.40	18.67	1.40	−4.03	−2.82	−1.25	−0.07	0.09	−3.54	0.95
	Productivity per employee	2000	1.06	1.6	4.61	2.57	7.75	6.09	130.78	2.66	2.93	3.28
		2020	3.94	10.01	19.24	7.18	23.13	19.31	955.38	7.92	12.27	7.37
		%Δ	269.78%	526.71%	317.41%	179.26%	198.39%	217.29%	630.53%	198.03%	319.49%	124.72%

BG425	Employment share by sector (%)	2000	25.55	25.89	3.35	14.23	1.14	0.64	0.08	1.33	26.18	1.59
		2020	35.57	19.14	5.16	18.83	0.24	0.27	0.17	2.45	16.15	2.03
		Δ	10.02	−6.75	1.80	4.59	−0.90	−0.37	0.09	1.12	−10.03	0.43
	GVA share by sector (%)	2000	24.46	15.57	3.12	14.08	2.81	1.15	14.48	2.38	20.44	1.52
		2020	12.87	42.07	3.40	9.36	0.50	0.57	12.32	1.63	15.41	1.86
		Δ	−11.59	26.50	0.29	−4.72	−2.31	−0.58	−2.15	−0.75	−5.03	0.34
	Productivity per employee	2000	3.5	2.2	3.4	3.62	9.03	6.53	698	6.56	2.85	3.5
		2020	4.29	26.04	7.82	5.89	24.38	24.94	877.82	7.88	11.31	10.88
		%Δ	22.50%	1083.98%	130.17%	62.89%	169.83%	282.03%	25.76%	20.12%	296.09%	210.87%
RO211	Employment share by sector (%)	2000	60.82	16.55	3.90	9.72	0.49	0.62	0.18	1.03	5.35	1.34
		2020	39.51	14.36	14.80	18.21	0.64	0.57	0.11	1.72	8.76	1.33
		Δ	−21.31	−2.19	10.90	8.49	0.14	−0.05	−0.07	0.68	3.41	−0.01
	GVA share by sector (%)	2000	14.42	29.67	6.90	20.04	4.63	3.14	8.34	1.72	9.19	1.95
		2020	6.07	17.12	14.98	22.93	1.34	1.45	10.92	3.62	19.07	2.51
		Δ	−8.35	−12.55	8.07	2.88	−3.28	−1.69	2.57	1.90	9.88	0.57
	Productivity per employee	2000	0.55	4.19	4.14	4.82	21.98	11.85	107.65	3.89	4.02	3.39
		2020	2.13	16.54	14.05	17.48	29.27	35.35	1390.16	29.29	30.21	26.17
		%Δ	284.68%	294.65%	239.49%	262.31%	33.18%	198.39%	1191.38%	653.27%	652.49%	672.32%
RO212	Employment share by sector (%)	2000	67.82	12.31	3.31	7.31	0.33	0.54	0.07	0.78	6.60	0.93
		2020	43.66	12.97	11.97	16.92	0.33	0.51	0.09	1.34	11.01	1.19
		Δ	−24.15	0.66	8.66	9.61	0.00	−0.03	0.01	0.56	4.41	0.26
	GVA share by sector (%)	2000	31.53	19.39	4.38	15.80	2.70	3.51	4.11	1.03	15.23	2.30
		2020	11.47	20.23	5.83	20.54	0.72	1.13	9.07	3.93	24.35	2.74
		Δ	−20.06	0.84	1.45	4.73	−1.99	−2.39	4.96	2.90	9.12	0.44
	Productivity per employee	2000	0.92	3.13	2.63	4.29	16.27	12.83	109.81	2.65	4.58	4.9
		2020	3.63	21.55	6.73	16.77	29.65	30.51	1415	40.68	30.54	31.77
		%Δ	293.30%	589.27%	156.36%	290.98%	82.28%	137.79%	1188.56%	1437.14%	567.08%	548.99%

(Continued)

Table 4.4 (Continued)

		Sector	*A*	*B–E*	*F*	*G–I*	*J*	*K*	*L*	*M–N*	*O–Q*	*R–U*
RO214	Employment share by sector (%)	2000	70.82%	11.97%	2.34%	7.83%	0.27%	0.48%	0.14%	0.83%	4.47%	0.86%
		2020	51.41%	12.22%	8.33%	17.13%	0.50%	0.44%	0.14%	1.38%	7.35%	1.09%
		Δ	−19.40%	0.25%	6.00%	9.30%	0.23%	−0.04%	0.00%	0.56%	2.88%	0.23%
	GVA share by sector (%)	2000	18.52%	26.38%	5.37%	18.49%	5.10%	3.30%	8.39%	1.46%	11.65%	1.34%
		2020	9.82%	20.71%	5.78%	26.52%	1.07%	1.25%	8.38%	3.56%	20.54%	2.36%
		Δ	−8.70%	−5.67%	0.41%	8.03%	−4.03%	−2.05%	−0.01%	2.10%	8.90%	1.02%
	Productivity per employee	2000	0.45	3.8	3.96	4.07	31.98	11.81	106.37	3.05	4.49	2.7
		2020	2.12	18.8	7.69	17.17	23.55	31.4	665.78	28.54	31	24.04
		%Δ	369.88%	394.70%	94.19%	321.88%	−26.37%	165.91%	525.93%	835.38%	590.70%	790.11%
RO215	Employment share by sector (%)	2000	66.49	11.60	2.93	8.98	0.30	0.54	0.12	0.68	5.75	2.60
		2020	44.37	11.11	9.13	20.61	0.46	0.50	0.11	1.71	9.33	2.69
		Δ	−22.13	−0.49	6.20	11.62	0.15	−0.03	−0.02	1.03	3.58	0.08
	GVA share by sector (%)	2000	24.87	24.09	4.18	15.55	2.92	3.29	9.66	1.07	11.33	3.03
		2020	11.94	21.04	4.93	21.86	1.01	1.18	11.41	3.33	20.03	3.26
		Δ	−12.92	−3.05	0.76	6.31	−1.92	−2.11	1.75	2.26	8.70	0.23
	Productivity per employee	2000	0.78	4.35	2.99	3.62	20.24	12.85	163.8	3.28	4.12	2.44
		2020	3.75	26.34	7.52	14.76	30.68	32.73	1508.1	27.12	29.87	16.9
		%Δ	378.50%	506.07%	151.77%	307.41%	51.59%	154.84%	820.72%	727.62%	624.30%	592.18%

RO216	Employment share by sector (%)	2000	74.41	10.99	2.17	5.03	0.15	0.39	0.07	0.62	5.51	0.67
		2020	61.65	8.49	8.95	9.46	0.23	0.37	0.09	0.90	9.20	0.66
		Δ	−12.76	−2.50	6.79	4.43	0.08	−0.02	0.03	0.27	3.70	−0.01
	GVA share by sector (%)	2000	19.57	25.31	4.23	18.70	3.15	4.52	5.16	1.92	15.29	2.15
		2020	7.88	18.86	6.24	17.71	1.29	1.30	12.25	2.96	29.23	2.28
		Δ	−11.69	−6.46	2.01	−0.98	−1.86	−3.23	7.10	1.04	13.95	0.12
	Productivity per employee	2000	0.32	2.79	2.36	4.5	25.44	14.03	94.26	3.73	3.36	3.9
		2020	1.16	20.09	6.31	16.93	50.71	31.94	1208.11	29.9	28.73	31.33
		%Δ	263.33%	521.09%	166.65%	276.40%	99.32%	127.74%	1181.64%	701.15%	755.21%	704.08%

Source: Author's own elaboration based on the Eurostat database

Note: A: agriculture, forestry and fishing; B–E: industry (except construction); F: construction; G–I: wholesale and retail trade, transport, accommodation and food service activities; J: information and communication; K: financial and insurance activities; L: real estate activities; M+N: professional, scientific and technical activities and administrative and support service activities; O–Q: public administration, defence, education, human health and social work activities; R–U: arts, entertainment and recreation; other service activities; and activities of household and extra-territorial organisations and bodies

60%–75% in 2000 to 40%–62% in 2020; however, this is still 10–12 times more than the EU27 average. In Romania, a high share of employment was also found in the sector B–E, from 11% to 16.5% in 2000; this share was relatively stable over the 20 years under study. The share of Romania's services sector increased during the period under review, from 15%–22% in 2000 to 29%–46%, of which the most significant share was in sectors F and G–I, which are less knowledge-intensive. For Bulgaria, employment in agriculture varied in every region. In 16 of the 25 Bulgarian regions, agricultural employment decreased by 2% to 26% during the period under review; in the remaining 9, there was an increase from 0.4% to 10%. The increases and decreases were often correlated with changes in sectors B–E and F, which indicates a transfer of workers between these sectors. Bulgarian employment in the service sector was most often around 40%–50% of overall employment, with the highest share in sectors G–I and O–Q.

There was a slight increase in the share of sector A in the GVA for most regions. However, in 2020, the employees in sector A did not produce proportional GVA: the GVA share was much smaller than the employment share, in the range of 0.13–0.82. In the region with the highest share of sector A in employment, the value oscillated around 0.13–0.27 in 2020. Shares in employment in sectors B–E, F, G–I and R–U in most of the regions translated into almost proportional shares in GVA. The most significant changes in the share of GVA were recorded in most regions for sector B–E. The highest GVA share/employment share was recorded in sector L. In most regions, sectors J and K were also effective, although to a lesser extent. However, interpreting productivity indicators for sector L requires great care due to its nature. In 2000, many more sectors turned out to be effective (GVA share/employment share > 1), while in 2020, more sectors did not produce proportional GVA compared to employment share.

Productivity per employee, measured in thousands of EUR, increased between 2000 and 2020 for most sectors of the regions under study. There were only four cases where productivity decreased. The lowest value of productivity per employee was noted in sector A, while the highest was in sector L, followed by sectors J and K. On average, the increase in production was over 100% in all sectors. In Romania, even though productivity in sector A increased by almost 260%–380% over the study period, this sector was still characterised by the lowest productivity value. Over the 20-year period, the highest increase in the total value of productivity per employee was recorded in sector B–E (an average of 461%), followed by sector O–Q (an average of 382%) and sector K (an average of 290%). Again, it is difficult to find a common pattern for all analysed regions; where there was a few percent increase in one sector, it was a few hundred in the same sector for other regions.

The endogenous effect, static external effect and dynamic external effect are calculated based on Equation 1. Table 4.5 presents the productivity level for 2000 and 2020, the productivity growth rate and the shift-share breakdown of productivity growth for the 30 selected left-behind regions. In all these regions, productivity growth occurred over the period, though at greatly different rates. The highest

Table 4.5 Productivity and shift-share breakdown for 2000 and 2020 for selected left-behind NUTS 3 regions

Code	*Productivity in 2000 (thousands of EUR per employee)*	*Productivity in 2020 (thousands of EUR per employee)*	*Productivity growth rate 2020/2000 (%)*	*Shift-share breakdown of productivity growth rate for total economy (%)*		
				W	*S*	*D*
BG311	4.11	10.79	162	165	19	−21
BG312	3.86	11.79	205	192	28	−15
BG314	3.69	10.95	197	169	28	−1
BG315	3.20	12.00	275	247	17	11
BG321	3.19	11.33	255	221	22	11
BG322	3.34	13.47	303	288	14	2
BG323	3.66	12.14	231	219	33	−20
BG324	3.57	10.41	192	201	2	−11
BG325	3.34	8.66	159	143	15	1
BG331	4.34	15.40	255	223	31	2
BG332	3.96	10.62	168	170	14	−16
BG333	3.07	9.60	213	195	38	−21
BG334	3.23	10.10	213	222	3	−11
BG341	4.27	11.16	161	102	56	3
BG342	2.11	9.46	348	217	45	86
BG343	3.44	10.46	204	168	37	−1
BG344	4.09	15.46	278	239	16	24
BG413	3.44	9.74	183	159	57	−33
BG414	3.50	12.73	263	244	24	−5
BG415	3.84	11.93	210	195	15	0
BG421	3.38	12.77	278	251	16	12
BG422	3.31	9.72	193	186	15	−8
BG423	2.22	11.06	399	274	79	45
BG424	2.37	10.31	335	343	−1	−7
BG425	3.66	11.85	224	263	21	−60
RO211	2.34	13.88	494	389	33	72
RO212	1.98	13.82	596	429	34	133
RO214	1.72	11.09	543	377	44	122
RO215	2.09	13.92	565	453	28	84
RO216	1.21	9.04	648	481	35	131

Source: Author's own elaboration based on the Eurostat database

labour productivity growth occurred in Romanian regions RO211 (494%), RO212 (596%), RO214 (543%), RO215 (565%) and RO216 (648%). These regions started from the lowest productivity level in 2000. In 2020, RO215, RO211 and RO212 recorded a productivity rank of 3–5 in the surveyed sample of 30 regions. RO214 was in the middle of the 2020 productivity ranking, and RO216 remains in the penultimate place despite record productivity growth. The regions BG344 (278%) and BG331 (255%) also had a high productivity growth rate, which in 2020 turned out to be the best among the 30 analysed regions. These regions started with one of the highest levels of GVA per employee in 2000. In Bulgaria, BG322, BG424 and BG342 had an even faster growth rate of over 300%, but ultimately did not achieve outstanding productivity levels in 2020. In the breakdown of the productivity growth in all 30 regions, the endogenous effect (*W*) had the greatest impact on the overall productivity growth, which ranged from 102% to 481%. Therefore, there was an increase in technological progress in all analysed regions, which translated into more productive production. The static external effect (*S*) had a much smaller contribution to increasing productivity, which indicates low employee mobility to more productive sectors. The *S* value was positive in most regions, except for one region, BG424; therefore, the changes in employment share were positively correlated with productivity levels. The highest *S* value was noted in regions BG423 (79%), BG413 (57%) and BG341 (56%), while it was close to zero for BG334, BG324 and BG424. The dynamic external effect (*D*) had the most diverse values, varying from –60% to 133%. Regions where labour moved to sectors with relatively high productivity dynamics included all Romanian regions, as well as BG342 and BG423. An increase in the share of employment in sectors with relatively low labour productivity dynamics was noted in BG425, BG413, BG311, BG333 and BG323.

Since 21 of Greece's regions were the only ones out of 1,166 surveyed to experience a decline in productivity over the 20 years, an additional analysis was also conducted for them. Regions that are not currently last in terms of labour productivity but have the lowest growth rates may become the least productive in the near future. Figure 4.2 presents the productivity levels of 21 Greek regions from 2000 to 2020. Since 2000, there has been an upward trend, but from 2006 to

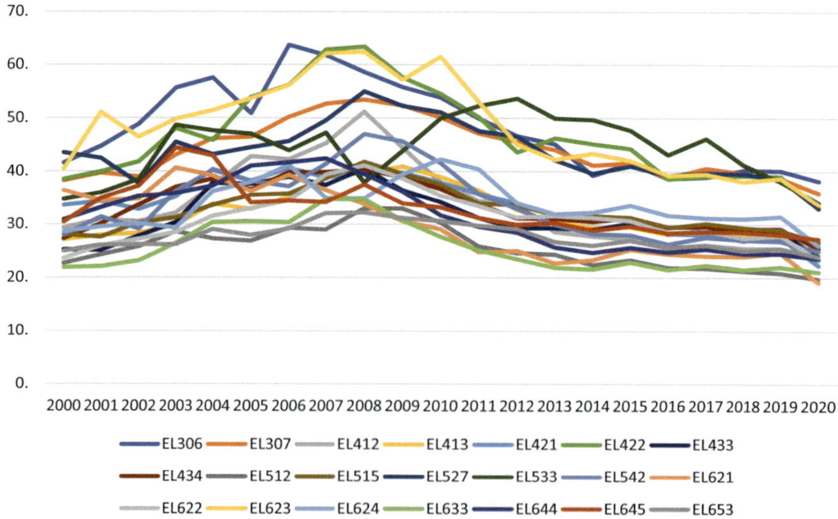

Figure 4.2 Productivity level for selected 21 NUTS 3 regions, thousands of EUR per employee

Source: Author's own elaboration based on the Eurostat database

2008, there was an apparent decline until 2013. Then, there was a period of relative stagnation, before another collapse in 2019. These turning points are related to the global crisis in 2008 and the COVID-19 pandemic in 2019. Over the period under review – five regions, EL527, EL306, EL623, EL422 and EL307 – dropped from above 100% of the EU average in 2000 to 50%–60% of the EU average in 2020. The most significant decline to the EU average was recorded in the tourist regions EL621 (Zakynthos) and EL527 (Chalkidiki).

Table 4.6 comprises employment, GVA and productivity statistics for 21 Geek regions. All regions were characterised by high employment in the sector G–I. In 2020, this share ranged from 26% in EL512 to 58% in EL622. A high share of employment also occurred in sector O–Q, rising from 9% to 31% in 2020. There were also regions with a significant share of employment in sector A in 2020, including EL653 (31%), EL527 (21%), EL633 (29%), EL644 (24%), EL512 (26%) and EL306 (23%). The labour force most often moved to sector O–Q, which reported a higher employment share in all regions. The highest GVA share/employment share indicator was recorded in sector L, while the lowest was in sector A. Sectors B–E, J and K also had a GVA/employment index value above 1. The highest decreases in GVA share were noted in sector G–I, with the highest increase in employment share. In most regions, GVA share increased in sectors B–E and O–Q. Changes in employment share in sectors O–Q and R–U in most of the areas translated into almost proportional changes in GVA share. Productivity per employee, measured in thousands of euros, increased between 2000 and 2020, mostly in sectors K, B–E and A. On average, productivity growth was only noted in sectors A (37%), B–E (56%) and K (60%), while the highest decline was noted in sectors L (−72%), F (−41%) and G–I (−41%).

Table 4.7 presents the productivity levels, productivity growth rate and shift-share breakdown of productivity growth for 2000 and 2020, calculated based on Equation 1, for the additional 21 regions. The highest productivity levels in 2020 were in regions EL306, EL307 and EL533, while the lowest were in EL512 and EL621. Regions EL306 and EL307 had high levels of productivity in 2000. EL621, which also had a high level of productivity in the base period after 20 years, was the worst one. All additionally selected regions had negative productivity growth rates. Detailed data for all regions with decreasing productivity can be found in the Appendix. 2. The most significant declines in productivity growth rate were recorded in EL621 (47%) and EL421 (33%). There were also regions that had only slightly decreasing productivity over the study period: EL533 (−1%), EL413 (−1%) and EL622 (−1%). All regions apart from EL306 noted a negative endogenous effect (*W*), which means that productivity due to technological progress decreased. The only positive indicator in the shift-share breakdown was for static external effect (*S*). Productivity growth is positively affected by the reallocation of labor to more productive sectors.The highest growth in this area was noted in sectors EL622 and EL413. The lowest value of *S* was for region EL306, which noted the highest *W* value. The dynamic external effect (*D*) was also negative for all regions, meaning that employment moved to sectors with relatively low-productivity dynamics.

Table 4.6 Productivity and shift-share breakdown for 2000 and 2020 for selected Greek NUTS 3 regions by sectors

		Sector	*A*	*B–E*	*F*	*G–I*	*J*	*K*	*L*	*M–N*	*O–Q*	*R–U*
EL306	Employment share by sector (%)	2000	6.18	25.48	8.67	30.03	2.81	0.91	0.06	4.33	18.36	3.15
		2020	2.70	23.29	2.57	41.12	0.81	0.59	0.26	7.18	19.18	2.31
		Δ	−3.47	−2.19	−6.10	11.09	−2.00	−0.32	0.20	2.84	0.81	−0.84
	GVA share by sector (%)	2000	2.05	21.65	24.17	20.20	5.94	1.35	6.64	3.70	12.85	1.46
		2020	1.57	27.66	12.52	26.03	0.56	1.68	7.38	4.63	16.95	1.02
		Δ	−0.48	6.01	−11.64	5.83	−5.38	0.34	0.74	0.93	4.10	−0.44
	Productivity per employee	2000	13.81	35.30	115.84	27.95	87.83	61.69	4485.25	35.46	29.07	19.27
		2020	22.21	45.40	186.28	24.20	26.36	109.85	1087.91	24.63	33.77	16.85
		%Δ	60.86%	28.58%	60.81%	−13.42%	−69.98%	78.05%	−75.74%	−30.55%	16.19%	−12.56%
EL307	Employment share by sector (%)	2000	2.12	12.68	5.55	41.93	3.02	2.28	0.08	5.60	21.29	5.44
		2020	0.94	8.07	2.22	45.88	1.55	1.49	0.43	8.98	25.64	4.81
		Δ	−1.19	−4.61	−3.33	3.95	−1.47	−0.79	0.35	3.38	4.35	−0.63
	GVA share by sector (%)	2000	0.77	10.78	14.00	31.16	6.97	3.68	8.85	4.96	16.09	2.75
		2020	0.58	11.06	0.32	36.99	2.19	4.53	12.90	6.03	23.14	2.25
		Δ	−0.19	0.29	−13.68	5.83	−4.78	0.85	4.05	1.07	7.04	−0.49
	Productivity per employee	2000	13.78	32.43	96.23	28.37	88.03	61.58	4400.19	33.84	28.86	19.27
		2020	22.30	49.28	5.19	29.00	50.70	109.51	1077.27	24.17	32.45	16.85
		%Δ	61.84%	51.93%	−94.61%	2.21%	−42.40%	77.83%	−75.52%	−28.56%	12.45%	−12.58%
EL412	Employment share by sector (%)	2000	17.03	8.76	6.89	33.98	0.81	2.35	0.08	7.22	19.38	3.57
		2020	10.19	5.96	6.12	41.25	0.70	0.98	0.33	4.99	26.72	2.82
		Δ	−6.84	−2.80	−0.77	7.26	−0.11	−1.38	0.24	−2.23	7.34	−0.75
	GVA share by sector (%)	2000	5.36	3.83	6.78	43.05	1.71	3.32	10.51	3.08	19.02	3.34
		2020	3.20	9.36	2.06	25.53	0.94	3.61	14.62	2.41	33.98	4.29
		Δ	−2.15	5.52	−4.72	−17.52	−0.77	0.29	4.11	−0.67	14.96	0.95
	Productivity per employee	2000	9.23	12.84	28.87	37.18	61.80	41.41	3805.00	12.53	28.80	27.45
		2020	7.34	36.62	7.85	14.44	31.08	86.28	1049.00	11.29	29.67	35.52
		%Δ	−20.52%	185.13%	−72.81%	−61.16%	−49.71%	108.33%	−72.43%	−9.85%	3.02%	29.37%

EL413	Employment share by sector (%)	2000	13.07	6.97	10.46	32.89	1.10	1.34	0.06	3.37	25.97	4.71
		2020	6.25	6.25	5.75	35.90	1.40	1.10	0.40	7.15	31.50	4.30
		Δ	−6.82	−0.72	−4.71	3.01	0.30	−0.24	0.34	3.78	5.53	−0.41
	GVA share by sector (%)	2000	14.51	4.64	6.22	30.42	2.49	3.39	11.34	2.60	19.73	4.66
		2020	5.82	8.81	2.00	18.28	1.60	6.40	16.58	3.41	34.84	2.25
		Δ	−8.70	4.17	−4.22	−12.13	v0.89	3.01	5.25	0.80	15.12	−2.40
	Productivity per employee	2000	30.04	18.00	16.10	25.03	61.16	68.65	5281.00	20.91	20.55	26.78
		2020	24.92	37.74	9.32	13.64	30.61	155.73	1110.00	12.76	29.61	14.03
		%Δ	−17.06%	109.64%	−42.10%	−45.53%	−49.95%	126.84%	−78.98%	−38.98%	44.07%	−47.59%
EL421	Employment share by sector (%)	2000	4.71	7.90	7.65	50.26	1.28	1.59	0.05	4.47	17.05	5.04
		2020	4.89	5.40	4.02	53.83	0.87	0.87	0.24	6.24	20.74	2.90
		Δ	0.18	−2.50	−3.62	3.57	−0.40	−0.72	0.19	1.77	3.68	−2.14
	GVA share by sector (%)	2000	3.27	6.07	8.58	51.96	1.47	2.31	6.19	2.50	14.58	3.08
		2020	3.16	9.13	1.70	39.03	1.37	3.00	11.59	5.13	22.05	3.83
		Δ	−0.11	3.07	−6.87	−12.93	−0.10	0.69	5.40	2.64	7.47	0.74
	Productivity per employee	2000	23.28	25.79	37.63	34.69	38.58	48.66	3944.00	18.71	28.68	20.53
		2020	14.45	37.80	9.44	16.19	35.14	76.79	1073.27	18.37	23.75	29.46
		%Δ	−37.96%	46.56%	−74.90%	−53.32%	−8.91%	57.80%	−72.79%	−1.86%	−17.20%	43.48%
EL422	Employment share by sector (%)	2000	12.50	9.04	16.92	42.23	1.05	1.27	0.09	2.28	11.17	3.46
		2020	8.18	6.00	8.83	53.72	0.81	0.79	0.47	5.87	12.23	3.08
		Δ	−4.32	−3.05	−8.09	11.49	−0.24	−0.47	0.38	3.59	1.07	−0.38
	GVA share by sector (%)	2000	3.65	7.78	8.60	53.05	1.06	1.85	9.46	2.18	10.16	2.22
		2020	2.74	5.92	4.97	48.13	0.87	2.82	15.79	3.10	11.31	4.36
		Δ	−0.91	−1.87	−3.64	−4.92	−0.19	0.97	6.34	0.92	1.15	2.14
	Productivity per employee	2000	11.24	33.13	19.56	48.34	38.65	56.03	4236.00	36.82	35.00	24.68
		2020	11.04	32.57	18.55	29.56	35.36	117.00	1108.90	17.44	30.50	46.67
		%Δ	−1.76%	−1.69%	−5.16%	−38.85%	−8.52%	108.80%	−73.82%	−52.62%	−12.87%	89.12%

(*Continued*)

Table 4.6 (Continued)

		Sector	*A*	*B–E*	*F*	*G–I*	*J*	*K*	*L*	*M–N*	*O–Q*	*R–U*
EL433	Employment share by sector (%)	2000	26.70	5.63	10.56	36.32	0.57	1.00	0.05	2.48	11.59	5.12
		2020	16.32	5.00	6.54	43.59	0.77	0.91	0.36	3.34	19.57	3.62
		Δ	−10.39	−0.63	−4.02	7.27	0.21	−0.09	0.31	0.86	7.99	−1.50
	GVA share by sector (%)	2000	14.26	6.25	8.54	40.58	1.13	2.16	8.35	2.31	11.46	4.96
		2020	8.27	8.16	4.03	33.14	1.58	4.47	15.65	3.07	17.54	4.09
		Δ	−5.99	1.90	−4.51	−7.45	0.45	2.32	7.31	0.76	6.08	−0.87
	Productivity per employee	2000	13.47	28.01	20.39	28.18	50.38	54.54	3905.50	23.47	24.95	24.45
		2020	12.21	39.33	14.84	18.31	49.29	118.27	1050.62	22.15	21.59	27.23
		%Δ	−9.36%	40.42%	−27.20%	−35.02%	−2.17%	116.85%	−73.10%	−5.62%	−13.49%	11.38%
EL434	Employment share by sector (%)	2000	25.00	9.12	6.94	32.11	0.66	1.43	0.05	4.62	16.03	4.03
		2020	13.46	6.04	5.01	41.87	0.81	0.91	0.29	5.48	22.89	3.24
		Δ	−11.53	−3.08	−1.94	9.76	0.14	−0.52	0.24	0.86	6.86	−0.79
	GVA share by sector (%)	2000	10.50	7.37	7.99	35.21	1.24	2.78	7.72	4.30	19.39	3.49
		2020	7.97	10.18	2.37	31.30	1.59	3.49	12.33	3.34	23.51	3.93
		Δ	−2.53	2.81	−5.62	−3.92	0.34	0.71	4.61	−0.96	4.12	0.44
	Productivity per employee	2000	11.48	22.07	31.44	29.95	51.24	53.10	4031.67	25.39	33.04	23.65
		2020	15.14	43.07	12.08	19.11	50.32	98.56	1096.10	15.58	26.27	31.01
		%Δ	31.88%	95.16%	−61.57%	−36.20%	−1.79%	85.61%	−72.81%	−38.62%	−20.50%	31.10%
EL512	Employment share by sector (%)	2000	33.48	14.92	12.86	15.85	0.64	0.96	0.02	1.54	18.44	1.32
		2020	25.76	7.64	4.75	25.73	1.23	0.61	0.20	8.71	22.28	3.07
		Δ	−7.72	−7.28	−8.11	9.89	0.59	−0.34	0.18	7.16	3.84	1.75
	GVA share by sector (%)	2000	11.16	18.46	9.09	20.54	1.83	2.29	5.34	3.70	23.95	3.62
		2020	9.58	18.39	1.66	17.00	2.34	2.30	11.03	4.18	31.07	2.43
		Δ	−1.58	−0.07	−7.43	−3.55	0.51	0.01	5.70	0.48	7.12	−1.19
	Productivity per employee	2000	7.55	28.04	16.02	29.37	65.23	54.38	4935.00	54.37	29.42	62.06
		2020	7.37	47.70	6.94	13.09	37.80	74.41	1068.56	9.52	27.64	15.72
		%Δ	−2.35%	70.13%	−56.67%	−55.43%	−42.06%	36.82%	−78.35%	−82.48%	−6.07%	−74.67%

EL515	Employment share by sector (%)	2000	16.94	14.22	6.63	31.64	0.95	1.77	0.04	4.06	19.74	4.01
		2020	12.81	10.28	3.66	38.44	0.95	1.48	0.31	6.31	22.80	2.95
		Δ	−4.13	−3.94	−2.97	6.81	0.00	−0.29	0.27	2.26	3.06	−1.07
	GVA share by sector (%)	2000	8.83	15.61	7.41	34.11	2.20	3.21	6.87	2.40	15.95	3.41
		2020	8.64	16.66	3.01	30.19	1.37	3.17	12.63	3.15	19.76	1.42
		Δ	−0.19	1.05	−4.40	−3.92	−0.83	−0.03	5.77	0.74	3.81	−1.99
	Productivity per employee	2000	14.62	30.78	31.37	30.24	65.26	50.79	4677.50	16.62	22.66	23.81
		2020	17.98	43.21	21.96	20.95	38.40	57.09	1083.24	13.30	23.12	12.83
		%Δ	23.02%	40.38%	−29.99%	−30.72%	−41.15%	12.40%	−76.84%	−19.98%	2.04%	−46.13%
EL527	Employment share by sector (%)	2000	28.08	15.43	9.56	26.36	0.99	0.99	0.13	6.43	8.79	3.26
		2020	21.43	6.53	4.38	44.32	0.69	0.57	0.60	5.06	13.34	3.06
		Δ	−6.65	−8.90	−5.18	17.96	−0.30	−0.42	0.47	−1.37	4.55	−0.20
	GVA share by sector (%)	2000	11.42	10.58	8.40	36.68	0.69	2.70	12.03	2.23	12.12	3.17
		2020	9.26	8.03	4.63	40.37	0.76	1.80	19.88	2.17	12.20	0.90
		Δ	−2.15	−2.54	−3.77	3.69	0.07	−0.90	7.85	−0.06	0.08	−2.27
	Productivity per employee	2000	17.67	29.79	38.21	60.47	30.26	118.87	4065.33	15.07	59.95	42.24
		2020	14.33	40.76	35.07	30.19	36.43	104.68	1099.15	14.19	30.33	9.75
		%Δ	−18.93%	36.85%	−8.22%	−50.08%	20.40%	−11.93%	−72.96%	−5.82%	−49.40%	−76.90%
EL533	Employment share by sector (%)	2000	22.92	12.33	14.92	18.53	0.42	1.08	0.06	5.17	21.84	2.77
		2020	14.65	13.61	3.83	27.67	0.60	0.60	0.22	4.92	30.18	3.77
		Δ	−8.27	1.28	−11.09	9.13	0.18	−0.48	0.16	−0.25	8.34	1.00
	GVA share by sector (%)	2000	14.19	37.01	8.92	11.34	1.52	1.88	5.01	1.65	13.08	5.39
		2020	13.97	35.72	3.69	9.49	1.18	1.94	7.36	1.80	22.59	2.26
		Δ	−0.22	−1.29	−5.23	−1.85	−0.34	0.06	2.35	0.14	9.51	−3.13
	Productivity per employee	2000	21.46	104.02	20.73	21.22	125.29	60.17	2887.00	11.08	20.77	67.57
		2020	32.58	89.64	32.97	11.72	67.09	110.09	1150.00	12.47	25.58	20.48
		%Δ	51.80%	−13.83%	59.08%	−44.78%	−46.45%	82.98%	−60.17%	12.50%	23.15%	−69.69%

(Continued)

Table 4.6 (Continued)

		Sector	*A*	*B–E*	*F*	*G–I*	*J*	*K*	*L*	*M–N*	*O–Q*	*R–U*
EL542	Employment share by sector (%)	2000	32.40	5.19	8.49	24.57	0.56	1.32	0.05	4.58	20.04	2.85
		2020	19.15	4.65	4.87	43.73	0.45	1.01	0.34	3.92	19.65	2.30
		Δ	−13.25	−0.54	−3.62	19.16	−0.11	−0.31	0.29	−0.66	−0.39	−0.55
	GVA share by sector (%)	2000	8.06	3.24	26.69	34.01	0.84	2.10	6.32	1.97	13.67	3.10
		2020	11.89	6.53	3.97	36.38	1.06	2.47	13.59	2.52	19.19	2.40
		Δ	3.83	3.29	−22.72	2.37	0.22	0.37	7.27	0.55	5.52	−0.69
	Productivity per employee	2000	6.96	17.48	87.95	38.74	42.09	44.42	3478.00	12.07	19.09	30.43
		2020	15.54	35.17	20.40	20.82	59.13	61.28	1012.50	16.11	24.44	26.22
		%Δ	123.16%	101.19%	−76.80%	−46.26%	40.47%	37.94%	−70.89%	33.54%	27.99%	−13.83%
EL621	Employment share by sector (%)	2000	31.25	6.62	6.75	29.97	0.90	1.29	0.06	5.08	14.15	4.05
		2020	18.34	4.82	5.63	42.43	0.50	0.81	0.27	8.67	14.57	3.97
		Δ	−12.91	−1.81	−1.13	12.46	−0.40	−0.48	0.21	3.59	0.42	−0.08
	GVA share by sector (%)	2000	8.06	3.98	11.05	51.63	1.45	1.60	7.06	2.26	9.90	3.01
		2020	4.63	5.65	3.75	45.51	0.98	2.69	15.12	3.35	14.32	3.99
		Δ	−3.43	1.67	−7.30	−6.12	−0.47	1.09	8.06	1.09	4.41	0.98
	Productivity per employee	2000	9.37	21.86	59.49	62.63	58.57	45.10	3992.00	16.15	25.45	27.03
		2020	4.83	22.45	12.75	20.52	37.38	63.57	1072.57	7.40	18.80	19.23
		%Δ	−48.48%	2.67%	−78.56%	−67.23%	−36.17%	40.96%	−73.13%	−54.21%	−26.11%	−28.85%
EL622	Employment share by sector (%)	2000	24.97	4.57	7.25	37.06	0.69	1.14	0.06	4.30	14.69	5.25
		2020	7.07	3.75	4.55	58.28	1.07	1.11	0.37	5.79	13.84	4.16
		Δ	−17.91	−0.82	−2.70	21.22	0.39	−0.03	0.31	1.49	−0.85	−1.09
	GVA share by sector (%)	2000	4.01	3.74	3.77	51.54	1.71	2.21	9.02	2.95	15.29	5.76
		2020	4.19	4.73	1.61	38.76	1.67	2.56	16.78	4.44	19.15	6.10
		Δ	0.18	1.00	−2.16	−12.78	−0.04	0.35	7.77	1.49	3.86	0.34
	Productivity per employee	2000	3.79	19.28	12.27	32.79	58.83	45.60	3723.00	16.17	24.53	25.87
		2020	13.90	29.58	8.29	15.59	36.56	53.91	1060.61	17.97	32.42	34.35
		%Δ	267.19%	53.44%	−32.48%	−52.46%	−37.86%	18.22%	−71.51%	11.12%	32.18%	32.79%

EL623	Employment share by sector (%)	2000	17.55	5.12	7.31	34.64	0.73	1.19	0.09	11.15	20.29	1.83
		2020	9.18	4.40	7.59	41.05	0.68	0.83	0.53	7.89	25.34	2.35
		Δ	−8.37	−0.72	0.27	6.40	−0.05	−0.35	0.44	−3.26	5.05	0.52
	GVA share by sector (%)	2000	6.10	2.19	9.87	52.44	1.10	2.09	9.95	1.45	13.40	1.41
		2020	12.09	7.06	1.84	41.40	0.78	2.42	18.30	2.09	12.64	1.38
		Δ	5.99	4.87	−8.03	−11.04	−0.32	0.33	8.35	0.64	−0.76	−0.03
	Productivity per employee	2000	14.06	17.32	54.59	61.25	60.75	71.31	4405.00	5.27	26.71	31.25
		2020	44.49	54.21	8.17	34.06	38.33	98.09	1163.71	8.96	16.85	19.84
		%Δ	216.47%	212.95%	−85.03%	−44.38%	−36.90%	37.56%	−73.58%	70.03%	−36.93%	−36.52%
EL624	Employment share by sector (%)	2000	15.86	8.79	8.48	38.15	0.31	1.41	0.16	4.08	19.62	3.30
		2020	7.19	4.31	7.43	44.07	0.24	0.84	0.48	7.43	22.40	5.75
		Δ	−8.67	−4.48	−1.05	5.92	−0.07	−0.57	0.32	3.34	2.77	2.45
	GVA share by sector (%)	2000	4.12	4.92	6.47	37.51	0.72	3.20	10.83	2.99	23.46	5.78
		2020	2.57	7.06	1.84	41.40	0.78	2.42	18.30	2.09	12.64	1.38
		Δ	−1.55	2.14	−4.63	3.89	0.06	−0.78	7.47	−0.89	−10.82	−4.40
	Productivity per employee	2000	7.44	16.00	21.81	28.10	65.50	64.78	1971.00	20.92	34.18	50.10
		2020	9.33	17.11	18.37	25.46	36.00	100.43	994.50	11.85	21.28	13.19
		%Δ	25.52%	6.94%	−15.79%	−9.42%	−45.04%	55.04%	−49.54%	−43.34%	−37.72%	−73.68%
EL633	Employment share by sector (%)	2000	52.38	6.67	6.49	17.97	0.66	0.83	0.03	1.91	10.23	2.81
		2020	29.07	5.95	4.96	30.34	0.57	0.64	0.25	4.37	19.52	4.31
		Δ	−23.31	−0.73	−1.53	12.36	−0.09	−0.19	0.21	2.46	9.29	1.50
	GVA share by sector (%)	2000	26.05	8.79	7.07	23.96	1.53	2.49	8.44	1.66	16.71	3.30
		2020	25.12	11.49	1.92	20.41	1.33	2.32	12.55	1.89	18.12	4.84
		Δ	−0.94	2.70	−5.15	−3.55	−0.20	−0.17	4.11	0.23	1.41	1.54
	Productivity per employee	2000	10.89	28.83	23.85	29.19	50.69	65.61	5455.00	18.96	35.75	25.67
		2020	18.26	40.84	8.20	14.22	49.56	76.41	1070.41	9.14	19.62	23.69
		%Δ	67.71%	41.66%	−65.63%	−51.28%	−2.23%	16.46%	−80.38%	−51.76%	−45.12%	−7.75%

(*Continued*)

Table 4.6 (Continued)

		Sector	*A*	*B–E*	*F*	*G–I*	*J*	*K*	*L*	*M–N*	*O–Q*	*R–U*
EL644	Employment share by sector (%)	2000	29.98	12.94	9.17	21.57	1.07	1.83	0.05	3.49	17.64	2.25
		2020	24.50	11.82	3.90	30.07	0.59	1.34	0.25	5.32	19.96	2.26
		Δ	−5.48	−1.12	−5.27	8.50	−0.49	−0.49	0.20	1.82	2.31	0.01
	GVA share by sector (%)	2000	19.21	23.72	4.23	21.03	1.47	2.00	6.79	2.35	15.54	3.65
		2020	12.31	25.30	1.11	19.73	0.96	2.58	11.74	2.52	20.16	3.59
		Δ	−6.91	1.58	−3.12	−1.30	−0.51	0.57	4.94	0.17	4.63	−0.06
	Productivity per employee	2000	19.77	56.56	14.24	30.08	42.28	33.81	4163.00	20.75	27.17	50.00
		2020	11.88	50.60	6.74	15.51	38.64	45.60	1093.47	11.22	23.89	37.56
		%Δ	−39.94%	−10.53%	−52.66%	−48.43%	−8.62%	34.88%	−73.73%	−45.93%	−12.07%	−24.88%
EL645	Employment share by sector (%)	2000	13.73	12.44	8.20	37.91	1.47	2.25	0.09	0.86	19.17	3.89
		2020	16.98	7.93	3.41	40.43	0.90	1.25	0.35	3.06	20.18	5.43
		Δ	3.25	−4.50	−4.79	2.52	−0.56	−0.99	0.26	2.20	1.01	1.54
	GVA share by sector (%)	2000	9.74	20.98	4.73	24.18	2.09	1.97	9.34	4.08	19.73	3.16
		2020	11.34	22.70	1.16	18.52	1.34	2.06	14.37	2.20	22.53	3.78
		Δ	1.60	1.73	−3.57	−5.67	−0.75	0.09	5.02	−1.88	2.80	0.63
	Productivity per employee	2000	21.57	51.28	17.52	19.39	43.35	26.65	3289.00	143.60	31.28	24.69
		2020	18.23	78.15	9.27	12.51	40.46	44.94	1127.40	19.64	30.48	19.04
		%Δ	−15.45%	52.40%	−47.10%	−35.51%	−6.67%	68.62%	−65.72%	−86.33%	−2.57%	−22.89%
EL653	Employment share by sector (%)	2000	39.70	7.08	6.35	22.88	1.04	1.67	0.07	2.86	15.30	3.04
		2020	31.35	5.53	4.31	31.49	0.68	1.01	0.40	4.14	16.82	4.27
		Δ	−8.35	−1.55	−2.03	8.61	−0.36	−0.66	0.33	1.28	1.52	1.22
	GVA share by sector (%)	2000	12.56	15.41	7.52	24.25	2.02	2.79	12.27	2.94	16.02	4.23
		2020	16.09	15.30	2.35	18.70	1.05	2.91	17.91	2.16	19.85	3.68
		Δ	3.53	−0.11	−5.17	−5.55	−0.96	0.12	5.64	−0.78	3.83	−0.56
	Productivity per employee	2000	7.90	54.31	29.56	26.44	48.36	41.62	4462.67	25.69	26.12	34.73
		2020	12.29	66.25	13.07	14.22	36.90	68.76	1064.19	12.51	28.27	20.65
		%Δ	55.69%	21.99%	−55.80%	−46.20%	−23.69%	65.19%	−76.15%	−51.31%	8.25%	−40.56%

Source: Author's own elaboration based on the Eurostat database

Table 4.7 Productivity and shift-share breakdown for 2000 and 2020 for selected Greek NUTS 3 regions

Code	*Productivity in 2000 (thousands of EUR per employee)*	*Productivity in 2020 (thousands of EUR per employee)*	*Productivity growth rate 2020/2000 (%)*	*Shift-share breakdown of productivity growth rate for total economy (%)*		
				W	*S*	*D*
EL306	41.55	38.22	−8	12	7	−27
EL307	38.18	35.96	−6	−13	32	−25
EL412	29.35	23.33	−20	−29	40	−32
EL413	27.07	26.77	−1	−14	65	−52
EL421	33.55	22.33	−33	−37	21	−18
EL422	38.48	32.99	−14	−27	52	−39
EL433	25.22	24.09	−4	−20	53	−38
EL434	27.32	25.57	−6	−15	44	−35
EL512	22.65	19.82	−13	−15	63	−60
EL515	28.05	26.67	−5	−12	45	−38
EL527	43.46	33.14	−24	−35	60	−49
EL533	34.67	34.17	−1	0	18	−19
EL542	27.99	25.03	−11	−22	45	−33
EL621	36.35	19.13	−47	−57	38	−29
EL622	23.57	23.44	−1	−15	74	−59
EL623	40.46	33.78	−17	−25	57	−49
EL624	28.58	26.09	−9	−21	31	−18
EL633	21.89	21.13	−3	−11	74	−67
EL644	30.85	23.64	−23	−31	30	−22
EL645	30.40	27.31	−10	−11	33	−32
EL653	24.95	23.95	−4	−15	63	−52

Source: Author's own elaboration based on the Eurostat database

4.4 Results and discussion

Europe has seen disparate prosperity among its regions over the past decades. Industrial production growth was stronger in rural and urban areas of Western Europe and was evenly distributed across the regions of Central and Eastern Europe. The largest cities, including capital cities, and the regions near them often replaced industrial production with high-value services, especially tradable services such as finance, technology, culture and advertising, or with high-tech manufacturing. Today, company profits are no longer tied as strongly to size or market power, but to the sector in which the company operates. The literature on the subject needs more analyses of how structural economic changes have led to regional disparities. Profitable companies and highly skilled people are concentrated in successful cities, leaving less prosperous areas behind (Odendahl et al., 2019).

I analysed productivity levels for the period 2000–2020, which confirmed the slow process of equalising productivity levels between NUTS 3 regions in the EU. The number of outlier regions, the worst- and best-performing in terms of productivity, decreased over the study period. The productivity distribution among EU regions was more concentrated closer to the EU average. This aligns with the findings of Cuadrado-Roura et al. (2000) and Gardiner et al. (2006). Taking into account the EU average, employment in the period under study decreased in agriculture, forestry and fishing (A) and industry (excluding construction) (B–E), and slightly in construction (F) and financial and insurance activities (K), while it increased most notably in professional, scientific and technical activities and administrative and support service activities (M–N) and in public administration, defence, education, human health and social work activities (O–Q). The EU continues to increase the share of the services sector in its economic structure, reallocating labour from the agricultural and industrial sectors. While the GVA share/employment share ratio is unfavourable for agriculture, the B–E sector is effective. The dominant sectors in the economy did not change during the period under study: wholesale and retail trade, transport, accommodation and food service activities (G–I) and public administration, defence, education, human health and social work activities (O–Q), which together constituted almost half of all employment. The effective sectors, i.e. those in which the GVA share/employment share ratio was above 1, as well as those sectors with the highest labour productivity per employee, were the service sectors, real estate activities (L), information and communication (J), financial and insurance activities (K) and the previously mentioned industry sector (B–E).

The main objective of this study is to identify the regions left behind in the EU countries and to analyse the structural and productivity changes taking place in them. The analysis identified left-behind regions in terms of productivity. From the 1,166 NUTS 3 regions under study, the 30 with the lowest productivity per employee in 2020 were selected for more detailed analysis. Of these, 25 are located in Bulgaria. These constitute almost all of Bulgaria's regions; the three which are excluded are the capital, its agglomeration and Vratsa Province, which includes the Kozloduy nuclear power plant – crucial for the production of electricity for the entire country. This demonstrates that the level of the whole country is still lower than other EU countries. The remaining five regions, RO211 (Bacau), RO212 (Botosani), RO214 (Neamt), RO215 (Suceava) and RO216 (Vaslui), are located in the north-eastern part of Romania. All 30 regions were characterised by an overall upward trend in productivity per employee over the 20-year study period. However, Romania's regions had better growth than Bulgaria's, with a much lower starting point in 2000. Despite favourable growth rates, these regions have not managed to make up the difference between themselves and the EU average; they continue to lag behind.

The analysis allowed me to answer whether all left-behind regions in the EU have similar economic structures. Overall, the worst-performing sector was agriculture, so the expectation was that left-behind regions would have a significant share of employment in this area. This relationship was also confirmed by studies by McMillan and Rodrik (2011), Mundlak et al. (2008) and Thurlow and Wobst (2004). However, these regions are very diverse in terms of employment structure. It is impossible to point to a single pattern of employment structure common to all

30 regions. Five Romanian regions are similar and can be characterised by a high share of employment in agriculture, forestry and fishing. This sector saw the most significant decline in employment, but the employment share is still at least tenfold higher than the EU average. Employees from sector A moved to less advanced service sectors, such as construction and wholesale and retail trade, transport, accommodation and food service. In the Romanian regions, a few percent of employees work in industry. This percentage was relatively stable in the period under study and is dominated by the wood, pulp and paper, textile, food and furniture industries.

Bulgaria's regions can be divided into four groups in terms of employment structure. The first group contains regions dominated by agriculture, with a similar share of industry; wholesale and retail trade, transport, accommodation and food service; and public administration, defence, education, human health and social work. These are regions BG325 (Silistra), BG332 (Dobrich), BG334 (Targovishte), BG324 (Razgrad), BG425 (Kardzhali), BG342 (Sliven), BG343 (Yambol), BG311 (Vidin) and BG333 (Shumen). These regions are not located next to each other, but are scattered throughout the country. The next group contains regions with a similar share of employment in agriculture; industry; wholesale and retail trade, transport, accommodation and food service; and public administration, defence, education, human health and social work. These include regions BG423 (Pazardzhik), BG312 (Montana), BG314 (Pleven), BG422 (Haskovo), BG315 (Lovech), BG321 (Veliko Tarnovo), BG413 (Blagoevgrad) and BG414 (Pernik). Again, the regions are not concentrated in one area. The third group consists of regions with a predominance of the industry sector: BG424 (Smolyan), BG323 (Ruse), BG344 (Stara Zagora), BG415 (Kyustendil), BG421 (Plovdiv) and BG322 (Gabrovo). The last group includes regions with predominant wholesale and retail trade, transport, accommodation and food service activities. These are BG341 (Burgas) and BG331 (Varna), located on the Black Sea and home to the popular tourist destinations Golden Sands and Sandy Beach. It is also worth noting that employment in more advanced sectors – like information and communication, financial and insurance activities; professional, scientific and technical activities; and administrative and support service activities – is negligible in all 25 regions.

In the 30 surveyed regions, the least productive sector was agriculture, while the most productive was real estate, but the specific nature of this sector should be taken into account. Information and communication and financial and insurance activities, which are advanced service sectors, also achieved high GVA per employee. In the case of Romania, other sectors were also characterised by high productivity: professional, scientific and technical activities; administrative and support service activities; public administration, defence, education, human health and social work activities; arts, entertainment and recreation; other service activities; and activities of household and extra-territorial organisations and bodies. These sectors, with few exceptions, were largely characterised by a GVA share/employment share ratio above 3, which proves their high efficiency. The least effective sectors in all 30 surveyed regions were agriculture and construction.

In all 30 regions, productivity increased in the period 2000–2020, but the growth dynamics varied. The highest increase in labour productivity (above 500%) was noted in Romanian regions, which is partly due to these regions starting from the lowest level of productivity in 2000. In Bulgaria, the regions BG322 (Gabrovo), BG424 (Smolyan) and BG342 (Sliven) recorded a growth rate of over 300%, but did not achieve outstanding levels of productivity in 2020, as their high growth rate, similar to Romania's regions, resulted mainly from a low initial level rather than a spectacular increase in productivity. Among Bulgarian regions, high growth rates (above 250%) were recorded for BG344 (Stara Zagora) and BG331 (Varna). In 2000, these regions had some of the highest productivity levels in the study group, and thanks to high growth, they maintained their leading position.

The shift-share analysis linked structural changes and productivity in selected NUTS 3 regions. The study provides the division of productivity growth into three sub-indices: the endogenous effect (*W*), the static external effect (*S*) and the dynamic external effect (*D*). In all 30 regions, the endogenous effect significantly impacted overall productivity growth over the period under study. Its value ranged from 102% to 481%, indicating an increase in technological progress that translated into more productive production. The static externality contributed much less to productivity growth. No significant migrations of workers to more productive sectors were recorded. Only in the case of the Romania's regions was there a more substantial outflow of labour from the least productive sector (agriculture) to other, more productive sectors. The value of *S* was positive in most regions, except for BG424, which recorded −1%. Therefore, it can be concluded that the changes in the economic structure were positively correlated with the level of productivity. The dynamic externality had the most diverse impact on productivity growth. The regions where the labour force moved to sectors with relatively dynamic productivity were all regions of Romania, as well as BG342 (Sliven) and BG423 (Pazardzhik). However, an increase in the share of employment in sectors with relatively low labour productivity dynamics was recorded in the regions BG425 (Kardzhali), BG413 (Blagoevgrad), BG311 (Vidin), BG333 (Shumen) and BG323 (Ruse).

Another interesting finding was that over a relatively long period of 20 years, 21 out of the 52 Greek NUTS 3 regions recorded a decline in productivity per employee. Therefore, an additional analysis was performed for those regions to identify the structural changes that may have led to this unfavourable productivity trend. Greek regions are not last in terms of labour productivity, but they have the lowest growth rates. If this trend continues, they may become the least productive in the near future.

Greece's regions noted a decline in productivity levels between 2006–2008 and 2013. The financial crisis in Greece, which officially began in 2010, was rooted in several factors. The first was an excessive budget deficit and public debt. Furthermore, Greece has a history of mismanaging public finances, i.e. unreliable data reporting, insufficient control over public spending and overspending in the public sector. The subprime crisis that began in 2008 affected many countries, including Greece. The economic slowdown and restrictions on access to credit on international markets worsened Greece's financial situation. All those events significantly impacted the Greek economy and its productivity growth until 2013. After a period of relative stagnation from 2013 to 2019, the COVID-19 pandemic caused another downturn in the global economy. The COVID-19 pandemic reduced tourism revenues in Greek regions. Restrictions on the entry and exit of citizens, the obligation to quarantine and uncertainty related to potential restrictions on movement and hotel operations led to a sharp decline in tourism.

Over the study period, five regions – EL527 (Chalkidiki), EL306 (Dytiki Attiki), EL623 (Ithaki, Kefallinia), EL422 (Andros, Thira, Kea, Milos, Mykonos, Naxos, Paros, Syros and Tinos) and EL307 (Peiraias and Nisoi) – dropped from above the EU average in 2000 to 50%–60% of it in 2020. The most significant decrease compared to the EU average was recorded in the tourist regions EL621 (Zakynthos) and EL527 (Chalkidiki). All of Greece's regions were characterised by high employment in wholesale and retail trade, transport, accommodation and food service (from 26% to 58% in 2020), followed by public administration, defence, education, human health and social work; some regions also had a high share in agriculture. The increase in labour reallocation in all regions was noted in public administration, defence, education, human health and social work. As with the 30 left-behind regions, the highest GVA share/employment share value was recorded in the real estate sector, while the lowest was in agriculture. In the study period, the highest decreases in GVA share were noted in wholesale and retail trade, transport, accommodation and food service activities, along with the highest increases in employment share. Productivity growth was only noted in the agriculture, industry and finance and insurance sectors. The highest decrease in productivity level was recorded in real estate, construction, wholesale and retail trade, transport, accommodation and food service. The most significant decline in productivity growth rate was recorded in EL621 (Zakynthos) and EL421 (Kalymnos, Karpathos, Kasos, Kos and Rodos). All regions apart from EL306 (Dytiki Attiki) had a negative endogenous effect (*W*) index, which means that productivity due to technological progress decreased. For Greek regions, only the static external effect (*S*) was positive in the shift-share breakdown, so the labour force was generally reallocated to more productive sectors. The highest growth in this area was noted in EL622 (Kerkyra), where labour moved from agriculture to wholesale and retail trade, transport, accommodation and food service. Also, the dynamic external effect (*D*) was negative for 21 regions, meaning that employment was reallocated to sectors with relatively low-productivity changes.

References

Arcelus, F. (1984). An extension of shift-share analysis. *Growth and Change*, *15*,3–8.

Bah, E. M., & Brada, J. C. (2009). Total factor productivity growth, structural change and convergence in the new members of the European Union. *Comparative Economic Studies*, *51*(4), 421–446. doi:10.1057/ces.2009.8

Barff, R. A., & Knight III, P. L. (1988). Dynamic shift-share analysis. *Growth and Change*, *19*(2), 1–10. https://doi.org/10.1111/j.1468-2257.1988.tb00465.x

Bronzini, R., & Piselli, P. (2009). Determinants of long-run regional productivity with geographical spillovers: The role of R&D, human capital and public infrastructure. *Regional Science and Urban Economics*, *39*(2), 187–199.

Carrascal-Incera, A., McCann, P., Ortega-Argilés, R., & Rodríguez-Pose, A. (2020). UK interregional inequality in a historical and international comparative context. *National Institute Economic Review*, *253*, R4–R17.

Corrado, L., Martin, R., & Weeks, M. (2005). Identifying and interpreting regional convergence clusters across Europe. *Economic Journal*, *115*(3), C133–C160.

Cuadrado-Roura, J. R. (2001). Regional convergence in the European Union: From hypothesis to the actual trends. *Annals of Regional Science*, *35*, 333–356.

Cuadrado-Roura, J., Mancha-Navarro, T., & Garrido-Yserte, R. (2000). Regional productivity patterns in Europe: An alternative approach. *The Annals of Regional Science*, *34*, 365–384. https://doi.org/10.1007/s001680000019

De Noni, I., Orsi, L., & Belussi, F. (2018). The role of collaborative networks in supporting the innovation performances of lagging-behind European regions. *Research Policy*, *47*(1), 1–13. doi:10.1016/j.respol.2017.09.006

Dobrzański, P. (2019). Productivity performance of the Czech Republic: Shift-Share analysis. In T. Loster & T. Pavelka (Eds.), *The 13th International days of statistics and economics: conference proceedings* (pp. 317–326). Melandrium. http://doi.org/10.18267/pr.2019.los.186.31

Dobrzański, P., & Grabowski, W. (2019). Structural and productivity changes of Central and Eastern Europe. *Zbornik Radova Ekonomskog Fakulteta U Rijeci-Proceedings of Rijeka Faculty of Economics*, *37*, 427–471. https://doi.org/10.18045/zbefri.2019.2.427

Dobrzański, P., & Olszewski, L. (2019). Structural change path and economic growth performance of polish economy. In *New challenges of economic and business development—2019: Incentives for sustainable economic growth. Proceedings*. 230–39, University of Latvia.

Dowrick, S. (1989). Sectoral change, catching up and slowing down. *Economics Letters*, *31*(4), 331–335. doi:10.1016/0165–1765(89)90024-4

Duarte, M., & Restuccia, D. (2010). The role of the structural transformation in aggregate productivity. *Quarterly Journal of Economics*, *125*(1), 129–173. doi:10.1162/qjec.2010.125.1.129

Enflo, K., & Hjertstrand, P. (2009). Relative sources of European regional productivity convergence: A bootstrap frontier approach. *Regional Studies*, *43*(5), 643–659. https://doi.org/10.1080/00343400701874198

Esteban-Marquillas, J. M. (1972). A reinterpretation of shift-share analysis. *Regional and Urban Economics*, *2*, 249–255.

Ezcurra, R., & Pascual, P. (2007). Spatial disparities in productivity in Central and Eastern Europe. *Eastern European Economics*, *45*(3), 5–32. doi:10.2753/EEE0012-8775450301

Fabricant, S. (1942). *Employment in manufacturing, 1899–1939*. New York: NBER.

Fagerberg, J. (2000). Technological progress, structural change and productivity growth: A comparative study. *Structural Change and Economic Dynamics*, *11*(4), 393–411.

Feder, G. (1986). *Growth in semi-industrial countries: A statistical analysis. Industrialization and growth: A comparative study*. Oxford: Oxford University Press.

Friesenbichler, K., & Peneder, M. (2016). Innovation, competition and productivity. *Economics of Transition*, *24*(3), 535–580. doi:10.1111/ecot.12100

Gardiner, B., Martin, R., & Tyler, P. (2006). Competitiveness, productivity and economic growth across the European regions. In R. Martin, M. Kitson, & P. Tyler (Eds.), *Regional competitiveness* (pp. 61–84). Cheltenham: Routledge.

Habib, M., Abbas, J., & Noman, R. (2019). Are human capital, intellectual property rights, and research and development expenditures really important for total factor productivity? An empirical analysis. *International Journal of Social Economics*, *46*(6), 756–774. doi:10.1108/IJSE-09-2018-0472

Havlik, P. (2015). Patterns of structural change in the new EU member states. *DANUBE: Law and Economics Review*, *6*(3), 133–157. doi:10.1515/danb-2015-0009

Hegerty, S. W. (2016). Regional convergence and growth clusters in Central and Eastern Europe: An examination of sectoral-level data. *Eastern European Business and Economics Journal*, *2*(2), 95–110.

Kaldor, N. (1966). *Causes of the slow rate of economic growth in the United Kingdom.* Cambridge: University Press.

Keil, S. R. (1992). On the value of homotheticity in the shift-share framework. *Growth and Change*, *23*(4), 469–493. doi:10.1111/j.1468-2257.1992.tb00945.x

Knudsen, D. C. (2000). Shift-share analysis: Further examination of models for the description of economic change. *Socio-Economic Planning Sciences*, *34*(3), 177–198. doi:10.1016/s0038-0121(99)00016-6

Kutan, A. M., & Yigit, T. M. (2009). European integration, productivity growth and real convergence: Evidence from the new member states. *Economic Systems*, *33*(2), 127–137. doi:10.1016/j.ecosys.2009.03.002

Kuznets, S. (1973). Modern economic growth: Findings and reflections. *American Economic Review*, *63*, 247–258.

Le Gallo, J., & Dall'erba, S. (2008). Spatial and sectoral productivity convergence between European regions, 1975–2000. *Papers in Regional Science*, *87*(4), 505–525. doi:10.1111/j.1435-5957.2007.00159.x

Lewis, W. A. (1954). Economic development with unlimited supplies of labour. *The Manchester School*, *22*(2), 139–191. doi:10.1111/j.1467-9957.1954.tb00021.x

Loveridge, S., & Selting, A. C. (1998). A review and comparison of shift-share identities. *International Regional Science Review*, *21*, 37–58.

McMillan, M. & Rodrik, D. (2011) Globalization, Structural Change, and Productivity Growth, NBER Working Paper 17143.

Marrocu, E., Paci, R., & Usai, S. (2012). Productivity growth in the old and new Europe: The role of agglomeration externalities. *Journal of Regional Science*, *53*(3), 418–442. doi:10.1111/jors.12000

Martin, R. (2001). EMU versus the regions? Regional convergence and divergence in Euroland. *Journal of Economic Geography*, *1*(1), 51–80.

Mcmillan, M., Rodrik, D., & Verduzco-Gallo, Í. (2014). Globalization, structural change, and productivity growth, with an update on Africa. *World Development*, *63*, 11–32. doi:10.1016/j.worlddev.2013.10.012

Mundlak, Y., Butzer, R. & Larson, D. F. (2008). Heterogeneous technology and panel data: the case of the agricultural production function, *Policy Research Working Paper Series 4536*, The World Bank.

Naveed, A., & Ahmad, N. (2016). Labour productivity convergence and structural changes: Simultaneous analysis at country, regional and industry levels. *Economic Structures*, *5*(19). https://doi.org/10.1186/s40008-016-0050-y

Nazara, S., & Hewings, G. J. D. (2004). Spatial structure and taxonomy of breakdown in shift-share analysis. *Growth and Change*, *35*(4), 476–490.

Odendahl, C., Springford, J., Johnson S., & Murray, J. (2019). *The big sort? The diverging fortunes of Europe's regions*. London: Centre for European Reform.

O'Leary, E., & Webber, D. J. (2014). The role of structural change in European regional productivity growth. *Regional Studies*, *49*(9), 1548–1560. doi:10.1080/00343404.2013.839868

Radosevic, S. (2017). Upgrading technology in Central and Eastern European economies. *IZA World of Labor*, 338. doi: 10.15185/izawol.338

Rosés, J., & Wolf, N. (2021). Regional inequality in the long-run: Europe 1900–2015. *Oxford Review of Economic Policy*, *37*, 17–48.

Skorupinska, A. & Torrent-Sellens, J. (2015). The role of ICT in the productivity of Central and Eastern European countries: Cross-Country comparison. *Revista de Economía Mundial*, *39*, 201–221.

Sondermann, D. (2012). Productivity in the euro area: Any evidence of convergence? *Working Paper Series*, 1431. European Central Bank.

Stevens, B. H., & Moore, C. L. (1980). A critical review of the literature on shift-share as a forecasting technique. *Journal of Regional Science*, *20*(4), 419–437. doi:10.1111/j.1467-9787.1980.tb00660.x

Stojcic, N., Aralica, Z., & Anic, I.-D. (2019). Spatio-temporal determinants of the structural and productive transformation of regions in Central and East European countries. *Economic Systems*, *43*(3), 1–12, Online first. doi:10.1016/j.ecosys.2019.100715

Stojcic, N., Vojinic, P., & Aralica, Z. (2018). Trade liberalization and export transformation in new EU member states. *Structural Change and Economic Dynamics*, *47*, 114–126.

Thurlow, J. & Wobst, P. (2004). The road to pro-poor growth in Zambia: past lessons and future challenges, DSGD discussion papers 16, International Food Policy Research Institute (IFPRI).

Timmer, M. P., & Szirmai, A. (2000). Productivity growth in Asian manufacturing: The structural bonus hypothesis examined. *Structural Change and Economic Dynamics*, *11*(4), 371–392. doi:10.1016/s0954-349x(00)00023-0

Tondl, G. (2001). *Convergence after divergence: Regional growth in Europe*. Vienna—New York: Springer.

Verdoorn, P. J. (2002). Fattori che Regolano lo Sviluppo della Produttivita' del Lavoro.′ L'industria (A. P. Thirlwall, Trans.). In J. S. L. McCombie, M. Pugno, & B. Soro (Eds.), *Productivity growth and economic performance: Essays in Verdoorn's law* (pp. 28–36). Basingstoke: Palgrave MacMillan. Original work published 1949

Villaverde, J., & Maza, A. (2008). Productivity convergence in the European regions, 1980–2003: A sectoral and spatial approach. *Applied Economics*, *40*(10), 1299–1313. doi:10.1080/00036840600771361

Appendix

Table A1 Productivity for 30 selected NUTS 3 left-behind regions (thousands of EUR per employee)

NUTS code	*NUTS name*	*2000*	*2001*	*2002*	*2003*	*2004*	*2005*	*2006*	*2007*	*2008*	*2009*	*2010*	*2011*	*2012*	*2013*	*2014*	*2015*	*2016*	*2017*	*2018*	*2019*	*2020*	*Percent of EU27 in 2000*	*Percent of EU27 in 2020*
BG311	Vidin	4.11	4.56	4.84	4.39	4.97	5.43	5.53	6.4	7	7.16	8.02	7.76	7.65	7.4	8.15	8.13	7.98	9.05	9.71	10.62	10.79	6	18
BG312	Montana	3.86	4.35	4.9	4.33	4.51	5.09	5.19	6.07	6.87	6.85	7.79	7.77	7.99	8.46	8.37	8.86	9.15	10.13	10.62	11.26	11.79	6	20
BG314	Pleven	3.69	4.02	4.45	4.09	3.93	4.53	4.79	5	5.38	6.23	6.62	7.56	7.55	7.58	7.53	7.7	8.13	8.82	9.68	10.57	10.95	6	19
BG315	Lovech	3.2	3.76	4.11	4.18	4.35	4.54	4.72	5.99	6.55	6.84	7.32	8.12	8.29	8	8.49	8.59	9.71	9.73	10.03	10.67	12	5	20
BG321	Veliko Tarnovo	3.19	3.68	4.1	4.01	4.21	4.38	4.73	5.17	5.64	6.4	7.04	7.83	8.25	8.3	8.24	8.36	8.81	9.59	10.69	10.94	11.33	5	19
BG322	Gabrovo	3.34	3.62	4.11	4.28	4.25	4.7	5.05	6.23	6.57	7.43	8.01	8.57	9.08	8.55	9.36	9.82	10.22	11.23	12.17	12.54	13.47	5	23
BG323	Ruse	3.66	4.04	4.47	4.16	4.29	4.53	4.97	6.06	6.68	7.38	6.83	8.09	8.73	8.75	9.57	9.9	10.13	10.49	11.06	11.93	12.14	6	21
BG324	Razgrad	3.57	4.63	5.24	4.27	4.23	4.63	4.77	5.65	6.39	6.47	6.81	7.36	8.83	8.81	9.14	7.21	8.22	8.48	9.94	10.32	10.41	5	18
BG325	Silistra	3.34	3.72	3.63	3.55	3.88	3.62	3.64	4.28	4.85	5.07	5.19	6.1	5.65	6.18	6.41	6.58	6.44	7.06	7.62	8.25	8.66	5	15
BG332	Dobrich	3.96	3.95	4.42	4.31	4.43	4.6	4.68	5.15	6.53	6.05	7.11	7.5	7.69	7.54	7.59	7.99	8.32	8.48	8.9	9.66	10.62	6	18
BG333	Shumen	3.07	3.48	3.9	3.75	3.97	4.14	4.58	5.33	5.9	6.55	6.71	7.14	7.43	7.72	7.58	7.62	8.18	8.63	8.91	9.77	9.6	5	16
BG334	Targovishte	3.23	3.61	3.82	3.56	3.81	4.36	4.91	5.53	6	5.81	6.19	7.09	7.69	8.07	7.51	7.69	8.8	8.68	9.33	9.75	10.1	5	17
BG341	Burgas	4.27	3.81	4.06	4.46	4.32	5.65	5.95	7	7.72	8.25	8.99	9.8	9.91	9.55	8.62	9.99	10.84	11.73	11.84	12.57	11.16	7	19
BG342	Sliven	2.11	2.44	2.59	2.83	3.16	4.77	4.69	4.99	5.22	5.75	6.65	7.06	7.65	7.27	7.94	7.62	7.97	7.85	8.9	9.02	9.46	3	16
BG343	Yambol	3.44	3.38	3.7	3.38	4.1	3.86	4.14	3.99	4.64	5.17	5.71	6.36	7.04	6.98	7.79	7.73	7.7	8.64	9.54	10.06	10.46	5	18
BG413	Blagoevgrad	3.44	3.76	3.96	4.27	4.63	4.94	4.95	5.13	5.72	5.92	5.77	6.44	6.76	6.85	7.02	7.31	7.57	8.03	8.9	9.14	9.74	5	17
BG414	Pernik	3.5	3.7	4.34	4.62	5.41	5.52	5.95	8.15	10.03	8.34	8.95	9.33	8.51	7.86	8.23	8.46	9.77	10.5	11.62	11.85	12.73	5	22
BG415	Kyustendil	3.84	3.31	4.92	5.02	4.62	5.06	5.21	6.43	6.26	6.4	7.25	7.34	7.57	7.42	7.98	8.7	8.85	9.05	9.92	10.25	11.93	6	20
BG421	Plovdiv	3.38	3.83	3.94	4.09	4.58	4.95	5.28	5.99	6.13	7.05	7.42	8.37	8.73	8.99	8.83	9.67	10.4	10.43	11.61	12.64	12.77	5	22
BG422	Haskovo	3.31	4.57	4.64	4.51	4.86	4.93	4.84	5.2	5.67	5.49	5.66	6.61	6.89	6.38	6.64	7.32	7.67	8.09	9.05	9.33	9.72	5	17
BG423	Pazardzhik	2.22	2.86	3.84	4.13	4.39	5.14	6.75	6.38	6.9	5.49	6.39	7.33	8.18	7.71	6.98	8.13	7.97	8.24	9.48	10.17	11.06	3	19
BG424	Smolyan	2.37	3	3.25	2.88	3.19	3.47	3.62	4.79	5.97	5.9	7.29	7.69	7.96	7.44	8.26	8.86	8.81	9.57	9.95	10.41	10.31	4	18

(*Continued*)

Table A1 (Continued)

NUTS code	*NUTS name*	*2000*	*2001*	*2002*	*2003*	*2004*	*2005*	*2006*	*2007*	*2008*	*2009*	*2010*	*2011*	*2012*	*2013*	*2014*	*2015*	*2016*	*2017*	*2018*	*2019*	*2020*	*Percent of EU27 in 2000*	*Percent of EU27 in 2020*
BG425	Kardzhali	3.66	3.77	4.09	4.82	5.48	6.35	6.79	5.72	6.22	5.66	6.06	5.2	5.68	5.49	5.55	5.98	6.59	7.27	8.23	9.93	11.85	6	20
RO211	Bacau	2.34	2.69	3.45	3.5	4.53	5.49	6.53	8.29	9.55	9.04	9.03	8.48	9.24	8.93	9.25	9.62	10.4	11.21	12.52	13.65	13.88	4	24
RO212	Botosani	1.98	2.24	3	2.96	3.46	4.46	5.37	7.49	8.69	8.09	8.86	9.19	8.18	9.68	8.95	9.17	9.46	10.99	13.3	13.76	13.82	3	24
RO214	Neamt	1.72	1.99	2.51	2.39	3.28	4.18	5.11	6.23	6.93	5.89	6.33	6.38	7.03	6.89	6.78	6.76	8	8.9	10.02	10.41	11.09	3	19
RO215	Suceava	2.09	2.31	3.15	3.21	4.04	4.95	5.84	7.82	8.32	8.09	8.38	8.43	8.54	8.84	8.93	9.29	9.97	10.69	12.01	13.5	13.92	3	24
RO216	Vaslui	1.21	1.54	1.97	2.21	2.64	3	3.93	4.81	6.28	5.44	5.44	6.01	6.31	6.2	6.3	5.81	6.82	7.49	8.26	8.84	9.04	2	15
RO312	Calarasi	1.56	2.05	2.23	2.36	3.32	3.36	4.15	5.19	7.35	6.64	7.38	8.31	7.21	7.96	8.02	8.63	9.45	10.3	11.54	12.42	12.33	2	21
RO315	Ialomita	1.44	1.75	2.18	2.33	3.03	3.46	4.09	4.43	6.04	5.4	5.79	7.49	6.49	7.17	7.03	8.25	9.21	10.64	11.56	13.18	12.99	2	22
EU27_2020	European Union, 27 countries (from 2020)	64.97	39.24	40.74	41.69	43.36	44.65	46.24	48.13	49.4	48.23	50.3	51.81	52.25	53	53.71	55.16	55.89	57.27	58.39	59.84	58.59	100	100

Source: Author's own elaboration based on the Eurostat database

Table A2 Productivity for 21 selected NUTS 3 Greek regions (thousands of EUR per employee)

NUTS code	*NUTS name*	*2000*	*2001*	*2002*	*2003*	*2004*	*2005*	*2006*	*2007*	*2008*	*2009*	*2010*	*2011*	*2012*	*2013*	*2014*	*2015*	*2016*	*2017*	*2018*	*2019*	*2020*	*Percent of EU27 in 2000*	*Percent of EU27 in 2020*
EL306	Dytiki Attiki	41.55	44.67	48.84	55.63	57.54	50.34	63.72	61.79	58.6	55.77	53.84	49.89	46.64	45.13	39.22	41.56	38.62	38.93	40.22	40.13	38.22	110	65
EL307	Peiraias and Nisoi	38.18	39.68	38.92	43.05	46.08	46.39	50.16	52.62	53.41	52.31	50.13	47.1	45.55	44.05	41.12	41.56	38.75	40.59	39.59	38.72	35.96	101	61
EL412	Ikaria and Samos	29.35	30.87	30.48	32.08	37.26	42.78	42.22	45.24	51.14	44.45	37.97	34.47	33.86	28.59	27.78	27.25	25.66	26.17	25.54	25.53	23.33	78	40
EL413	Chios	27.07	27.95	28.29	29.84	33.8	32.34	35.06	38.85	39.75	40.86	38.98	36.36	32.74	30.46	29.4	29.48	28.13	28.71	27.64	28.07	26.77	72	46
EL421	Kalymnos, Karpathos, Kasos, Kos and Rodos	33.55	34.31	32.8	35.16	40.37	38.17	40.56	38.84	40.03	39.73	37.89	35.76	34.02	31.83	31.39	31.07	28.25	28.02	26.96	27.51	22.33	89	38
EL422	Andros, Thira, Kea, Milos, Mykonos, Naxos, Paros, Syros and Tinos	38.48	39.91	41.79	48.07	45.79	53.9	56.19	62.86	63.44	57.6	54.53	50.16	43.6	46.22	45.16	44.24	38.56	39.09	39.22	39.11	32.99	102	56
EL433	Rethymni	25.22	25.1	27.77	30.3	37.76	37.59	38.92	37.42	40.48	36.41	34.22	31.21	29.27	29.3	28.97	30.2	28.3	28.95	28.82	28.58	24.09	67	41
EL434	Chania	27.32	30.01	33.62	36.98	38.56	36.49	39.76	39.85	40.34	38.9	36.67	33.77	31.14	31.1	30.48	31.23	29.45	29.62	29.16	29.21	25.57	73	44
EL512	Xanthi	22.65	24.26	25.78	28.59	27.32	26.36	29.28	28.97	32.98	32.95	30.36	25.89	24.62	24.36	22.43	23.34	21.89	21.76	21.31	20.91	19.82	60	34
EL515	Thasos and Kavala	28.05	27.62	30.24	31.23	33.58	35.48	35.78	38.66	41.75	39.53	37.56	33.91	33.66	31.79	31.58	31.3	29.35	30.15	29.38	28.95	26.67	75	46
EL527	Chalkidiki	43.46	42.43	37.71	45.46	43.12	44.45	45.64	49.58	54.94	52.26	51.06	47.56	46.54	42.12	39.6	41.02	39.24	39.7	39.52	38.66	33.14	115	57
EL533	Florina	34.67	35.95	38.44	48.64	47.63	[illegible]	43.9	47.21	37.88	43.8	49.97	52.3	53.66	49.94	49.67	47.69	43.11	46.14	41.24	38.17	34.17	92	58
EL542	Thesprotia	27.99	31.36	29.12	36.22	40.2	[illegible]	37.14	41.4	46.98	45.59	41.55	35.71	32.95	29.98	28.2	27.97	26.32	27.54	27.1	26.87	25.03	74	43
EL621	Zakynthos	36.35	34.41	34.74	40.61	39.16	36.26	39.26	36.47	33.78	30.58	29.09	24.79	25.02	22.73	23.31	25.28	24.42	24.04	23.96	24.65	19.13	97	33
EL622	Kerkyra	23.57	25.94	27.2	28.47	31.49	[illegible]	34.48	39.36	41.1	38.67	35.49	33.43	31.31	31.57	31.25	30.66	28.44	28.83	27.45	27.88	23.44	63	40
EL623	Ithaki and Kefallinia	40.46	51.03	46.41	49.76	51.37	53.66	56.15	62.18	62.43	57.18	61.55	53	45	42.21	43.35	42	39.21	39.5	38.06	38.74	33.78	107	58
EL624	Lefkada	28.58	29.52	30.17	29.28	36.22	37.93	41.17	34.96	34.9	39.46	42.26	40.39	33.98	31.93	32.24	33.59	31.65	31.21	31.07	31.5	26.09	76	45
EL633	Ileia	21.89	22.08	23.14	26.44	30.38	30.56	30.38	34.75	34.68	30.71	27.67	25.14	23.5	21.89	21.58	22.91	21.53	22.32	21.53	22.02	21.13	58	36
EL644	Fthiotida	30.85	33.13	35.27	35.84	37.22	41.01	41.64	42.39	39.45	36.21	31.73	29.54	28.45	25.7	24.7	25.64	24.79	25.37	24.52	24.52	23.64	82	40
EL645	Fokida	30.4	34.86	37.18	44.38	42.88	34.04	34.38	34.12	37.5	33.92	33.17	31.17	29.94	30.28	28.84	29.61	28.32	28.59	28.5	28.08	27.31	81	47
EL653	Lakonia and Messinia	24.95	26.1	26.19	26.2	29.04	27.93	29.14	32.04	32.18	31.19	30.61	29.76	29.13	26.76	26.05	27.02	25.64	26.09	25.07	25.54	23.95	66	41

Source: Author's own elaboration based on the Eurostat database

5 Effectiveness of EU cohesion policy in left-behind places – data envelopment analysis

5.1 Literature review

The effectiveness of EU funds in eliminating differences between regions remains debatable. The literature is dominated by studies confirming that the Cohesion Policy contributes to eliminating differences between regions. However, empirical research also points to the imperfections of the Cohesion Policy and the ineffective use of funds. The differences in the results are related to the Cohesion Policy programmes, their implementation and the different levels of development of the regions. Researchers also use different research methodologies, variables, study periods and groups of regions. The aim of this chapter is to verify whether EU funding is used efficiently in EU regions. Measuring the efficiency of EU funds and its impact on the economic situation of the regions is not a new area of research. However, empirical analysis still requires further investigation, especially for the most recent statistics.

Some studies have confirmed the positive impact of EU funds on regional growth and on reducing differences between regions. Fiaschi et al. (2017) proved the EU Cohesion Policy's effectiveness in its two main objectives in the period 1989–2006. The increase in regional competitiveness, measured by additional annual growth in GDP per employee, was estimated at a median annual growth of 1.4%. The reduction in regional disparities, measured by the Gini index, decreased by 0.08%. Moreover, it was confirmed that strong spatial effects influenced this efficiency. This research confirmed the two objectives of the EU Cohesion Policy: to increase overall economic growth and to reduce inequality. Maynou et al. (2014) studied convergence between Eurozone countries from 1990 to 2010. The results of the spatiotemporal econometric model show that EU funds positively contributed to the growth of GDP per capita in recipient regions, thus enabling them to achieve (conditional) convergence. Beugelsdijk and Eijffinger (2005) also confirmed that the Structural Funds have had a positive impact and that poorer countries seem to be catching up with more prosperous countries. In addition, they also examined the problem of abuse and substitution effects, as in some cases, the recipients may use the funds inefficiently. More corrupt EU15 countries do not achieve less economic growth from Structural Funds. Dall'erba (2005) examined the relationship between the spatial distribution of regional income and regional development

DOI: 10.4324/9781032615516-6

funds among 145 European regions from 1989 to 1999. The results indicate that rich/poor regions tend to cluster close to other rich/poor regions in a regional distribution of growth rates and regional funds. Secondly, the local indicators of spatial association (LISA) statistics indicate spatial heterogeneity over the decade in the form of two spatial clusters of rich and poor regions, highlighting the persistence of a significant core–periphery pattern among European regions. The research also shows a positive relationship between regional growth and Structural Funds. Rodriguez-Pose and Fratesi (2004) state that despite the concentration of development resources on infrastructure and, to a lesser extent, business support, the returns on liabilities on these axes are not significant. Support for agriculture has a short-term positive impact on economic growth. Only investment in education and human capital – accounting for just one eighth of the total commitments – deliver positive and significant returns in the medium term. Scotti et al. (2022) studied the sectoral impact of the Structural and Cohesion Funds at the NUTS 2 level in the period 2007–2014. Their findings confirm that spending in the energy, R&D and transport sectors results in higher GDP per capita growth rates with consistent, lasting effects, reduced production costs and greater accessibility and innovation in the recipient regions. Moreover, these effects are amplified when spending is more diversified across sectors. Spatial panel models show that the transport sector generates the greatest spillover effects by exploiting agglomeration and proximity, while geographically we find significant spillover effects across national borders. Crucitti et al. (2023) examined the macroeconomic impacts of Cohesion Policy investments in the EU in the period 2007–2013. They confirmed that Cohesion Policy programmes positively and significantly impact the economies of EU Member States and regions, especially the EU's poorest regions. Spatial effects mean that programmes implemented by the policy's primary beneficiaries also benefit its main contributors. For some Member States, the primary source of benefits is the spillover effects from the Cohesion Policy. In their study, Becker et al. (2010) confirmed that the expenditure on Objective 1 caused an increase in real GDP per capita by, on average, about 1.6%. However, they found no significant effects on employment over the funding period, unless we include spillover effects from treatment regions up to 200 km away. The positive impact of GDP growth and the lack of an effect from employment growth may have various reasons. This may be because transfers under Objective 1 mainly increase the volume and change the investment structure. Another reason may be that job creation takes longer than the programming period of five to seven years. Therefore, financing Objective 1 does not have an immediate impact. Still, over the medium programming period and across the region, it will take at least four years to see the effect of growth on GDP per capita.

Other research shows a negative or no significant impact from EU funds on reducing regional disparities. Boldrin and Canova (2001) summarised their research by concluding that there is no clear sign that EU policies, unlike other social and economic factors, are reducing regional disparities. Regional and structural policies are mainly redistributive, motivated by the nature of the political balance on which the European Union is built, and have little connection with supporting economic growth. Moreover, they looked for the main factors that explain such discrepancies and, in particular, found that they should have been considered in the economic models adopted by the Commission to justify the policy. Dall'Erba and Le Gallo (2008) assessed the impact of the Structural Funds on the convergence process between 145 European regions in the period 1989–1999. Spillover effects are examined using spatial econometric methods that evaluate the impact of funds on a given region and its neighbours. The results confirmed the convergence process, but found that EU funds do not influence it. Moreover, investments directed to peripheral regions never spill over to neighbours. Esposti and Bussoletti (2008) examined the impact of Objective 1 structural fund spending on EU regions by estimating an econometric model of extended conditional convergence. According to this model, economic growth convergence is influenced by policymaking, which controls the regional rate of initial investment by interacting with other regional structural variables and ultimately affecting its constant level. The results confirm that estimates of the conditional convergence rate range from 1.9% to 4.9%. In terms of determinants, the positive impact of ESIFs on Objective 1 regions is confirmed across the EU, although the statistical significance and magnitude of this impact may vary depending on alternative estimators. However, the effect of Objective 1 policies on economic growth is generally quite limited and may become negligible or even negative in some regional cases. Moreover, Esposti and Bussoletti (2008) drew attention to the fact that the delayed effect of funds over time is essential, which is often ignored in empirical work on this topic.

Breidenbach et al. (2019) noted that EU policymakers' goal in the coming years is to make the Cohesion Policy more effective and focussed on measurable results. It was emphasised that although significant progress had been made in solving this problem, particularly through the use of regression discontinuity design, the shift to semi-parametric and non-parametric approaches at the national and regional levels has weakened the link with the theory-based causality that underpins the intervention logic of the Cohesion Policy programmes. Therefore, analyses should consider the transmission mechanisms from public investment to output and impact. To identify these mechanisms, combining different approaches and methods in a convergent, synergistic and eclectic way would be necessary to provide information on how territorial policies can promote economic and social cohesion. The evidence needs to be analysed systematically and embedded in data collection and project selection, as well as project management and evaluation systems related to cohesion. Based on the analysis of transmission channels from Cohesion Policy to economic growth, Breidenbach and colleagues concluded that the best approach is to focus on the effects at the company level. To support research and innovation, we should look for direct transmission channels. In addition, trade theory and the new economics of geography emphasise other productivity-enhancing effects of better transportation infrastructure: market expansion, increased trade, specialisation and agglomeration. Kersan-Škabić and Tijanić (2017) noted that the absorption of financial resources from EU funds is a very important aspect, and they examined the impact of selected territorial economic conditions on EU regions' effective absorption of money. The analysis is based on 86 regions whose GDP per capita is below 75% of the EU average (convergence regions) and 186 regions with GDP per capita above 75% of the EU average (developed regions). Thanks to the analysis of panel data, it was confirmed that regional economic characteristics conditionally influence the absorption of EU funds, and that they differ between convergence regions and developed regions. They indicated the characteristics of the labour force, institutional quality, public investments, fiscal decentralisation and infrastructure as key factors contributing to the greater absorption of EU funds. Moreover, the need to give regions and their sub-national authorities greater responsibility in managing their development was emphasised.

5.2 Methodology

The effectiveness of EU funds is assessed using the data envelopment analysis methodology. DEA is a non-parametric methodology that measures the efficiency of units with multiple outputs and inputs with determined weights. DEA was introduced by Farrell (1957) and further developed by Charnes et al. (1978). It assesses each decision-making unit's (DMU) effectiveness, comparing it to other DMUs involved in the same process. DEA measures technical efficiency, which is relative, as it measures efficiency concerning units that are compared with each other. Because DEA is not an absolute measure of efficiency, when interpreting the results it must be taken into account that units which are efficient according to DEA may be able to improve their performance even further. Efficient DMUs are not necessarily the production frontier, but rather the best practice frontier (Cook et al., 2014). DEA uses data points to create production efficiency limits that serve as benchmarks for efficiency measures. It determines which DMUs represent the efficiency frontier and which do not.

The first step in applying the DEA method is to select appropriate inputs and outputs that can be measured in different units. The results depend on the choice of variables. Identifying exogenous variables is essential, and it is necessary to remove output data that may be duplicative (Jenkins & Anderson, 2003).

In DEA, relative efficiency is calculated as the ratio of the weighted sum of outputs to the weighted sum of inputs (Cooper et al., 2000). The CRS model maximises this ratio (Equations 1–3):

$$\text{Max}\theta_0 = \frac{\sum_{s=1}^{S} u_r\, y_{rj}}{\sum_{m=1}^{M} v_m x_{mj}}, \tag{1}$$

subject to

$$\frac{\sum_{s=1}^{S} u_r\, y_{rj}}{\sum_{m=1}^{M} v_m x_{mj}} \leq 1, \tag{2}$$

$$u_r\ ,\ v_m \geq 0; s = 1,\ldots, S; m = 1,.., M$$

where u_s is the weight of the output
v_m is the weight of the input,
y_{rj} is the output and
x_{mj} is the input.

A variable returns to scale (VRS) calculation requires an additional constraint equation:

$$\sum n_{i=1}\lambda j = 1, \tag{3}$$

where θ is the efficiency score calculated for each DMU,
λ is the corresponding solution vector for the optimisation and
n is the number of DMUs.

The application of DEA should follow the principle below with respect to the selection of variables (Zhang & Bartels, 1998):

$$n \geq 3 * (s + m), \tag{4}$$

where s is the number of inputs,
m is the number of outputs and
n is the number of DMUs.

DEA can use either input- or output-orientated models. The input-orientated model aims to equate technical efficiency with a proportional reduction in the consumption of inputs while keeping the results unchanged. Efficiency in the output-orientated model is represented by a proportional increase in outputs, while the proportion of inputs remains unchanged. DEA methodology may use constant returns to scale (CRS) or variable returns to scale. Interpreting VRS is much more complex than CRS; therefore, VRS is only used to control increasing or decreasing returns.

The DEA methodology is easy to use because it does not require definition of the functional form of the relationship between the inputs and the results (Thanassoulis, 2003). This makes it useful for analysing the complex and often unknown nature of the relationship between variables. Moreover, DEA allows for the analysis of many inputs and outputs simultaneously. DEA does not require a priori information about which inputs and outputs are most important in assessing efficiency (Wober, 2007). The DEA methodology also has some limitations, several of which can be identified in this study. The input and output data were selected based on available statistics. It should be remembered that the selection of these variables has a decisive impact on the results for efficiency. The analysis would have been more complex if additional indicators for environmental protection or innovation had been included in this study. However, increasing the number of indicators would have also reduced the discriminatory power of the DEA. Additionally, DEA does not consider qualitative variables, which may result in some critical factors being omitted from the analysis. There is also a negative correlation between efficiency and the number of DMUs (Zhang & Bartels, 1998). DEA requires a full understanding of its potential and limitations, and thus careful interpretation of the results (Molinero & Woracker, 1996).

5.3 Data and empirical analysis

This study examines the effectiveness of EU policy and therefore the relationship between EU payments (input) and achieving Cohesion Policy goals. The calculations were performed in Microsoft Excel and DEAFrontier. The study covers 233 EU NUTS 2 regions between 2007 and 2018. This scope yielded enough DMUs to obtain a comparable peer group.

One of the main limitations of the study was the availability of data for EU regions. The EU publishes its statistics according to NUTS, which subdivides the economic territory of the EU into regions at three different levels (NUTS 1, 2 and 3, moving from larger to smaller territorial units). Eurostat established the NUTS classification as a single, coherent system for dividing up the EU's territory in order to produce regional statistics for the Community. Since 2010, the NUTS classification has changed three times. Unfortunately, these changes are not automatically applied to all historical statistics. In my study, this meant that some data, such as payments from EU funds, were available in the old NUTS division and data on outputs were available in the latest breakdown. In practice, this implied that payments were presented for some cumulative regions. This, in turn, required that NUTS codes be manually changed in input output data and data for the accumulated regions be recalculated (see all changes in Table 5.1). Moreover, I originally intended to use NUTS 3 data for the study, but most of the statistics I was looking for were not available. In addition, other indicators could have been included in the study, such as statistics related to environmental protection or innovation, which are also

Table 5.1 Changes made to NUTS codes in input and output indicators

NUTS code in CPP indicator	*NUTS code in output indicators*	*NUTS in CPP indicator*	*NUTS code in output indicators*
PL11	PL71	FR41	FRF3
PL12	PL91&PL92	FR42	FRF1
PL31	PL81	FR43	FRC2
PL32	PL82	FR51	FRG0
PL33	PL72	FR52	FRH0
PL34	PL84	FR53	FRI3
LT00	LT01&LT02	FR61	FRI1
IE01&IE02	IE04&IE05&IE06	FR62	FRJ2
HU10	HU11&HU12	FR63	FRI2
HR04	HR02&HR05&HR06	FR71	FRK2
FR21	FRF2	FR72	FRK1
FR22	FRE2	FR81	FRJ1
FR23	FRD2	FR82	FRL0
FR24	FRB0	FR83	FRM0
FR25	FRD1	FR91	FRY1
FR26	FRC1	FR92	FRY2
FR30	FRE1	FR93	FRY3
		FR94	FRY4

Source: Author's own elaboration based on the Eurostat database (2023a)

primary goals of the Cohesion Policy, but these statistics were not available for all years or at the regional level.

The diagnostic variables were selected based on available statistics from Eurostat. The input indicators were EU payments (in EUR) by NUTS 2 regions, represented by Cohesion Policy Payments (CPP). Those payments were from the ERDF, ESF, CF, YEI and FEAD and are subject to the Cohesion Policy. Over the years, the funds' names have changed, but their primary goal remains to equalise inequalities in the EU. The YEI and FEAD funds were also selected for analysis because they are related to the ESF, and from 2021, they were integrated into the European Social Fund+(ESF+). All EU regions are eligible for ERDF and ESF funding, but only the less developed ones can receive support from the Cohesion Fund. The data come from the database called 'Historic EU payments – regionalised and modelled' (REGIO.B2; Walsh, 2023). This data set answers the deceptively difficult question of how much a given region/country received under the regional policy. This question is difficult because many programmes are actually national rather than regional in nature and because there are many EU funding sources. The dataset shows the volume of EU payments per fund, programme period and year. From 2007 to 2013, before full EU membership, Croatia received funding from the Instrument for Pre-Accession Assistance, which is presented under the CF, ERDF and ESF. In this study, I did not incorporate any time lag for inputs and outputs. It is assumed that the funds received from the EU are allocated immediately to investments and that they stimulate the economy and the labour market. The five output indicators chosen for analysis are productivity, measured as GVA per employee (GVApE), GDP per capita (GDPpC), compensation per employee (CpE), disposable income in PPS per capita (DIpC) and unemployment rate (UNE). Because the unemployment rate is a destimulant, it should be converted into a stimulant for the DEA; I therefore used the employment rate in the labour force (EMP) as the final variable. Malta was excluded from the study due to missing data for the output variable DIpC. Table 5.2 presents the final set of selected variables and their descriptions.

Table 5.2 Indicators and sources

Input/output	*Variable*	*Full indicator name*	*Units*	*Source*
Input	CPP	Cohesion Policy payments	mln EUR	Eurostat
Output	GVApE	Productivity per employee (GVA per employee)	thousands of EUR per person	Eurostat
Output	GDPpC	Gross domestic product per capita	thousands of EUR per person	Eurostat
Output	CpE	Compensation per employee	thousands of EUR per person	Eurostat
Output	DIpC	Disposable income in PPS per capita	thousands of EUR per person	Eurostat
Output	EMP	Employment rate	% of labour force	Eurostat

Source: Author's own elaboration based on Eurostat (2023b)

Table 5.3 Descriptive statistics for diagnostic input and output indicators in 2007 and 2018

	2007			2018		
Variable	*Average*	*Min*	*Max*	*Average*	*Min*	*Max*
CPP	145.66	–	1257.66	182.91	0.74	1536.20
GVApE	46.12	5.52	101.00	54.55	10.41	136.02
GDPpC	23.77	2.80	78.30	28.74	5.30	98.80
CpE	23.53	2.09	51.76	28.97	4.93	66.36
DIpC	13.53	4.40	23.50	16.03	6.70	26.50
EMP	92.30	75.90	97.60	92.44	71.00	98.70

Source: Author's own elaboration based on Eurostat (2023b)

Table 5.3 consists of descriptive statistics for the input and output indicators. There was a significant difference between the minimum and maximum values for all indicators. The minimum value for the 2007 CPP indicator was zero for Croatia's regions. In 2007 the country was a participant of the Instrument for Pre-Accession Assistance programme, but did not receive any payments in the first year; therefore, the efficiency for the regions HR03 and HR02&HR05&HR06 in 2007 may be overestimated. This is also true for regions DE50 in 2015 and FI20 in 2012, which did not receive EU payments in a particular year. The average CPP increased by 25% between 2007 and 2018, while the output indicators increased accordingly by 18%, 20%, 23% and 16%. Only the employment rate was quite stable, though the minimum value decreased over the study period.

Finally, efficiency for the 233 NUTS 2 regions was calculated using DEAFrontier. I used two DEA models: input-orientated and output-orientated. The EU strives to increase the effects of the Cohesion Policy as much as possible while reducing payments. With the input-orientated model, one can test whether a given DMU can reduce its inputs while keeping its outputs at their current levels. Therefore, it can be used to determine whether Cohesion Policy payments may be decreased while maintaining output indicators at the same level. Output-orientated models are also assessed to validate whether constant inputs may cause a proportional increase in outputs. Both models use VRS, which reflects the fact that production can exhibit increasing, constant or decreasing returns to scale. The results of these calculations are presented in Table 5.4 for the input-orientated model and in Table 5.5 for the output-orientated model.

In the input-orientated model, productive units with objective function values equal to 1 are efficient, while all values below 1 are inefficient. Among the 233 NUTS 2 EU regions in the input-orientated model, only one was efficient in all years under the VRS assumption: LU00 (Luxembourg). FI20 (Åland) was efficient in 11 out of 12 years and AT32 (Salzburg) was efficient in 10 out of 12 years. ITH1 (Provincia Autonoma di Bolzano/Bozen) was efficient for 8 of the years, similar to DE21 (Oberbayern), which has maintained an efficiency index of 1 since 2011. The remaining regions in most of the years under analysis scored between 0 and 1;

Table 5.4 Efficiency of EU funds for selected NUTS 2 regions in 2007–2018 (input-orientated VRS model)

DMU name	*2007*	*2008*	*2009*	*2010*	*2011*	*2012*	*2013*	*2014*	*2015*	*2016*	*2017*	*2018*	*Average*	*Rank*
LU00	1.00	1.00	1.00	1.00	1.00	1.00	1.00	1.00	1.00	1.00	1.00	1.00	1.000	1
FI20	1.00	1.00	1.00	1.00	1.00	1.00	1.00	1.00	0.84	1.00	1.00	1.00	0.985	2
AT32	1.00	1.00	0.83	1.00	1.00	1.00	1.00	0.74	1.00	1.00	1.00	1.00	0.961	3
ITH1	1.00	1.00	1.00	1.00	0.60	0.59	1.00	0.83	1.00	1.00	1.00	0.79	0.893	4
DE21	0.24	0.22	0.45	0.33	1.00	1.00	1.00	1.00	1.00	1.00	1.00	1.00	0.818	5
AT33	0.93	1.00	0.57	0.88	1.00	1.00	1.00	1.00	0.39	0.50	0.51	1.00	0.804	6
AT34	0.70	0.59	0.30	0.63	0.87	0.55	0.92	1.00	0.90	1.00	1.00	1.00	0.796	7
DEB2	0.21	0.13	0.36	0.37	0.36	1.00	0.41	0.72	0.88	1.00	1.00	1.00	0.658	8
DE14	0.23	0.11	0.22	0.43	0.33	1.00	0.48	1.00	0.84	0.37	1.00	1.00	0.616	9
BE24	1.00	0.37	0.22	1.00	1.00	0.87	0.30	1.00	0.45	0.13	0.34	1.00	0.608	10
BE10	0.54	0.47	0.31	0.60	1.00	1.00	0.93	1.00	0.16	0.06	0.33	0.18	0.550	11
NL34	1.00	0.09	1.00	1.00	0.47	1.00	0.29	0.20	0.08	0.15	0.76	1.00	0.548	12
DE25	0.13	0.09	0.23	0.18	0.27	0.30	0.47	0.43	0.62	1.00	1.00	1.00	0.507	13
DE22	0.12	0.09	0.25	0.20	0.21	0.24	0.20	0.33	1.00	1.00	1.00	0.78	0.481	14
DK01	0.26	1.00	0.35	0.47	0.36	0.60	0.28	0.14	0.22	1.00	0.33	0.56	0.481	14
DE13	0.19	0.10	0.26	0.50	0.29	0.47	0.46	0.67	1.00	0.20	0.27	0.62	0.441	16
DE26	0.12	0.09	0.28	0.20	0.22	0.31	0.25	0.45	0.36	0.63	0.83	0.86	0.408	17
DE27	0.16	0.10	0.41	0.29	0.30	0.41	0.39	0.48	0.48	0.54	0.51	0.51	0.403	18
DE11	0.17	0.10	0.14	0.27	0.27	0.30	0.20	0.73	0.84	0.16	0.38	1.00	0.399	19
BE25	0.61	0.90	0.17	0.61	0.19	0.39	0.26	0.61	0.19	0.01	0.25	0.53	0.373	20
ES11	0.01	0.00	0.00	0.00	0.00	0.00	0.00	0.00	0.00	0.00	0.00	0.00	0.001	225
ITF3	0.00	0.00	0.00	0.00	0.00	0.00	0.00	0.00	0.00	0.00	0.00	0.00	0.001	225
PT16	0.01	0.00	0.00	0.00	0.00	0.00	0.00	0.00	0.00	0.00	0.00	0.00	0.001	225
ITG1	0.00	0.00	0.00	0.00	0.00	0.00	0.00	0.00	0.00	0.00	0.00	0.00	0.001	225
PL22	0.00	0.00	0.00	0.00	0.00	0.00	0.00	0.00	0.00	0.00	0.00	0.00	0.001	225
PL91&PL92	0.00	0.00	0.00	0.00	0.00	0.00	0.00	0.00	0.00	0.00	0.00	0.00	0.001	225
LT01&LT02	0.01	0.00	0.00	0.00	0.00	0.00	0.00	0.00	0.00	0.00	0.00	0.00	0.001	225
ES61	0.00	0.00	0.00	0.00	0.00	0.00	0.00	0.00	0.00	0.00	0.00	0.00	0.001	225
PT11	0.00	0.00	0.00	0.00	0.00	0.00	0.00	0.00	0.00	0.00	0.00	0.00	0.001	225

Source: Author's own calculations based on the Eurostat data in the DEAFrontier software

Table 5.5 Efficiency of EU funds for selected NUTS 2 regions in 2007–2018 (output-orientated VRS model)

DMU name	*2007*	*2008*	*2009*	*2010*	*2011*	*2012*	*2013*	*2014*	*2015*	*2016*	*2017*	*2018*	*Average*	*Rank*
LU00	1.00	1.00	1.00	1.00	1.00	1.00	1.00	1.00	1.00	1.00	1.00	1.00	1.000	1
AT32	1.00	1.00	1.00	1.00	1.00	1.00	1.00	1.00	1.00	1.00	1.00	1.00	1.000	1
FI20	1.00	1.00	1.00	1.00	1.00	1.00	1.00	1.00	1.01	1.00	1.00	1.00	1.001	3
AT33	1.00	1.00	1.00	1.00	1.00	1.00	1.00	1.00	1.00	1.00	1.00	1.00	1.002	4
DE21	1.01	1.00	1.01	1.00	1.00	1.00	1.00	1.00	1.00	1.00	1.00	1.00	1.002	4
ITH1	1.00	1.00	1.00	1.00	1.01	1.01	1.00	1.01	1.00	1.00	1.00	1.01	1.003	6
CZ01	1.00	1.00	1.00	1.01	1.01	1.00	1.01	1.00	1.00	1.00	1.00	1.00	1.003	6
BE24	1.00	1.00	1.01	1.00	1.00	1.00	1.01	1.00	1.01	1.01	1.01	1.00	1.005	8
AT34	1.01	1.01	1.03	1.01	1.01	1.01	1.00	1.00	1.00	1.00	1.00	1.00	1.007	9
DE14	1.02	1.01	1.02	1.02	1.00	1.00	1.00	1.00	1.00	1.00	1.00	1.00	1.007	9
NL34	1.00	1.00	1.00	1.00	1.01	1.00	1.02	1.03	1.02	1.01	1.00	1.00	1.008	11
DE13	1.02	1.01	1.02	1.01	1.00	1.00	1.00	1.00	1.00	1.01	1.01	1.01	1.008	11
BE25	1.00	1.00	1.01	1.01	1.00	1.01	1.01	1.01	1.02	1.01	1.01	1.00	1.008	11
DE22	1.02	1.02	1.03	1.01	1.00	1.01	1.01	1.00	1.00	1.00	1.00	1.00	1.008	11
DEB2	1.03	1.03	1.02	1.01	1.01	1.00	1.00	1.00	1.00	1.00	1.00	1.00	1.009	15
DE23	1.03	1.02	1.03	1.01	1.01	1.01	1.01	1.00	1.00	1.00	1.00	1.00	1.010	16
DE27	1.02	1.02	1.02	1.01	1.01	1.01	1.01	1.00	1.00	1.01	1.00	1.01	1.010	16
DE11	1.02	1.01	1.02	1.02	1.01	1.01	1.01	1.00	1.00	1.01	1.01	1.00	1.010	16
BE23	1.02	1.01	1.01	1.02	1.01	1.01	1.01	1.00	1.02	1.02	1.01	1.00	1.011	19
AT31	1.01	1.00	1.01	1.01	1.01	1.01	1.02	1.02	1.02	1.02	1.01	1.01	1.011	19
DE26	1.03	1.02	1.03	1.02	1.01	1.01	1.01	1.00	1.00	1.00	1.00	1.00	1.012	21
DE25	1.04	1.03	1.03	1.03	1.01	1.01	1.01	1.01	1.00	1.00	1.00	1.00	1.014	22
DE12	1.03	1.02	1.03	1.02	1.01	1.01	1.01	1.01	1.00	1.01	1.01	1.01	1.015	23
NL31	1.00	1.00	1.00	1.01	1.01	1.02	1.03	1.03	1.03	1.03	1.01	1.00	1.015	23
CZ02	1.01	1.01	1.02	1.03	1.03	1.02	1.03	1.03	1.01	1.01	1.00	1.01	1.016	25

(*Continued*)

Table 5.5 (Continued)

DMU name	*2007*	*2008*	*2009*	*2010*	*2011*	*2012*	*2013*	*2014*	*2015*	*2016*	*2017*	*2018*	*Average*	*Rank*
ES62	1.05	1.12	1.22	1.26	1.30	1.34	1.37	1.33	1.29	1.22	1.20	1.19	1.241	223
EL63	1.08	1.09	1.08	1.10	1.18	1.31	1.36	1.37	1.36	1.39	1.33	1.30	1.247	224
ES42	1.06	1.11	1.20	1.23	1.27	1.36	1.39	1.37	1.32	1.28	1.24	1.20	1.253	225
FRY1	1.25	1.24	1.25	1.26	1.25	1.25	1.30	1.26	1.26	1.27	1.24	1.25	1.257	226
EL53	1.11	1.12	1.11	1.15	1.27	1.38	1.43	1.35	1.41	1.43	1.38	1.35	1.290	227
FRY4	1.27	1.28	1.32	1.35	1.37	1.35	1.36	1.32	1.27	1.26	1.27	1.29	1.309	228
ES43	1.12	1.16	1.23	1.26	1.30	1.45	1.48	1.39	1.37	1.35	1.33	1.29	1.311	229
ES64	1.19	1.22	1.27	1.25	1.25	1.33	1.44	1.36	1.47	1.41	1.35	1.32	1.323	230
ES70	1.09	1.18	1.31	1.36	1.38	1.44	1.47	1.44	1.37	1.32	1.28	1.23	1.324	231
ES63	1.23	1.18	1.19	1.27	1.34	1.53	1.49	1.43	1.34	1.30	1.26	1.38	1.329	232
ES61	1.12	1.19	1.30	1.34	1.39	1.48	1.53	1.50	1.42	1.38	1.32	1.28	1.354	233

Source: Author's own calculations based on the Eurostat data in the DEAFrontier software

according to the DEA methodology, they can be identified as inefficient. These regions can improve their efficiency or reduce their inefficiencies proportionately by reducing inputs. A total of 220 NUTS 2 regions received an efficiency index below 0.5, which means that they can improve their efficiency by reducing their inputs by 50%. Moreover, 168 NUTS 2 regions had an efficiency below 0.1, meaning that 90% of their inputs do not produce the desired outputs. An average efficiency of 0.001 was noted for ES11 (Galicia), ITF3 (Campania), PT16 (Centro), ITG1 (Sicilia), PL22 (Śląskie), PL91&PL92 (Mazowieckie), LT01&LT02 (Lietuva), ES61 (Andalucía) and PT11 (Norte). The DEA methodology also allows for the identification of benchmarks (Benchmark Decision Making Unit (BDMU)), i.e. efficient units. Inefficient units should follow the example of BDMUs or should develop organisational solutions to recognise best practices and possibly adapt them so as to improve the expenditure transformation processes. The benchmark for almost all analysed NUTS regions in 2007, 2008, 2012 and 2013 was AT32. It was FI20 in 2009; AT32, FI20 and BE24 (Prov. Vlaams-Brabant) in 2010; AT32, FI20 and BE10 (Région de Bruxelles-Capitale/Brussels Hoofdstedelijk Gewest) in 2011; AT33 (Tirol) and FI20 in 2014; AT32 and DE50 (Bremen) in 2015; AT12 (Niederösterreich) and DEB1 (Koblenz) in 2016; FI20, BE31 (Prov. Brabant Wallon) and AT34 (Vorarlberg) in 2017; and AT34 and FI20 in 2018.

In the output-orientated model, DMUs with an efficiency value equal to 1 are efficient, and all values above 1 are inefficient. LU00 and AT32 were efficient under the VRS assumption in all years. FI00 was efficient in 11 out of 12 years. AT33 and DE21 had an average efficiency slightly above 1. The remaining regions in most of the study period scored between 1 and 1.35 and were identified as inefficient. The output-orientated model says that in order to attain efficiency, productive units must increase their outputs, so regions should produce more outputs with unchanged inputs. A total of 59 NUTS 2 regions achieved an efficiency index above 1.1. The regions with the lowest output-orientated efficiency index were mostly located in Spain – ES62 (Región de Murcia), ES42 (Castilla-La Mancha), ES43 (Extremadura), ES64 (Ciudad Autónoma de Melilla), ES70 (Canarias), ES63 (Ciudad Autónoma de Ceuta), ES61 (Andalucía) – as well as Greece, EL63 (Dytiki Ellada) and EL53 (Dytiki Makedonia), and overseas regions of France, FRY1 (Guadeloupe) and FRY4 (Réunion). Benchmarks, or effective units, were identified for each year. In 2007, the BDMUs for almost all NUTS regions were CZ01 (Praha) and BE24 (Prov. Vlaams-Brabant). For 2008, these were CZ01, ITH1 (Provincia Autonoma di Bolzano/Bozen) and AT32 (Salzburg); for 2009 ITH1, LU00 (Luxembourg) and NL34 (Zeeland); for 2010 ITH1; for 2011 AT33 (Tirol); for 2012 DE21 (Oberbayern), AT32 and DEB2 (Trier); for 2013 DE21, AT32 and AT33 (Tirol); for 2014 DE21 and AT33; for 2015 DE13 (Freiburg), DE21 and AT32; for 2016 DE22 (Niederbayern) and DE21; for 2017 CZ01 and AT32; and for 2018 CZ01, AT33 and AT32 (Table 5.6).

The calculations allowed me to rank the NUTS 2 regions in both the input-orientated and output-orientated models. Both models singled out the productive unit LU00. Other units were inefficient: they fell short of the efficiency curve. In both models, the regions AT32 and FI20 were at the top of the efficiency ranking.

Table 5.6 Efficiency rank for selected NUTS 2 regions

DMU name	*Input-orientated rank*	*Output-orientated rank*	*Overall rank*
LU00	1	1	1
AT32	3	1	2
FI20	2	3	3
DE21	5	4	4
AT33	6	4	5
ITH1	4	6	5
AT34	7	9	7
BE24	10	8	8
DE14	9	9	8
DEB2	8	15	10
NL34	12	11	10
DE22	14	11	12
DE13	16	11	13
BE25	20	11	14
DE27	18	16	15
DE11	19	16	16
DE25	13	22	16
CZ01	30	6	18
DE26	17	21	19
DE23	27	16	20
EL63	192	224	223
PT11	225	191	223
EL30	206	217	225
ES70	192	231	225
ES52	206	222	227
ES11	225	204	228
ES42	206	225	229
ES43	206	229	230
ITF3	225	211	231
ITG1	225	213	232
ES61	225	233	233

Source: Author's own calculations based on the Eurostat data in the DEAFrontier software

The worst-performing regions were mostly located in Spain (ES70, ES52, ES11, ES42, ES43 and ES61) and Italy (ITF3 and ITG1). There was no single pattern as to whether the countries at the top of the ranking were more efficient in the input- or output-orientated model. Similarly, for the regions ranked lowest, some fared better in either the input-orientated model or the output-orientated model.

5.4 Malmquist index

The Malmquist index measures the ratio of DEA efficiencies in two different time periods with shifting DEA efficiency frontiers, so it can assess the change in efficiency over time. The Malmquist index is divided into two components: catch-up (efficiency change) and frontier shift (technical change) (Fare & Grosskopf, 1992). Equation 4 presents the formula for the Malmquist index:

$$n \geq 3*(s+m) \tag{4}$$

The Malmquist index can be the product of two indices. The first component measures the efficiency change, which is the change between the distance of the observed production from the maximum potential production between periods t and t+1. The second component of the Malmquist formula is the technical change between periods t and t+1 measured along an array through period t+1 data.

$$\text{efficiency change} = \frac{D_o^{t+1}\left(x^{t+1}, y^{t+1}\right)}{D_o^t\left(x^t, y^t\right)} \tag{5}$$

$$\text{technical change} = \sqrt{\left(\frac{D_o^t\left(x^{t+1}, y^{t+1}\right)}{D_o^{t+1}\left(x^{t+1}, y^{t+1}\right)}\right)\left(\frac{D_o^t\left(x^t, y^t\right)}{D_o^{t+1}\left(x^t, y^t\right)}\right)} \tag{6}$$

Estimates of the Malmquist index (output-orientated), based on Equation (4), are presented in Table 5.7.

The 12 years were divided into three periods (2007–2009/2010–2012, 2010–2012/2013–2015, 2013–2015/2016–2018). This division was chosen because it is difficult to reconcile the inputs incurred in a given year (inputs) and the results received (outputs). One would have to consider which transition period to use in order to notice the inputs' benefits. Moreover, determining such a transition period for one country/region would not necessarily work in other countries/regions. One could also examine the two EU funding periods, i.e. 2007–2012 and 2013–2020, and compare them to each other. I would have opted for the proposed division if data were available for 2019 and 2020. In that case, it would have been possible to compare the two periods of EU funds, 2007–2013 and 2014–2020. Due to the lack of data for 2019–2020, it made more sense to divide the 12 years into the three periods mentioned above.

In an additional study, I also performed the analysis for 11 consecutive periods, which is not described in detail in this book. I observed 71 out of 2,563 cases that could cause problems with interpretation. With this approach, as mentioned above, the question arises as to whether the assumed effect is immediate or the result of previous inputs. In a small part of the study, the indicator's values were heavily inflated due to, for example, a lack of or minimal funding, so it would have to be counted as an outlier in order not to distort the regions' results. This sample represents only 2.78% of the total sample. Less than 3% would not result in much change, but with the proposed breakdown for more extended periods, the above cases were excluded, as no region received funding for several years.

The average Malmquist index value for all surveyed 233 NUTS 2 regions in the EU in the three periods from 2007 to 2018 was 34.49%. Forty-two regions obtained three-period averages below 1, indicating low-efficiency growth. The worst-performing regions were HR03 (0.510), RO21 (0.788), HU21 (0.805), RO11

Table 5.7 MI (output-orientated) based on Equation (4) for all NUTS 2 regions (change between time periods t and $t+1$)

DMU	*MI period I*	*Efficiency change (EC)*	*Frontier shift (FS)*	*MI period II*	*EC*	*FS*	*MI period III*	*EC*	*FS*	*Average all MI*	*Avg. all EC*	*Avg. all FS*
AT11	1.246	0.275	4.528	0.864	1.419	0.609	6.572	3.497	1.879	2.894	1.730	2.339
AT12	1.441	0.318	4.528	0.658	1.080	0.609	2.968	1.579	1.879	1.689	0.993	2.339
AT13	0.862	0.188	4.590	1.163	1.801	0.646	1.874	1.045	1.792	1.299	1.011	2.343
AT21	1.579	0.349	4.519	0.702	1.155	0.607	2.440	1.307	1.867	1.574	0.937	2.331
AT22	1.522	0.336	4.528	0.822	1.350	0.609	2.480	1.326	1.871	1.608	1.004	2.336
AT31	0.906	0.200	4.528	1.043	1.679	0.621	2.001	1.106	1.810	1.317	0.995	2.320
AT32	0.857	0.188	4.559	0.994	1.566	0.635	1.993	1.112	1.792	1.281	0.955	2.329
AT33	1.261	0.277	4.546	0.840	1.349	0.622	2.174	1.213	1.792	1.425	0.946	2.320
AT34	0.988	0.215	4.590	1.207	1.895	0.637	3.383	1.888	1.792	1.859	1.333	2.340
BE10	2.001	0.436	4.590	0.633	0.980	0.646	0.682	0.381	1.792	1.105	0.599	2.343
BE21	1.511	0.329	4.590	1.052	1.628	0.646	1.207	0.674	1.792	1.257	0.877	2.343
BE22	1.712	0.378	4.531	1.095	1.754	0.624	1.744	0.973	1.792	1.517	1.035	2.316
BE23	1.570	0.342	4.590	0.972	1.504	0.646	1.070	0.597	1.792	1.204	0.814	2.343
BE24	1.397	0.304	4.590	0.946	1.465	0.646	1.118	0.624	1.792	1.154	0.798	2.343
BE25	1.297	0.285	4.556	1.143	1.803	0.634	1.196	0.668	1.792	1.212	0.919	2.327
BE31	2.197	0.479	4.590	0.396	0.614	0.646	22.010	12.282	1.792	8.201	4.458	2.343
BE32	1.337	0.291	4.590	0.767	1.214	0.632	3.898	2.175	1.792	2.001	1.227	2.338
BE33	1.044	0.227	4.590	1.191	1.851	0.643	0.779	0.435	1.792	1.005	0.838	2.342
BE34	1.574	0.368	4.273	0.942	1.583	0.595	1.104	0.604	1.829	1.206	0.851	2.233
BE35	1.067	0.234	4.553	0.959	1.528	0.628	1.124	0.627	1.792	1.050	0.797	2.324
BG31	0.671	0.163	4.104	0.467	0.785	0.595	1.705	0.932	1.829	0.948	0.627	2.176
BG32	0.473	0.115	4.104	0.421	0.708	0.595	1.828	1.000	1.829	0.908	0.608	2.176
BG33	0.607	0.148	4.104	0.517	0.868	0.595	1.453	0.795	1.829	0.859	0.603	2.176
BG34	0.431	0.105	4.104	0.647	1.088	0.595	1.527	0.835	1.829	0.869	0.676	2.176
BG41	0.345	0.084	4.104	0.717	1.204	0.595	1.431	0.782	1.829	0.831	0.690	2.176

BG42	0.414	0.101	4.104	0.630	1.059	0.595	1.468	0.802	1.829	0.837	0.654	2.176
CY00	0.762	0.186	4.104	0.616	1.036	0.595	1.144	0.625	1.829	0.841	0.616	2.176
CZ01	0.730	0.178	4.104	0.599	1.007	0.595	1.674	0.915	1.829	1.001	0.700	2.176
CZ02	0.629	0.153	4.104	0.523	0.880	0.595	1.639	0.896	1.829	0.931	0.643	2.176
CZ03	0.635	0.155	4.104	0.644	1.083	0.595	1.507	0.824	1.829	0.929	0.687	2.176
CZ04	0.668	0.163	4.104	0.541	0.909	0.595	1.986	1.086	1.829	1.065	0.719	2.176
CZ05	0.583	0.142	4.104	0.647	1.088	0.595	1.466	0.802	1.829	0.899	0.677	2.176
CZ06	0.604	0.147	4.104	0.624	1.049	0.595	1.827	0.999	1.829	1.019	0.732	2.176
CZ07	0.628	0.153	4.104	0.686	1.153	0.595	1.615	0.883	1.829	0.976	0.730	2.176
CZ08	0.624	0.152	4.104	0.579	0.972	0.595	1.872	1.023	1.829	1.025	0.716	2.176
DE11	1.333	0.294	4.528	0.779	1.274	0.611	0.952	0.509	1.872	1.021	0.692	2.337
DE12	1.501	0.331	4.528	0.794	1.304	0.609	1.127	0.600	1.879	1.141	0.745	2.339
DE13	1.386	0.309	4.483	0.789	1.296	0.609	1.182	0.629	1.879	1.119	0.745	2.324
DE14	1.336	0.295	4.528	0.788	1.293	0.609	1.423	0.757	1.879	1.182	0.782	2.339
DE21	1.066	0.236	4.528	0.921	1.510	0.610	0.732	0.390	1.879	0.907	0.712	2.339
DE22	0.887	0.206	4.300	0.848	1.409	0.602	2.743	1.479	1.854	1.493	1.031	2.252
DE23	0.775	0.182	4.253	0.823	1.373	0.599	3.377	1.821	1.854	1.658	1.125	2.236
DE24	0.925	0.208	4.455	0.871	1.434	0.607	3.416	1.831	1.866	1.737	1.157	2.309
DE25	1.248	0.276	4.528	0.914	1.500	0.609	1.622	0.863	1.879	1.261	0.879	2.339
DE26	1.222	0.276	4.424	0.913	1.504	0.608	1.940	1.036	1.872	1.358	0.939	2.301
DE27	1.209	0.269	4.502	0.941	1.544	0.609	1.227	0.653	1.879	1.126	0.822	2.330
DE30	1.010	0.229	4.419	0.889	1.494	0.595	2.193	1.199	1.829	1.364	0.974	2.281
DE40	1.112	0.270	4.123	0.782	1.314	0.595	3.868	2.114	1.829	1.920	1.233	2.182
DE50	1.026	0.226	4.545	1.852	3.048	0.608	0.793	0.437	1.814	1.224	1.237	2.322
DE60	1.238	0.277	4.467	0.686	1.043	0.657	1.296	0.733	1.768	1.073	0.684	2.298
DE71	0.885	0.193	4.590	1.680	2.608	0.644	0.731	0.408	1.792	1.099	1.070	2.342
DE72	0.965	0.225	4.291	1.573	2.644	0.595	1.674	0.903	1.854	1.404	1.257	2.247
DE73	1.258	0.298	4.227	1.554	2.612	0.595	2.030	1.100	1.846	1.614	1.336	2.223

(Continued)

Table 5.7 (Continued)

DMU	*MI period I*	*Efficiency change (EC)*	*Frontier shift (FS)*	*MI period II*	*EC*	*FS*	*MI period III*	*EC*	*FS*	*Average all MI*	*Avg. all EC*	*Avg. all FS*
DE80	1.160	0.283	4.104	1.557	2.616	0.595	1.020	0.558	1.829	1.246	1.152	2.176
DE91	0.693	0.151	4.590	1.988	3.077	0.646	2.802	1.563	1.792	1.828	1.597	2.343
DE92	1.906	0.439	4.345	0.944	1.586	0.595	0.913	0.492	1.854	1.254	0.839	2.265
DE93	0.757	0.175	4.317	1.051	1.760	0.597	3.177	1.714	1.854	1.662	1.216	2.256
DE94	2.431	0.588	4.134	0.943	1.585	0.595	0.787	0.430	1.829	1.387	0.868	2.186
DEA1	1.392	0.304	4.577	0.731	1.194	0.612	1.390	0.752	1.847	1.171	0.750	2.345
DEA2	0.838	0.185	4.537	0.723	1.187	0.609	1.781	0.966	1.843	1.114	0.779	2.330
DEA3	1.448	0.346	4.184	0.721	1.212	0.595	1.726	0.941	1.834	1.298	0.833	2.205
DEA4	1.012	0.228	4.449	0.740	1.226	0.604	1.888	1.016	1.857	1.214	0.823	2.303
DEA5	1.425	0.321	4.443	0.719	1.209	0.595	1.936	1.045	1.853	1.360	0.858	2.297
DEB1	0.972	0.218	4.449	0.999	1.666	0.600	1.605	0.866	1.854	1.192	0.917	2.301
DEB2	1.230	0.286	4.294	1.014	1.705	0.595	2.155	1.171	1.841	1.466	1.054	2.243
DEB3	1.155	0.258	4.485	1.029	1.689	0.609	1.621	0.872	1.860	1.268	0.939	2.318
DEC0	2.772	0.659	4.206	0.244	0.409	0.595	2.766	1.512	1.829	1.927	0.860	2.210
DED2	1.342	0.327	4.107	0.834	1.401	0.595	3.856	2.108	1.829	2.011	1.279	2.177
DED4	1.156	0.281	4.112	0.843	1.416	0.595	3.877	2.119	1.829	1.958	1.272	2.179
DED5	1.125	0.270	4.163	0.872	1.466	0.595	5.812	3.177	1.829	2.603	1.638	2.196
DEE0	1.235	0.301	4.104	1.058	1.778	0.595	4.091	2.237	1.829	2.128	1.439	2.176
DEF0	1.170	0.263	4.441	1.068	1.770	0.604	1.875	1.010	1.856	1.371	1.015	2.300
DEG0	0.715	0.174	4.104	1.550	2.604	0.595	1.734	0.948	1.829	1.333	1.242	2.176
DK01	1.586	0.340	4.668	0.637	1.000	0.637	2.745	1.532	1.792	1.656	0.957	2.366
DK02	1.520	0.327	4.643	0.619	0.980	0.632	2.452	1.368	1.792	1.530	0.892	2.356

DK03	1.444	0.314	4.597	0.664	1.028	0.646	2.914	1.626	1.792	1.674	0.989	2.345
DK04	1.540	0.328	4.697	0.632	1.014	0.623	2.637	1.471	1.792	1.603	0.938	2.371
DK05	1.022	0.223	4.590	0.714	1.123	0.636	4.762	2.657	1.792	2.166	1.334	2.340
EE00	0.614	0.149	4.104	1.356	2.279	0.595	1.311	0.717	1.829	1.093	1.048	2.176
EL30	1.585	0.359	4.411	0.738	1.240	0.595	3.109	1.700	1.829	1.811	1.100	2.278
EL41	1.437	0.350	4.104	0.778	1.308	0.595	2.928	1.601	1.829	1.715	1.086	2.176
EL42	1.752	0.427	4.104	0.701	1.178	0.595	3.743	2.046	1.829	2.065	1.217	2.176
EL43	0.996	0.243	4.104	0.840	1.411	0.595	2.821	1.542	1.829	1.552	1.065	2.176
EL51	0.646	0.157	4.104	0.935	1.571	0.595	5.319	2.908	1.829	2.300	1.545	2.176
EL52	2.124	0.517	4.104	0.773	1.299	0.595	0.709	0.387	1.829	1.202	0.735	2.176
EL53	1.781	0.434	4.104	0.644	1.082	0.595	2.904	1.587	1.829	1.776	1.035	2.176
EL54	1.396	0.340	4.104	0.896	1.505	0.595	2.138	1.169	1.829	1.477	1.005	2.176
EL61	0.774	0.189	4.104	0.782	1.315	0.595	3.920	2.143	1.829	1.825	1.215	2.176
EL62	1.205	0.294	4.104	0.808	1.357	0.595	3.270	1.788	1.829	1.761	1.146	2.176
EL63	0.774	0.189	4.104	0.725	1.218	0.595	4.180	2.285	1.829	1.893	1.231	2.176
EL64	1.100	0.268	4.104	1.167	1.962	0.595	3.786	2.070	1.829	2.018	1.433	2.176
EL65	0.849	0.207	4.104	0.810	1.362	0.595	4.250	2.323	1.829	1.970	1.297	2.176
ES11	0.628	0.153	4.104	0.873	1.467	0.595	2.118	1.158	1.829	1.206	0.926	2.176
ES12	0.856	0.202	4.248	1.647	2.769	0.595	1.465	0.801	1.829	1.323	1.257	2.224
ES13	1.264	0.303	4.175	1.434	2.409	0.595	1.429	0.781	1.829	1.376	1.164	2.200
ES21	0.791	0.175	4.528	0.931	1.528	0.609	1.407	0.748	1.879	1.043	0.817	2.339
ES22	0.832	0.185	4.494	1.410	2.329	0.605	1.104	0.589	1.875	1.115	1.035	2.325
ES23	0.648	0.150	4.314	2.733	4.570	0.598	1.216	0.665	1.829	1.532	1.795	2.247
ES24	0.727	0.171	4.248	2.408	4.028	0.598	0.759	0.415	1.829	1.298	1.538	2.225
ES30	0.834	0.185	4.504	1.514	2.486	0.609	0.882	0.469	1.879	1.077	1.047	2.331

(Continued)

Table 5.7 (Continued)

DMU	*MI period I*	*Efficiency change (EC)*	*Frontier shift (FS)*	*MI period II*	*EC*	*FS*	*MI period III*	*EC*	*FS*	*Average all MI*	*Avg. all EC*	*Avg. all FS*
ES41	0.931	0.223	4.181	1.470	2.470	0.595	2.224	1.216	1.829	1.542	1.303	2.202
ES42	0.645	0.151	4.284	1.479	2.425	0.610	2.012	1.100	1.829	1.379	1.225	2.241
ES43	0.551	0.131	4.219	1.339	2.236	0.599	1.540	0.842	1.829	1.143	1.070	2.216
ES51	0.693	0.157	4.399	2.271	3.671	0.619	0.797	0.430	1.851	1.253	1.420	2.289
ES52	1.073	0.248	4.335	1.074	1.782	0.603	2.324	1.270	1.829	1.490	1.100	2.256
ES53	0.817	0.190	4.312	1.316	2.200	0.598	0.976	0.534	1.829	1.037	0.974	2.247
ES61	0.682	0.157	4.340	1.055	1.687	0.625	1.428	0.789	1.811	1.055	0.878	2.259
ES62	0.670	0.163	4.104	1.127	1.894	0.595	2.199	1.202	1.829	1.332	1.086	2.176
ES63	0.835	0.191	4.376	1.302	2.057	0.633	1.139	0.627	1.816	1.092	0.958	2.275
ES64	0.873	0.206	4.234	1.182	1.938	0.610	1.110	0.607	1.829	1.055	0.917	2.224
ES70	1.053	0.243	4.340	0.924	1.448	0.638	1.663	0.918	1.811	1.213	0.869	2.263
FI19	0.906	0.198	4.588	1.058	1.666	0.635	1.158	0.646	1.792	1.041	0.837	2.338
FI1B	1.413	0.308	4.590	1.089	1.686	0.646	2.027	1.131	1.792	1.509	1.041	2.343
FI1C	1.382	0.301	4.590	1.105	1.749	0.632	0.754	0.421	1.792	1.080	0.824	2.338
FI1D	0.808	0.177	4.578	1.155	1.839	0.628	1.620	0.904	1.792	1.194	0.973	2.333
FI20	4.412	1.000	4.412	0.625	1.000	0.625	1.823	1.000	1.823	2.287	1.000	2.287
FR10	1.954	0.426	4.590	0.559	0.865	0.646	1.632	0.911	1.792	1.382	0.734	2.343
FRB0	1.854	0.413	4.491	0.546	0.882	0.620	2.623	1.453	1.805	1.675	0.916	2.305
FRC1	1.804	0.401	4.503	0.541	0.886	0.611	1.879	1.035	1.816	1.408	0.774	2.310
FRC2	2.061	0.463	4.454	0.486	0.813	0.598	2.306	1.261	1.829	1.618	0.845	2.294
FRD1	1.510	0.348	4.335	0.666	1.120	0.595	1.774	0.970	1.829	1.317	0.813	2.253
FRD2	1.621	0.353	4.590	0.742	1.149	0.646	1.649	0.920	1.792	1.338	0.808	2.343
FRE1	1.506	0.328	4.590	0.652	1.027	0.635	2.113	1.179	1.793	1.424	0.845	2.339
FRE2	1.333	0.290	4.590	0.604	0.945	0.639	2.404	1.341	1.792	1.447	0.859	2.340

FRF1	1.004	0.219	4.590	0.923	1.448	0.637	2.347	1.310	1.792	1.425	0.992	2.340
FRF2	1.501	0.327	4.590	0.646	1.016	0.636	1.679	0.937	1.792	1.276	0.760	2.340
FRF3	1.129	0.247	4.563	0.909	1.460	0.623	1.610	0.896	1.796	1.216	0.868	2.327
FRG0	1.744	0.394	4.431	0.611	1.005	0.608	1.834	1.003	1.828	1.396	0.801	2.289
FRH0	1.385	0.323	4.283	0.608	1.020	0.596	1.907	1.043	1.829	1.300	0.795	2.236
FRI1	1.137	0.251	4.523	1.136	1.837	0.619	1.385	0.765	1.811	1.219	0.951	2.317
FRI2	1.427	0.347	4.114	0.690	1.160	0.595	1.757	0.960	1.829	1.291	0.822	2.180
FRI3	1.342	0.311	4.316	0.883	1.458	0.606	2.400	1.312	1.829	1.542	1.027	2.250
FRJ1	1.555	0.340	4.571	0.796	1.252	0.636	1.732	0.962	1.801	1.361	0.851	2.336
FRJ2	1.279	0.286	4.474	0.748	1.215	0.615	1.723	0.954	1.806	1.250	0.818	2.298
FRK1	1.334	0.313	4.265	0.944	1.586	0.595	1.091	0.596	1.829	1.123	0.832	2.230
FRK2	1.338	0.291	4.590	0.705	1.091	0.646	1.436	0.801	1.792	1.159	0.728	2.343
FRL0	2.040	0.444	4.590	0.482	0.746	0.646	1.711	0.955	1.792	1.411	0.715	2.343
FRM0	1.087	0.246	4.415	0.541	0.888	0.609	4.112	2.266	1.815	1.913	1.134	2.279
FRY1	1.640	0.357	4.590	0.481	0.745	0.646	4.710	2.628	1.792	2.277	1.243	2.343
FRY2	1.418	0.307	4.619	0.767	1.224	0.626	2.999	1.673	1.793	1.728	1.068	2.346
FRY3	0.991	0.216	4.590	0.726	1.124	0.646	1.602	0.894	1.792	1.106	0.745	2.343
FRY4	1.713	0.373	4.590	0.526	0.815	0.646	1.579	0.881	1.792	1.273	0.690	2.343
HR02& HR05& HR06	0.813	0.198	4.104	0.162	0.273	0.595	0.492	0.269	1.829	0.489	0.247	2.176
HR03	0.763	0.186	4.104	0.136	0.229	0.595	0.632	0.346	1.829	0.510	0.253	2.176
HU11& HU12	0.635	0.155	4.104	0.973	1.636	0.595	1.937	1.059	1.829	1.182	0.950	2.176
HU21	0.523	0.127	4.104	0.681	1.145	0.595	1.211	0.662	1.829	0.805	0.645	2.176
HU22	0.569	0.139	4.104	0.694	1.166	0.595	1.285	0.703	1.829	0.849	0.669	2.176
HU23	0.464	0.113	4.104	0.891	1.497	0.595	1.136	0.621	1.829	0.830	0.744	2.176
HU31	0.561	0.137	4.104	0.732	1.230	0.595	1.290	0.705	1.829	0.861	0.691	2.176

(*Continued*)

Table 5.7 (Continued)

DMU	*MI period I*	*Efficiency change (EC)*	*Frontier shift (FS)*	*MI period II*	*EC*	*FS*	*MI period III*	*EC*	*FS*	*Average all MI*	*Avg. all EC*	*Avg. all FS*
HU32	0.558	0.136	4.104	0.625	1.051	0.595	1.527	0.835	1.829	0.903	0.674	2.176
HU33	0.589	0.143	4.104	0.651	1.094	0.595	1.515	0.828	1.829	0.918	0.689	2.176
IE04& IE05& IE06	1.575	0.343	4.590	1.352	2.093	0.646	1.451	0.810	1.792	1.459	1.082	2.343
ITC1	0.715	0.158	4.528	1.012	1.655	0.611	1.095	0.588	1.862	0.940	0.800	2.334
ITC2	1.262	0.275	4.590	0.772	1.195	0.646	2.208	1.232	1.792	1.414	0.901	2.343
ITC3	1.298	0.285	4.549	0.708	1.141	0.621	1.629	0.881	1.849	1.212	0.769	2.339
ITC4	1.039	0.228	4.559	1.078	1.709	0.631	0.535	0.294	1.819	0.884	0.744	2.336
ITF1	2.236	0.541	4.132	0.343	0.577	0.595	2.055	1.123	1.829	1.545	0.747	2.185
ITF2	1.880	0.451	4.167	0.697	1.172	0.595	3.168	1.732	1.829	1.915	1.118	2.197
ITF3	1.627	0.395	4.124	0.371	0.624	0.595	1.786	0.977	1.829	1.262	0.665	2.183
ITF4	0.567	0.138	4.104	0.694	1.167	0.595	3.109	1.700	1.829	1.457	1.001	2.176
ITF5	1.607	0.389	4.127	1.342	2.255	0.595	2.789	1.525	1.829	1.913	1.390	2.184
ITF6	2.122	0.517	4.104	0.267	0.449	0.595	1.964	1.074	1.829	1.451	0.680	2.176
ITG1	1.518	0.368	4.126	0.384	0.646	0.595	1.377	0.753	1.829	1.093	0.589	2.183
ITG2	2.511	0.612	4.104	0.526	0.884	0.595	2.238	1.224	1.829	1.758	0.906	2.176
ITH1	0.984	0.217	4.528	2.723	4.436	0.614	0.718	0.383	1.876	1.475	1.679	2.339
ITH2	0.868	0.189	4.590	1.634	2.573	0.635	0.735	0.410	1.792	1.079	1.057	2.339
ITH3	1.010	0.232	4.350	1.115	1.865	0.598	0.878	0.480	1.829	1.001	0.859	2.259
ITH4	1.295	0.286	4.528	0.865	1.453	0.595	1.202	0.648	1.854	1.120	0.796	2.326
ITH5	1.087	0.240	4.528	1.095	1.798	0.609	0.864	0.460	1.879	1.015	0.833	2.339
ITI1	1.101	0.249	4.422	0.715	1.196	0.598	1.376	0.751	1.833	1.064	0.732	2.284
ITI2	1.256	0.295	4.250	0.661	1.111	0.595	2.020	1.104	1.829	1.312	0.837	2.225
ITI3	1.134	0.276	4.104	0.865	1.454	0.595	1.337	0.731	1.829	1.112	0.820	2.176

ITI4	1.255	0.273	4.590	0.741	1.147	0.646	1.904	1.062	1.792	1.300	0.828	2.343
LT01& LT02	0.724	0.177	4.104	1.372	2.305	0.595	1.178	0.644	1.829	1.091	1.042	2.176
LU00	0.891	0.203	4.400	1.312	1.996	0.657	1.278	0.723	1.768	1.161	0.974	2.275
LV00	0.672	0.164	4.104	0.978	1.643	0.595	2.173	1.188	1.829	1.274	0.998	2.176
NL11	1.686	0.367	4.590	1.079	1.671	0.646	3.878	2.164	1.792	2.215	1.401	2.343
NL12	1.576	0.384	4.104	1.087	1.827	0.595	3.361	1.837	1.829	2.008	1.350	2.176
NL13	2.170	0.529	4.104	0.890	1.496	0.595	4.646	2.540	1.829	2.569	1.522	2.176
NL21	1.454	0.354	4.104	0.772	1.297	0.595	2.106	1.151	1.829	1.444	0.934	2.176
NL22	1.815	0.439	4.138	0.835	1.404	0.595	1.742	0.952	1.829	1.464	0.931	2.187
NL23	0.675	0.153	4.405	1.044	1.717	0.608	2.880	1.591	1.811	1.533	1.154	2.275
NL31	1.412	0.308	4.590	0.840	1.300	0.646	1.946	1.086	1.792	1.400	0.898	2.343
NL32	1.687	0.368	4.590	0.817	1.265	0.646	1.862	1.039	1.792	1.455	0.890	2.343
NL33	1.379	0.300	4.590	0.845	1.308	0.646	1.779	0.993	1.792	1.334	0.867	2.343
NL34	3.474	0.839	4.141	0.592	0.996	0.595	4.437	2.426	1.829	2.834	1.420	2.189
NL41	1.231	0.276	4.462	0.775	1.257	0.617	2.040	1.133	1.801	1.349	0.889	2.293
NL42	1.673	0.393	4.258	0.784	1.311	0.598	3.501	1.914	1.829	1.986	1.206	2.228
PL21	0.560	0.136	4.104	0.911	1.531	0.595	1.284	0.702	1.829	0.918	0.790	2.176
PL22	0.583	0.142	4.104	0.910	1.530	0.595	1.415	0.773	1.829	0.969	0.815	2.176
PL41	0.542	0.132	4.104	1.076	1.809	0.595	0.990	0.541	1.829	0.869	0.827	2.176
PL42	0.571	0.139	4.104	1.053	1.769	0.595	1.368	0.748	1.829	0.997	0.885	2.176
PL43	0.610	0.149	4.104	1.191	2.001	0.595	1.428	0.781	1.829	1.076	0.977	2.176
PL51	0.510	0.124	4.104	1.035	1.739	0.595	1.484	0.811	1.829	1.010	0.891	2.176
PL52	0.548	0.134	4.104	1.354	2.276	0.595	0.830	0.454	1.829	0.911	0.954	2.176
PL61	0.512	0.125	4.104	1.003	1.686	0.595	1.358	0.742	1.829	0.958	0.851	2.176
PL62	0.482	0.117	4.104	0.908	1.527	0.595	1.626	0.889	1.829	1.005	0.844	2.176

(Continued)

Table 5.7 (Continued)

DMU	*MI period I*	*Efficiency change (EC)*	*Frontier shift (FS)*	*MI period II*	*EC*	*FS*	*MI period III*	*EC*	*FS*	*Average all MI*	*Avg. all EC*	*Avg. all FS*
PL63	0.530	0.129	4.104	0.965	1.622	0.595	1.466	0.801	1.829	0.987	0.851	2.176
PL71	0.640	0.156	4.104	0.912	1.532	0.595	1.571	0.859	1.829	1.041	0.849	2.176
PL72	0.418	0.102	4.104	1.289	2.167	0.595	1.190	0.651	1.829	0.966	0.973	2.176
PL81	0.440	0.107	4.104	1.045	1.756	0.595	1.240	0.678	1.829	0.908	0.847	2.176
PL82	0.414	0.101	4.104	0.965	1.621	0.595	1.449	0.792	1.829	0.943	0.838	2.176
PL84	0.496	0.121	4.104	0.935	1.571	0.595	1.351	0.739	1.829	0.927	0.810	2.176
PL91& PL92	0.604	0.147	4.104	0.830	1.394	0.595	2.295	1.255	1.829	1.243	0.932	2.176
PT11	0.589	0.144	4.104	1.200	2.016	0.595	1.282	0.701	1.829	1.023	0.954	2.176
PT15	0.859	0.209	4.104	1.463	2.459	0.595	3.204	1.752	1.829	1.842	1.473	2.176
PT16	0.594	0.145	4.104	1.334	2.242	0.595	1.191	0.651	1.829	1.039	1.013	2.176
PT17	0.833	0.201	4.150	1.602	2.692	0.595	1.571	0.859	1.829	1.335	1.251	2.191
PT18	0.537	0.131	4.104	1.170	1.965	0.595	2.269	1.240	1.829	1.325	1.112	2.176
PT20	0.463	0.113	4.104	1.872	3.145	0.595	0.878	0.480	1.829	1.071	1.246	2.176
PT30	0.691	0.168	4.104	1.396	2.345	0.595	1.297	0.709	1.829	1.128	1.074	2.176
RO11	0.999	0.243	4.104	0.291	0.490	0.595	1.140	0.623	1.829	0.810	0.452	2.176
RO12	1.080	0.263	4.104	0.266	0.446	0.595	1.682	0.920	1.829	1.009	0.543	2.176
RO21	0.915	0.223	4.104	0.373	0.627	0.595	1.076	0.588	1.829	0.788	0.479	2.176
RO22	1.043	0.254	4.104	0.266	0.447	0.595	1.637	0.895	1.829	0.982	0.532	2.176
RO31	1.065	0.260	4.104	0.356	0.598	0.595	1.141	0.624	1.829	0.854	0.494	2.176
RO32	1.261	0.307	4.104	0.250	0.420	0.595	1.432	0.783	1.829	0.981	0.503	2.176
RO41	0.862	0.210	4.104	0.438	0.736	0.595	1.144	0.625	1.829	0.815	0.524	2.176
RO42	0.965	0.235	4.104	0.264	0.443	0.595	1.983	1.084	1.829	1.071	0.587	2.176

SE11	0.661	0.144	4.590	0.839	1.298	0.646	0.975	0.544	1.792	0.825	0.662	2.343
SE12	2.071	0.451	4.590	0.917	1.420	0.646	1.206	0.673	1.792	1.398	0.848	2.343
SE21	2.093	0.470	4.458	0.659	1.020	0.646	1.633	0.911	1.792	1.462	0.800	2.299
SE22	1.992	0.434	4.590	0.727	1.125	0.646	1.474	0.823	1.792	1.398	0.794	2.343
SE23	0.677	0.147	4.590	0.818	1.267	0.646	1.194	0.666	1.792	0.897	0.694	2.343
SE31	0.826	0.180	4.580	1.420	2.198	0.646	1.290	0.720	1.792	1.179	1.033	2.339
SE32	0.921	0.201	4.590	0.979	1.516	0.646	1.602	0.894	1.792	1.168	0.870	2.343
SE33	0.907	0.198	4.590	1.039	1.608	0.646	1.408	0.786	1.792	1.118	0.864	2.343
SI03	0.488	0.119	4.104	0.779	1.309	0.595	3.488	1.907	1.829	1.585	1.112	2.176
SI04	0.473	0.115	4.104	0.930	1.562	0.595	2.120	1.159	1.829	1.174	0.945	2.176
SK01	0.537	0.129	4.167	0.584	0.978	0.597	2.984	1.631	1.829	1.368	0.913	2.198
SK02	0.467	0.114	4.104	0.720	1.210	0.595	1.275	0.697	1.829	0.821	0.674	2.176
SK03	0.600	0.146	4.104	0.695	1.169	0.595	1.835	1.003	1.829	1.044	0.773	2.176
SK04	0.541	0.132	4.104	0.814	1.368	0.595	1.365	0.746	1.829	0.907	0.749	2.176
Average	1.125	0.259	4.320	0.907	1.487	0.610	2.015	1.106	1.824	1.349	0.951	2.251

Source: Author's own calculations based on the Eurostat data in the DEAFrontier software

Note: period I: avg. (2007–2009)/avg. (2010–2012); period II: avg. (2010–2012)/avg. (2013–2015); period III: avg. (2013–2015)/avg. (2016–2018)

(0.810), RO41 (0.815), SK02 (0.820), SE11 (0.825), HU23 (0.830), BG41 (0.830), BG42 (0.837), CY00 (0.841) and HU22 (0.849). Twelve of these regions did not exceed a value of 0.85. Of the 12 least efficient regions, 3 each came from Romania and Hungary, 2 from Bulgaria and 1 each from Croatia, Slovakia, Sweden and Cyprus. One of these regions, HR03, significantly lagged behind the weakest by obtaining an MI value of 0.510, which was 0.278 lower than the second-weakest region (RO21). The remaining 191 regions scored a three-period average above 1, meaning they improved in efficiency. Sixteen of the best-performing regions obtained averages of more than 2.0, and 57 regions obtained averages of more than 1.5 for the periods under review, meaning that the average three-year period productivity was higher than 33.33% for the 16 best-performing regions and more than 16.67% for 57 regions. These 16 best-performing regions were BE31 (8.201), AT11 (2.894), NL34 (2.834), DED5 (2.601), NL13 (2.569), EL51 (2.300), FI20 (2.287), FRY1 (2.227), NL11 (2.215), DK05 (2.166), DEE0 (2.130), EL42 (2.065), EL64 (2.018), DED2 (2.011), NL12 (2.008) and NL32 (2.001). Five of them were from the Netherlands, three each from Germany and Greece, two from Belgium and one each from Austria, Finland and France. The performance of the regions is not surprising except for the three regions in Greece. It is worth noting that the efficiency scores for EL51 were not the highest in the first two periods (0.646 and 0.935). Still, the efficiency score for the third period of 5.319 significantly increased the region's average. The situation was more stable in the other Greek regions, particularly EL64, which proved efficient over all three periods (1.099, 1.167 and 3.786). Nevertheless, a trend was revealed that the situation is changing in the right direction in these three Greek regions, as the highest efficiency values were achieved in the final period under review, which may indicate a good outlook for these regions.

Eighteen of the analysed 233 NUTS 2 regions were efficient in every period studied. Six of these regions are in Germany, three in Belgium, two each in the Netherlands and Spain and one each in Finland, Greece, Italy, France and Ireland. These regions are shown in Table 5.8.

In period I, in which the change in efficiency between 2007 and 2012 was studied, 124 out of 233 regions were efficient (i.e. achieved values above 1), and 109 scored below 1. The average MI for this period was 1.125. The analysis revealed that 146 regions were above average and 87 below average. The lowest MI value was 0.345 (BG41), and the highest was 4.412 (FI20). In period II, which examined the change in efficiency between 2010 and 2015, 72 out of 233 regions were efficient, while 161 scored below 1. The average MI for this period was 0.907. The analysis showed that 102 regions were above average and 131 below average. The lowest MI value was 0.136 (HR03), and the highest was 2.733 (ES23). In period III, in which the change in efficiency between 2013 and 2018 was studied, as many as 208 out of the 233 regions were efficient, while only 25 were not efficient. This was connected with the high average MI in this period, which was 2.015. As many as 158 regions were above the average, and 75 were below the average. The lowest MI value was 22.010 (BE11), and the highest was 0.492 (HR02&HR05&HR06).

Table 5.8 Regions that were efficient in each of the three periods studied, according to the Malmquist index (production-orientated) based on Equation (4) for all NUTS 2 regions (change between time periods *t* and *t*+1)

	NUTS 2	*Malmquist index, output-orientated CRS (period I)*	*Malmquist index, output-orientated CRS (period II)*	*Malmquist index, output-orientated CRS (period III)*	*Average*
1	BE21	1.511	1.052	1.207	1.257
2	BE22	1.712	1.095	1.744	1.517
3	BE25	1.297	1.143	1.196	1.212
4	DE73	1.258	1.554	2.030	1.614
5	DE80	1.160	1.557	1.020	1.246
6	DEB2	1.230	1.014	2.155	1.466
7	DEB3	1.155	1.029	1.621	1.268
8	DEE0	1.235	1.058	4.091	2.128
9	DEF0	1.170	1.068	1.875	1.371
10	EL64	1.100	1.167	3.786	2.018
11	ES13	1.264	1.434	1.429	1.376
12	ES52	1.073	1.074	2.324	1.490
13	FI1B	1.413	1.089	2.027	1.509
14	FRI1	1.137	1.136	1.385	1.219
15	IE04&IE05&IE06	1.575	1.352	1.451	1.459
16	ITF5	1.607	1.342	2.789	1.913
17	NL11	1.686	1.079	3.878	2.215
18	NL12	1.576	1.087	3.361	2.008

Source: Author's own calculations based on the Eurostat data in the DEAFrontier software

Note: period I: avg. (2007–2009)/avg. (2010–2012); period II: avg. (2010–2012)/avg. (2013–2015); period III: avg. (2013–2015)/avg. (2016–2018)

5.5 Results and discussion

Despite EU efforts to reduce differences between regions, there is still wide variation in economic development within the EU. Therefore, it is reasonable to ask whether the billions of EUR pumped into the Cohesion Policy are spent properly and whether they bring the expected results. Do the least developed regions have the appropriate absorption capacity to spend these funds effectively?

The study presented in this chapter examines the relationship between EU payments (input) and the outputs, which describe the level of development and the standard of living in EU regions. Output indicators include GVA per employee, GDP per capita, compensation per employee, disposable income in PPS per capita and employment rate. The input and output variables were selected based on available statistics from Eurostat. No time lag between input and output production is taken into consideration. It was assumed that funds received from the EU are allocated immediately to investments and that they stimulate the economy and the labour market. The study covers 233 EU NUTS 2 regions for the period 2007–2018.

Between 2007 and 2018, Cohesion Policy funding increased by 25%. However, these payments relate to specific programming periods. The amounts received by a region may vary significantly from year to year, depending on the payment schedule and the number of financing programmes submitted by the region and accepted for implementation. During the 12 years under review, the largest beneficiary of EU payments was ES61, with EU payments totalling 15 billion EUR. Second place went to PL91&PL92, with total payments of 13.6 billion EUR; this was followed by PT11 with 12.6 billion EUR. The most minor support was received by FI20 (12 million EUR), followed by AT32 (59 million EUR) and AT34 (75 million EUR). The Bulgarian regions with the worst output indicators were in the middle of the EU payment list.

Sizable increases were also noted in four output indicators. The average GVA per employee increased from 46,120 EUR to 54,550 EUR. The highest percentage increase was noted in all Bulgarian regions, from 78% to 101%, while a decrease was found in all Greek regions. The highest value of GVA per employee was in 2018 in IE04&IE05&IE06 (136,000 EUR), LU00 (122,000 EUR) and BE31 (107,000 EUR), while the lowest was in Bulgaria's BG33, BG31, BG32 and BG42 (less than 12,000 EUR). The average GDP per capita increased by 21%, from 23,770 EUR to 28,740 EUR. The highest growth was in regions of Bulgaria and Romania, while growth decreased in those of Greece. The highest values of the indicator in 2018 were achieved by LU00 (99,000 EUR), BE10 (69,000 EUR) and DK01 (69,000 EUR), while the lowest were in BG42, BG32 and BG31 (less than 6,000 EUR). Compensation per employee grew by 23%, with the highest value in 2018 being posted for LU00, BE10 and FR10 and the lowest for BG31, BG42 and RO21. Average disposable income in PPS per capita increased by 18% on average in the study period. LU00, DE21 and DE11 had the highest values, while five Bulgarian regions had the lowest: BG34, BG42, BG32, BG33 and BG31. The highest employment rate values were recorded for CZ01, CZ03 and DE25. However, it decreased in 98 out of the 233 regions, most notably in EL53, EL41, EL63 and EL30.

The least developed regions are catching up in terms of the selected macroeconomic indicators, but the pace is slow. Bulgarian and Romanian regions can boast record percentage increases, but the nominal values show that they still occupy the last positions among the 233 analysed NUTS regions for output indicators 1–4. For example, the weakest region, BG31, recorded an 89% percentage increase in GDP per capita in the study period; however, the ratio of GDP per head to the EU average increased from 27% to 34% of the EU average. Greek regions dominated in terms of the worst employment rates. During the period under review, employment decreased from 15% to 8% in Greece's regions. Since the outbreak of the 2008 financial crisis, the Greek labour market has faced major problems. Labour market reform was one of the main conditions for loans granted to the Greek government by the EU and the International Monetary Fund (IMF). The Greek government has agreed to a series of reforms, including the deregulation of the collective bargaining system, the standardisation of a flexible workforce, the individualisation of employment contracts, the abolition of the Labor Inspectorate and the reduction of the national minimum wage from €751 gross per month to €586. However, these changes did not positively affect the labour market, and unemployment increased (Poulimenakos et al., 2021).

Efficiency for the 233 NUTS 2 regions was calculated using DEAFrontier. DEA input-orientated and output-orientated models were used. The EU strives to maximise the effects of the Cohesion Policy while limiting payments. The input-orientated model verifies whether payments under the Cohesion Policy can be reduced while maintaining output indicators at the same level. The output-orientated models confirm whether fixed inputs can bring about a proportional increase in the results. Both models use variable returns to scale (VRS). The evidence presented in this study documents the relatively poor efficiency of EU funding. The results indicate that the outputs do not produce proportional inputs, which confirms that higher Cohesion Policy spending does not generate proportional effects for EU regions. These results showing little or no impact of EU funds on regional development are consistent with those of Boldrin and Canova (2001), Dall'Erba and Le Gallo (2008) and Eposti and Bussoletti (2008). The average efficiency change for all 233 NUTS 2 regions surveyed in the EU from 2007 to 2018 was 34.49%. Discarding a trend in the Malmquist index is difficult because the proportion of efficiency change and technological change components varies from period to period.

The only effective region in both input-orientated and output-orientated models was LU00 (Luxembourg). FI20 was effective in 11 of the 12 years, and AT32 was effective in 10 of the 12 years. LU00 was 228th out of 233 regions in terms of EU funding, receiving a total of only 88 million EUR over the 12-year period, which represents only 0.02% of all payments during the study period. For outputs 1–3, it achieved one of the highest indicators in the group. LU00 fared worse regarding disposable income per capita in the indicator PPS; it ranked 209th out of 233 due to the high cost of living. LU00 ranks 113th for the employment rate. This does not change the fact that it achieved very good results despite receiving relatively limited funding from the EU. LU00 is generally one of the most developed EU economies; the economy is in good condition and is able to ensure further development on its own. EU funds are rather an additional stimulus for development and the manifesto of EU membership. The situation with FI20 and AT32 is slightly different. These regions receive the least funds of all regions: 0.003% and 0.01%, respectively, of all payments during the period under review. In the case of outputs for FI20, they are usually in the middle of the group, apart from GDP per capita (where they are in 33rd place) and compensation per employee (57th place). AT32 outperforms FI20 on most metrics. However, considering that FI20 has lower expenditure, the efficiency is at a comparable level.

ES61, PL91&PL92 and PT11 received the most EU funds, each accounting for almost 3% of all payments paid during the period under review. However, this does not translate into a large increase in outputs for all those regions. For example, in ES61, GVA per employee increased by 17%, while, on average, it increased by 22%. The GDP per capita was only 4% in the 12-year period, while the average for all regions was 21%. For compensation per employee, the increase was 14%, while the average was 23%. Only in terms of disposable income per capita in PPS, ES61 increases by 31%, with the average for all regions being at level of 25%. In the case of employment rate, there was a decline of over 10%. Such slight changes in outputs compared to high inputs put this region last in the ranking of the efficiency index. It can be concluded that the significant funds received from the EU are not used effectively and do not result in a significant improvement in macroeconomic indicators. PT11 achieved an increase in outputs close to the average for all regions, which, combined with one of the highest total inputs, makes it inefficient. The PL91&92 region is characterised by much greater efficiency, as evidenced by a significant improvement in all output indicators in the study period: for output 1, a 54% increase with an average of 22%; for output 2, a 63% increase with an average of 21%; for output 3, a 61% increase with an average of 23%; for output 4, 85% with an average of 20%; and for output 5, 5% with an average of 0.14%. The increases in all indicators were above the EU average. However, with such large inputs compared to other units, the DEA methodology requires much larger effects to indicate the unit as effective. Still, this does not change the fact that, compared to the region ES61, the Polish region made much better use of the funds received and translated them positively into improved macroeconomic conditions.

The regions with the worst output indicators, i.e. Bulgaria and Romania, were in the middle of the ranking, where we can also observe regions that use EU funds for better or worse. The regions BG41, BG42 and BG34 received more funding than BG31, BG32 and BG33 and achieved a lower performance index. Overall, BG41 and BG31 performed better than other Bulgarian regions, but the results were not commensurate with the funds these regions received. The situation is similar in the case of Romania's regions. They received a total of 1.8 billion out of 3.3 billion EUR, which did not translate into significantly better results. In terms of funds received from the EU, they were between 54th and 82nd place, but in terms of efficiency achieved, they were in between 116th and 173rd place. This indicates the low absorption capacity of these regions for the effective use of EU funds.

The results indicate a relationship in which the more EU funding a region receives, the lower its effectiveness. It is not a linear relationship and a few points do stand out, but such a general relationship can be noticed in Figure 5.1. Two Czech regions (CZ02

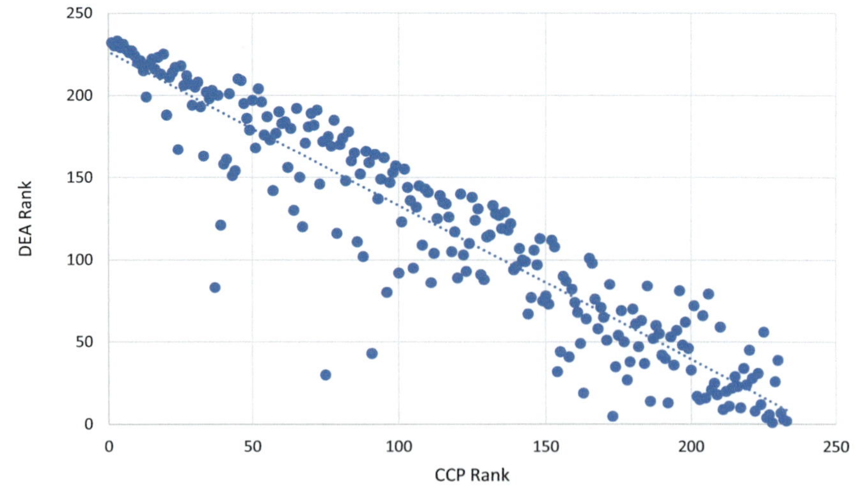

Figure 5.1 Relationship between CCP rank and DEA rank

Source: Author's own elaboration based on the Eurostat database

and CZ03) were characterised by a relatively low efficiency index with relatively large expenditures. However, CZ01 and IE04&IE05&IE06 achieved much better positions in the efficiency ranking despite their lower position in terms of funds received.

The DEA model determines how a productive unit should change its behaviour to become efficient and rise to the efficiency curve. The analysis confirmed that more than half of the studied NUTS 2 regions had an efficiency below 0.1, which means that 90% of their inputs do not generate the desired results. The DEA methodology indicates benchmarks, which in this study were most often AT32 and FI20. Inefficient units should follow the example of the BDMUs or develop organisational solutions to recognise best practices and possibly adapt them to improve expenditure transformation processes. In this study, the BDMUs are those regions which received the least support from the EU. This is another confirmation of the thesis that EU funds are not used effectively. With reduced EU funding, regions would likely generate very similar results and achieve better efficiency.

One of the largest limitations of the study was the availability of data for EU regions. The EU changes the NUTS classification every few years. These changes are not automatically applied to all historical statistics, which in practice means that data for older periods follow the old NUTS division, and newer data follow the new one. This requires additional effort to obtain comparable data – often manually changing NUTS codes from old to new or accumulating values for NUTS regions that have been divided into smaller units. The European Union provides more and more data for smaller territorial units, but there is still a lack of longer historical data for NUTS 3 units. By incorporating more reliable inputs and outputs into the DEA methodology, a better overview of the effectiveness of EU funds can be obtained. Moreover, in order to present results for the main objectives of the Cohesion Policy, other indicators should also be included in the outputs, such as statistics related to environmental protection or innovation, but such statistics were not available for all years or at the regional level. Furthermore, an analysis over a longer period may allow for more general conclusions and recommendations for planning the Cohesion Policy.

References

Becker, S. O., Egger, P. H., & von Ehrlich, M. (2010). Going NUTS: The effect of EU structural funds on regional performance. *Journal of Public Economics*, *94*(9–10), 578–590. doi:10.1016/j.jpubeco.2010.06.006

Beugelsdijk, M., & Eijffinger, S. C. W. (2005). The effectiveness of structural policy in the European Union: An empirical analysis for the EU-15 in 1995–2001. *Journal of Common Market Studies*, *43*(1), 37–51. doi:10.1111/j.0021-9886.2005.00545.x

Boldrin, M., & Canova, F. (2001). Inequality and convergence in Europe's regions: Reconsidering European regional policies. *Economic Policy*, *16*(32), 206–253. doi:10.1111/1468-0327.00074

Breidenbach, P., Mitze, T., and Schmidt, C. M. (2019) EU regional policy and the neighbour's curse: Analyzing the income convergence effects of ESIF funding in the presence of spatial spillovers. *JCMS: Journal of Common Market Studies*, *57*, 388–405. https://doi-org.ezp-prod1.hul.harvard.edu/10.1111/jcms.12807

Charnes, A., Cooper, W. W., & Rhodes, E. (1978). Measuring the efficiency of decision making units. *European Journal of Operational Research*, *2*, 429–444. doi:10.1016/0377–2217(78)90138-8

Cook, W. D., Tone, K., & Zhu, J. (2014). Data envelopment analysis: Prior to choosing a model. *Omega*, *44*, 1–4. doi:10.1016/j.omega.2013.09.004

Cooper, W. W., Seiford, L. M., & Tone, K. (2000). *Data envelopment analysis: A comprehensive text with models, applications, references and DEA-Solver software*. Boston, MA: Kluwer Academic Publishers.

Crucitti, F., Lazarou, N.-J., Monfort, P., & Salotti, S. (2023). Where does the EU Cohesion policy produce its benefits? A model analysis of the international spillovers generated by the policy. *Economic Systems*, *47*(3). doi:10.1016/j.ecosys.2023.101076

Dall'erba, S. (2005). Distribution of regional income and regional funds in Europe 1989–1999: An exploratory spatial data analysis. *The Annals of Regional Science*, *39*(1), 121–148. doi:10.1007/s00168-004-0199-4

Dall'erba, S., & Le Gallo, J. (2008). Regional convergence and the impact of European structural funds over 1989–1999: A spatial econometric analysis. *Papers in Regional Science*, *87*(2), 219–244. doi:10.1111/j.1435–5957.2008.00184.x

Esposti, R., & Bussoletti, S. (2008). Impact of objective 1 funds on regional growth convergence in the European Union: A panel-data approach. *Regional Studies*, *42*(2), 159–173. doi:10.1080/00343400601142753

Eurostat. (2023a). *NUTS—nomenclature of territorial units for statistics: history*. Retrieved December 26, 2023 from https://ec.europa.eu/eurostat/web/nuts/history

Eurostat. (2023b). *Regional statistics*. Retrieved December 26, 2023 from https://ec.europa.eu/eurostat/databrowser/explore/all/economy?lang=en&subtheme=na10.nama10.nama_10reg&display=list&sort=category

Fare, R., & Grosskopf, S. (1992). Malmquist productivity indexes and fisher ideal indexes. *The Economic Journal*, *102*(410), 158. doi:10.2307/2234861

Farrell, M. J. (1957). The measurement of productive efficiency. *Journal of the Royal Statistical Society. Series A (General)*, *120*, 253–290. doi:10.2307/2343100

Fiaschi, D., Lavezzi, A. M., & Parenti, A. (2017). Does EU cohesion policy work? Theory and evidence. *Journal of Regional Science*, *58*(2), 386–423. doi:10.1111/jors.12364

Jenkins L., Anderson M. (2003). A multivariate statistical approach to reducing the number of variables in data envelopment analysis, *European Journal of Operational Research*, *147*(1), 51–61, doi.org/10.1016/S0377-2217(02)00243-6

Kersan-Škabić, I., & Tijanić, L. (2017). Regional absorption capacity of EU funds. *Economic Research-Ekonomska Istraživanja*, *30*(1), 1191–1208. doi: 10.1080/1331677X.2017.1340174

Maynou, L., Saez, M., Kyriacou, A., & Bacaria, J. (2014). The impact of structural and cohesion funds on Eurozone convergence, 1990–2010. *Regional Studies*, *50*(7), 1127–1139. doi:10.1080/00343404.2014.965137

Molinero, C. M., & Woracker, D. (1996). Data envelopment analysis. *OR Insight*, *9*(4), 22–28. doi: http://dx.doi.org/10.1057/ori.1996.21

Poulimenakos, G., Della Puppa, A. G., Alexandridis, A., Pavlopoulos, D., & Dalakoglou, D. (2021). The Greek crisis ends here tonight: A qualitative study of labor market deregulation in Greece beyond the "crisis" paradigm. *Journal of Labor and Society*, *24*(2), 261–281. https://doi.org/10.1163/24714607-bja10004

Rodriguez-Pose, A., & Fratesi, U. (2004). Between development and social policies: The impact of European structural funds in objective 1 regions. *Regional Studies*, *38*(1), 97–113. doi:10.1080/0034340031001632226

Scotti, F., Flori, A., & Pammolli, F. (2022). The economic impact of structural and cohesion funds across sectors: immediate, medium-to-long term effects and spillovers. *Economic Modelling*, *111*(C), 105833. doi: 10.1016/j.econmod.2022.105833

Thanassoulis, E. (2003). *Introduction to the theory and application of data envelopment analysis*. Norwell, MA: Kluwer Academic Publishers. doi:10.1007/978-1-4615-1407-7

Wober, K. W. (2007). Data envelopment analysis. *Journal of Travel & Tourism Marketing*, *21*, 91–108. doi:10.1300/j073v21n04_07

Zhang, Y., & Bartels, R. (1998). The effect of sample size on the mean efficiency in DEA with an application to electricity distribution in Australia, Sweden and New Zealand. *Journal of Productivity Analysis*, *9*, 187–204.

Index

Note: **Bold** page numbers refer to tables and *italic* page numbers refer to figures.